THE SOCIAL MEDIA INDUSTRIES

Edited by Alan B. Albarran

Routledge
Taylor & Francis Group

NEW YORK AND LONDON

First published 2013
by Routledge
711 Third Avenue, New York, NY 10017

Simultaneously published in the UK
by Routledge
2 Park Square, Milton Park, Abingdon, Oxon OX14 4RN

Routledge is an imprint of the Taylor & Francis Group, an informa business

Library of Congress Cataloging-in-Publication Data
The social media industries / edited by Alan B. Albarran.
p. cm. – (Media management and economics series)
Includes bibliographical references and index.
1. Internet industry. 2. Internet marketing–Social aspects. 3. Social
media–Economic aspects. 4. Mass media–Economic aspects. 5. Electronic
commerce–Social aspects. I. Albarran, Alan B.
HD9696.8.A2S63 2012
384'.33–dc23
2012033109

ISBN: 978-0-415-52318-9 (hbk)
ISBN: 978-0-415-52319-6 (pbk)
ISBN: 978-0-203-12105-4 (ebk)

Typeset in Bembo
by Keystroke, Station Road, Codsall, Wolverhampton

Certified Sourcing
www.sfiprogram.org
SFI-00453

Printed and bound in the United States of America
by Edwards Brothers, Inc.

THE SOCIAL MEDIA INDUSTRIES

This volume examines how social media is evolving as an industry—it is an extension of the traditional media industries, yet it is distinctly different in its nature and ability to build relationships among users. Examining social media in both descriptive and analytical ways, the chapters included herein present an overview of the social media industries, considering the history, development, and theoretical orientations used to understand social media. Topics covered are:

- Business models found among the social media industries and social media as a form of marketing.
- Social media as a form of entertainment content, both in terms of digital content, and as a tool in the production of news.
- Discussions of ethics and privacy as applied to social media.
- An examination of audience uses of social media considering differences among Latinos, African Americans, Asian Americans, and people over the age of 35.

Overall, *The Social Media Industries* provides a timely and innovative look at the business aspects of social media, and has much to offer scholars, researchers, and students in media and communication, as well as media practitioners.

Alan B. Albarran is Professor and Chair of the Department of Radio, Television and Film at the University of North Texas. His teaching and research interests revolve around the management and economics of the communication industries. *The Social Media Industries* is the fifteenth book he has written/edited during his career.

Series: Media Management and Economics
Alan B. Albarran, Series Editor

This book is dedicated to our grandson,
Nathaniel Dean Lloyd
"Nate"

CONTENTS

FIGURES

TABLES

CONTRIBUTORS

Alan B. Albarran, Ph.D., is Professor and Chair of the Department of Radio, Television and Film at the University of North Texas. His teaching and research interests revolve around the management and economics of the communication industries. *The Social Media Industries* is the 15th book he has written/edited during his career.

Berrin Beasley, Ph.D., is an Associate Professor of Communication at the University of North Florida. Her research areas include media ethics, gender studies, and media history, and her work has been published in numerous journals and books. She is also co-editor of the book *Social Media and the Value of Truth*.

Jiyoung Cha, Ph.D., is an Assistant Professor in the Film and Video Studies program at George Mason University. Her research focuses on adoption of new media, business models of new media, and interrelationships between new technologies and traditional media from management and marketing perspectives. She received her Ph.D. in mass communication with a minor in marketing from the University of Florida and her Master's degree in Television, Radio, and Film at the S.I. Newhouse School of Communications at Syracuse University.

David H. Goff, Ph.D., is Professor and Chair, Department of Communication, University of North Florida. His research interests are centered on the profound changes affecting media as a result of digital technology, deregulation, and globalization. His work has examined the convergence of the media, telecommunications, and information technology industries; the increasingly global scope of these industries; the impact of the Internet and other new media technologies; and the social, political, and economic implications of these phenomena.

Laurie Thomas Lee, Ph.D., is Professor of Broadcasting at the University of Nebraska-Lincoln. Her research interests include privacy law, new technologies, media law, and media economics.

Paige Miller, M.A.J., is President of MultiPlanet Marketing, Inc., an interactive agency based outside Philadelphia that focuses on fast-paced, innovative companies. For 14 years, she has helped start-up and mid-sized software companies market their products through traditional media and emerging social media. From her experiences, she has gained valuable insights into the channels, techniques and best practices for successful marketing campaigns.

Francisco J. Pérez-Latre, Ph.D., is Director of International Relations and Assistant Professor of Advertising at the School of Communication of the University of Navarra, Spain. He has written 8 books, 20 book chapters and 53 articles on media management, advertising, and communication strategy. His research has been published in international journals such as the *Journal of Media Business Studies*, *Journal of Spanish Language Media* and *The International Journal on Media Management*. His research work now focuses on social responsibility and social media technologies.

Daniel Schackman, Ph.D., was an Assistant Professor in Media and Communication at the State University of New York-New Paltz where he taught courses and conducted research in the areas of new media and media management and programming. Daniel died suddenly of a heart attack in November 2011.

Tracy Collins Standley, Ph.D., is an Assistant Professor of Mass Communication at McNeese State University in Lake Charles, LA. She received her doctorate from the University of Alabama in Tuscaloosa in 1999. Her research interests include the news industry and children and the media.

Aimee Valentine, M.A., holds a Bachelor's in Advertising from Texas Tech University and a Master's in Radio, Television and Film at the University of North Texas. She is a seasoned marketing and advertising professional with six years of experience as a media planner across both traditional and interactive platforms. Currently, Aimee is focused on market research in the area of digital media. As a technical account manager for Nielsen, she is involved in innovative online audience measurement studies and services.

Jacqueline Ryan Vickery, Ph.D., is an Assistant Professor in the Department of Radio, Television and Film at the University of North Texas. She conducts qualitative research on teens' digital media practices as they intersect with issues such as digital equity, school policies, identity politics, privacy, and digital literacy. She has worked as a Research Assistant for the MacArthur Foundation's

Connected Learning Research Network in Austin, Texas, and was a 2012 Digital Media & Learning Summer Research Fellow. Additionally she has served as a Managing Editor for the online journal *FlowTV.org*.

Maria Williams-Hawkins, Ph.D., is an Associate Professor of Telecommunications at Ball State University. Her teaching, speaking, and community efforts focus on representations of ethnicity, culture, gender, and age in the media and medical settings. Her publications have examined ethnic use of new technology. Her international efforts have focused on China, Korea, and Taiwan.

FOREWORD

What an exciting time to be researching social media! As a digital media scholar I often tell people I study a moving target: as soon as academics identify a phenomenon, people have likely already moved onto the next platform, meme, slang, or device. In less than a decade of research I have followed young people as they move from blogs, to Myspace, to Facebook, and onto Tumblr; the dynamic nature of social media is both stimulating and challenging. Platforms such as blogs, Facebook, YouTube, wikis, LinkedIn, and Twitter increasingly complement and challenge so many aspects of our lives—as citizens, consumers, educators, family members, researchers, friends, and colleagues. Fundamentally, social media sites were developed as a way to connect people to other people, be it friends to friends or as a way for like-minded people to find community. However, even in its brief and ever-changing history, social media and social networking sites have become so much more than just a way to connect friends: they serve to connect people to ideas, journalists to breaking news, businesses to customers, politicians to citizens, employers to jobs, consumers to advertisers, students to teachers, content to revenue, and the global to the local. It is because of the far-reaching and increasingly expanding influence of social media that I am so delighted about this book.

When Alan Albarran first told me he was working on an edited book about social media industries, I knew it was a much needed contribution to the developing field of social media. As an emerging scholar myself, I know firsthand the extent to which we need grounded research which brings together historical, theoretical, empirical, and analytical perspectives of social media from an industry perspective. My research primarily focuses on ethnographic work which relies heavily on the viewpoints of users, in particular educators', parents', and young people's experiences with social media. Through my own research I find it is so important to connect users' everyday lived experiences with broader issues and implications of industry. This is why I am so excited about the significant contribution *The Social Media Industries* makes to the scholarly field of social media.

With more than 25 years of international experience working with and in the fields of media management and economics, Alan brings into conversation the unique perspectives of diverse scholars who contribute to our understanding of social media as industries. Much of the existing research related to social media industries resides in the domain of "how-to" but generally lacks a more nuanced scholarly contribution to social media as an emerging academic field. What this book brings to the table is both theoretical and empirical discussions of the ways social media function in the United States and in an international context. Through real-world examples such as Twitter's capacity for breaking news to Pixar's innovative viral marketing campaign, this book provides insights into the complexities and functions of social media industries. As a researcher constantly striving to connect users' experiences with industry's perspectives, this book provides a bridge for understanding how industry develops, operates, functions, and contributes to social media engagement.

Contributions in this book trace the history of social networking sites but also consider the social and media landscapes that led to the emergence of new modes of engagement. Other chapters address the developing and evolving business models and expand our understanding of the role social media are playing in broader economic and revenue models. Arguably privacy is one of the most contentious issues related to social media and this book discusses a variety of ethical considerations and explores how these issues affect the overall growth of the industry. Beyond issues of privacy, this book implores us to think critically about the morality and ethics of social media from an industry perspective and calls into question the value of "truth" in the age of always-on and viral media. Significantly, at a time when social media research still tends to focus on young, affluent, white consumers, this book also considers the unique perspectives and experiences of Latinos, African and Asian Americans, older adults, and international audiences.

Trying to avoid the trap of celebratory discourse around the opportunities afforded by social media, this book successfully addresses the strengths, limitations, and challenges social media present from an industry perspective. I recognize the difficulty of bringing theoretical, historical, analytical, and empirical perspectives together; as such, I am so excited about the contribution this book makes to the field. Far from solely contributing to an economic understanding of media industries, this book brilliantly considers social media industries through an historical lens, within an entertainment framework, from the perspective of news and citizenship, as well as marketers and business, and all the while acknowledges the paradoxes, challenges, and ethical dilemmas industries and consumers encounter on a daily basis. It is in this spirit that this book contributes to the developing field of social media and industry studies. Social media will undoubtedly continue to evolve as audiences and industries continue to find new ways to engage online.

At times, I worry that studying a moving target will render my research obsolete one day ("Wait, what was Friendster?"), yet as this book demonstrates, quality research is both timely and timeless. While audiences will evolve, new platforms will develop, and different business practices will emerge, there still remain questions to which the answers are always significant. How have social media evolved historically? What are the moral and ethical dilemmas industries must always be mindful of? How do economics and industries contribute to audiences' experiences as consumers and citizens? This edited volume significantly contributes to social media scholarship while simultaneously demonstrating the need for future research. It is my hope that our research target never stops moving and that as scholars we will always question the challenges and opportunities afforded by social media.

Jacqueline Ryan Vickery
Department of Radio, Television and Film
The University of North Texas

PREFACE

On behalf of the contributors who help make this edited volume possible, thanks for your interest in *The Social Media Industries*. This project came about because of my own curiosity and fascination with social media, coupled with my lifelong passion of studying the managerial and economic aspects of the communication industries. Like many of you, I've invested time and energy in social media with profiles on Facebook and LinkedIn, as well as a couple of Twitter accounts. I use YouTube a lot in finding video material for my courses and just watching old video material. I had a good run at Mafia Wars before I got tired of the game. I use social media a lot, but I am by no means an expert. I'm still learning the full use of hashtags and retweets.

Back in 2009, the idea for this project came to me when I noticed the plethora of material on "how to" do social media, but virtually nothing on social media as a set of markets and industries from a business and economic perspective. The scholarly journals were starting to publish articles on social media, much of it devoted to usage, others to psychological and sociological considerations. The closest I found to any sort of "business" aspect was how TV stations were using social media, mostly with a focus on Facebook and Twitter. All interesting material, but a gap in the market remained.

I have had the good fortune as an author to have a long-standing relationship with Linda Bathgate at Taylor & Francis. Over dinner at an academic conference I broached the idea of an edited volume devoted to social media from an industry perspective. My ideas were pretty sketchy, but Linda was intrigued, and encouraged me to prepare a proposal. The proposal was met with both praise and deserved criticism from the reviewers, who shared their own insights and ideas that ultimately developed into a refined proposal and the work you either hold in your hands, or your appropriate e-reader, whatever the case.

Social media has captured the attention and interest of consumers, marketers, advertisers, and businesses. While the number of social media users grows literally by the hour, it is clear millions of people are using these sites around the world. Social media is impacting everything from a media and non-media standpoint. Social media is now a key source for news and information. Social media has greatly impacted politics and the political process. Social media is a must for marketers and advertisers. Non-profits and entrepreneurs are using social media to find start-up capital in new and innovative ways. In short, social media is a game changer.

This volume looks at how social media is evolving as an industry—an extension of the basic "media" industries, yet very different in terms of the nature of social media and its ability to connect people and build relationships. This book looks at social media from multiple perspectives.

Overview of the Book

While the chapters are presented independently and can be read in any order, readers are encouraged to review the first four chapters to provide a foundation on which to examine social media from an industry perspective, especially if they are new to social media.

In the first chapter, my focus is on introducing social media as a set of industries using the industrial organization model, a tool widely used in the study of media economics. The IO model is applied to the social media industries, and the chapter investigates the early sub-markets emerging across the space.

Chapter 2 reviews the history of the social media industries. My long-time friend and colleague David Goff authors this chapter. A comprehensive researcher, Goff's history of the development of social media is critical to understanding social media as an industry.

In Chapter 3, Francisco "Quico" Pérez-Latre of the University of Navarra in Spain discusses theoretical issues associated with social media. Quico was one of the first scholars to fully embrace social media, and he does an excellent job discussing the relevant theoretical issues.

Which business models are associated with social media? That is the focus of Chapter 4, written by Jiyoung Cha. This chapter helps clarify how social media is being monetized and making plans for further development of revenue streams.

Social media is an important marketing tool, and for this work it was important to get a perspective from someone outside academe. Paige Miller is the President of Multiplanet Marketing, and helps clients in developing their social media strategy and campaigns. Miller is the author of Chapter 5 on social media marketing, and for the record is also my sister-in-law.

Chapter 6 examines social media content, written by the late Dan Schackman of SUNY-New Paltz. Dan died suddenly of a heart attack in November 2011, and I was very saddened by his loss. I'm pleased his chapter is represented here, a brief glimpse of the type of scholarship our field will miss by his passing.

Berrin Beasley, at the University of North Florida, authors Chapter 7 examining the role of social media and morality. The chapter gives readers a lot to think about regarding social media's role in society.

Social media has influenced mainstream media in many ways. In Chapter 8, Tracy Standley Collins examines how traditional news media is using social media, presenting an interesting early picture of this topic.

Chapter 9 is concerned with privacy and social media, a topic that could fill an entire book. Laurie Thomas Lee of the University of Nebraska has been studying legal and privacy issues associated with the media for several years; her examination of privacy and social media is first-rate.

Chapters 10–12 focus on the demand side by examining how different demographic groups are using social media. Another industry professional and former graduate student, Aimee Valentine examines how people over the age of 35 are using Facebook in Chapter 10. Chapter 11, written by the Editor, examines social media use among young Latinos, using data from a large-scale project involving six different nations. In Chapter 12, Maria Williams-Hawkins of Ball State University reviews social media use from the perspective of African Americans and Asian Americans, and discusses the state of the "digital divide" in this new era of social media.

Chapter 13 is a synthesis of the book prepared by the Editor. Upon reviewing the contents, we expect readers will find they have gained many insights, but many questions will remain about the social media industries.

ACKNOWLEDGMENTS

A few acknowledgments are in order. First, my sincere thanks to Linda Bathgate for championing this proposal all the way through this finished product. I hope she is as pleased as I am with the outcome. My thanks to each of the contributors for their work and insights presented in this volume. My wife and best friend Beverly is a constant source of support and encouragement, and I appreciate her so much.

During the development of this project our first grandchild was born in August 2010—Nathaniel D. "Nate" Lloyd. Nate has added so much joy to our lives, and we've enjoyed our new roles as grandparents. In some philosophical moments while writing and editing this volume, I've often wondered how Nate's life and other children's lives are going to be impacted and influenced by social media. At what age will he and his peers have a profile on Facebook or some other SNS? How will social media be used in their education? How will it impact choices they will make as consumers? How will social media influence them on issues of their day? Or will social media be a short-lived phenomenon, only to be replaced by some other yet-to-be-developed innovation now being shaped by some young entrepreneur?

This book is dedicated to Nate, and his generation, and the hope that they will use the social media industries in many positive ways to better their world and their lives.

1

INTRODUCTION

Alan B. Albarran

This chapter, as well as this volume, centers on the complicated and fascinating topic of social media examined from an industry perspective. There is a growing body of books and scholarly literature on social media. On the practical side, many of the early works discuss how to use social media in areas such as marketing and public relations, ideally to help a business reach existing and new customers (e.g., Li & Bernoff, 2008). On the scholarly side, early research on social media has concentrated on areas such as uses and gratifications, psychological impact, and communication patterns and preferences (e.g., Ellison, Steinfield, & Lampe, 2007; Hargittai, 2007; Pempek, Yermolayeva, & Calvert, 2009).

Missing from the literature is scholarship addressing social media from what can be called an industry perspective. That is the goal of this volume and the contributors whose work is published here—to look at social media using a different set of lens. Our goal is to consider social media as an evolving and unique communications-based industry, one that is dynamic and growing, and one that has generated a number of interesting markets of activity. To begin this approach, we should first have clear definitions as to the topic at hand in order to guide our exploration in examining social media from an industry perspective.

Key Definitions

boyd and Ellison offer a widely-cited definition of *social networking sites*. The authors identify social network sites (SNS) as:

> web-based services that allow individuals to (1) construct a public or semi-public profile within a bounded system, (2) articulate a list of other users with whom they share a connection, and (3) view and traverse their list of connections and those made by others within the system.
>
> *(boyd & Ellison, 2008, p. 211)*

This early definition was helpful in understanding the role of social networks, although the emphasis was on the construction of a public profile. There is, of

course, a differentiation that now exists between the broad content-sharing applications such as YouTube, Flickr, Reddit, and Pinterest, compared to relationship-building applications such as Facebook, Twitter, LinkedIn and Google+.

Utilizing the boyd and Ellison (2008) definition for social networking sites, how then do we define social media? A search on the Internet and trade literature will generate hundreds of definitions for social media, offered by bloggers, industry analysts, and various types of wikis. For the purposes of this volume, *social media* represents the *technologies* or *applications* that people use in developing and maintaining their social networking sites. This involves the posting of multimedia information (e.g., text, images, audio, video), location-based services (e.g., Foursquare), gaming (e.g. Farmville, Mafia Wars), and many aspects explored throughout this volume.

This book is about the social media industries. An *industry* is traditionally defined in a business and economic sense as a group of sellers offering related products and services to buyers in different markets (Albarran, 2002). In looking at social media from an industry perspective, these "sellers" are represented by the individual companies such as Facebook, Twitter, LinkedIn and YouTube, while the "buyers" are a combination of consumers who create their sites with social media technologies and advertisers, who purchase access to these audiences with the hopes of selling their own products and services. While most people may think of social media as a 21st-Century phenomenon, the roots of social media actually are deeper. In Chapter 2, Goff details the history of the social media industries.

Buyers and sellers interact with one another to exchange goods and services in a *market*. Traditionally, markets determine the price for products, and are based on supply and demand characteristics of the market. Markets have evolved over time across the communication industries. While markets used to involve physical transactions, today many markets, including the social media industries, function via the Internet and digital platforms (Albarran, 2010b).

The traditional hybrid market structure—offering the same product (social media or social networking sites or platforms) to audiences and advertisers—is known as a dual product market, and is found in many of the "traditional" media industries, such as newspapers, radio and television broadcasting, and magazines (Albarran, 2010a; Picard, 1989).

The social media industries follows this hybrid approach, with businesses trying to reach consumers (e.g., Facebook as a platform attracting new users), and businesses transacting with other businesses (e.g. advertisers like Dell buying online advertising from Facebook and other sites). Social media also adds another dimension involving consumers directly able to reach other consumers. These markets are further detailed in Table 1.1.

The three markets in Table 1.1 all have the ability to generate revenue, but advertising is the dominant business model. One of the biggest challenges for the social media is how to monetize their efforts, the topic of Chapter 4, by Cha. This

TABLE 1.1 Social media tri-product market

Market	Types of products	Main business model
Business-to-Business (B2B)	Advertising in different formats/platforms	Built on audience impressions
Business-to-Consumer (B2C)	Attract users/followers	Premium services, add-ons, subscriptions, other payments
Consumer-to-Consumer (C2C)	Various types of products and services	Direct transactions among consumers

is particularly true for large sites like Facebook and Google's YouTube, which both have millions of users, but still rely on advertising as the primary form of economic support.

Having defined a few key terms, we can now turn our attention to an analysis of the social media industries from a business and economic perspective. One helpful tool is the well-established industrial organization (IO) model, explicated by Bain (1956) and expanded upon by Scherer and Ross (1990) and others. Adding to its utility is the fact that the IO model has been applied extensively to the media industries by other scholars (e.g. Albarran, 2010b; Chan-Olmsted, 2005: Gomery, 1989; Wirth & Block, 1995).

The IO model is simple to understand in that it follows a tri-partite formula for analyzing any group of firms or industry by considering the structure, conduct, and performance characteristics of the subjects. As such, the IO model is also referred to as the SCP model or simply the SCP model in the literature. By understanding the underlying economic structure of an industry, one can then anticipate the likely conduct of the firms involved which, in turn, influence the performance of the industry. We will utilize the IO/SCP model in the next three sections as we apply this framework to the social media industries.

Structure of the Social Media Industries

In assessing the structure of an industry, scholars utilizing the IO model have traditionally sought data to address five different variables which together provide a clear picture of the structure of the market. These five variables are listed below:

1   The number of sellers, useful in determining the level of concentration that exists in a market/industry.
2   How products are differentiated from one another.
3   The barriers to entry for new firms wishing to enter a market.
4   The cost structures that exist among the firms in a market.
5   Vertical and horizontal integration among firms in the market.

Number of Sellers

The number of sellers in a market typically tells us a great deal about the level of concentration that exists in a market. From neoclassical economics we know that a single seller is a monopolist, and sets prices in a market, while at the other end of a continuum is perfect competition, where an unlimited number of sellers provide a similar product, and price is determined by the market. In the middle are the theorized oligopoly (3–10 sellers each offering homogeneous products) and monopolistic competition (multiple sellers offering slightly differentiated products) market structures (Albarran, 2010a).

In applying this framework to the social media industries, we immediately find a challenge in that the social media industries—at least in its nascent stage in the 21st Century—consists of multiple markets that are differentiated by their individual "products" or what they offer to audiences and advertisers (in a dual product market). For example, we could begin to classify the broader social media industries using several sub-markets of activity:

- *Social networking.* Popular sites such as Facebook, Myspace, LiveJournal, and Tagged allow users to create personal profiles to share with their own network. Businesses and non-profit organizations also create profiles on these sites.
- *Professional networking sites.* These would include Linkedin and Google+ which target the business and professional community. Slideshare is a related site which allows for sharing presentations.
- *Community/microblogging.* Twitter is the killer application in this arena. Kaboodle and Fark are also popular, while Pinterest has been called "Twitter with pictures."
- *Social tagging.* Tagging allows users a system of bookmarks and tags to help organize content. Golder and Huberman (2003, p. 198) define social tagging as "the process by which many users add metadata in the form of keywords to shared content." StumbleUpon, Del.icio.us, and Technorati are among the well-known sites in this sector.
- *Image/photo sites.* Pinterest has emerged as a powerful new site where users "pin" photos and other content to different "boards" organized by themes (e.g. cooking, scrapbooking, etc.). Flickr was among the early leaders in the photo sharing sub-market. Instagram, another competitor, was purchased by Facebook in 2012.
- *Video sites.* These would include YouTube, Vimeo, and Socialcam.
- *Social news.* Popular sites in this area include Digg, Reddit, Newsvine, and Yahoo Buzz.
- *Gaming sites.* Zynga, the maker of the popular Farmville, Mafia Wars, and Words with Friends is the market leader in this sector. Other firms involved in gaming include Pogo, Yahoo! Games, Big Fish, and PopCap.

- *Consumer shopping.* Sites like Groupon, Living Social, Dealster, and Social Buy offering daily digital coupons or special offers.
- *Review sites.* Designed primarily for local businesses, sites like Yelp, Citysearch, and Epinions offer customer reviews for others to share.
- *Wikis.* Wikipedia is the best known, but there are many other wikis on the Internet that allow for the sharing and editing of information/content posted online. Investopedia is a popular site for personal finance and investing. Other popular wikis are Wikitravel, Wikia, and ShopWiki.
- *Social publishing.* Scribd is a popular publishing site.
- *Location based services (LBS).* Foursquare was the first to capture wide attention, and is often used in combination with review and shopping sites.

Given the large number of sub-markets (and this listing is by no means exhaustive), we can conclude that in terms of market structure, the various sub-markets within the social media industries are for the most part competitive in that there are multiple firms involved in every sub-market, although the sizes of the firms differ greatly in terms of their market share, as measured just by the number of users/subscribers/accounts in force.

Facebook is the classic example; reaching over 900 million people in 2012, Facebook is easily the largest social networking site in the world. Other SNS like Myspace, LiveJournal, and Orkut pale in comparison to visitors to Facebook. Most of these sub-markets reveal a hybrid-type structure, with an oligopoly found on one end evidenced by a small number of firms leading the sector, and a set of smaller firms vying for the remaining market share. However, if we have learned anything about the emerging social media industries to date it is that trends can change almost overnight, as evidenced by the rapid growth of Pinterest and Groupon, to offer just two examples.

Another distinction we note about the social media industries is that the term "price" only applies at this initial examination of the market for advertisers. The majority of the social media sites listed previously are available for free to consumers, so price is not a consideration. The price to advertise—largely based in social media on audience impressions—varies based on usage and the number of consumers who have formed profiles or accounts, whatever the case. Facebook, LinkedIn, and YouTube can charge more for advertising than comparable sites based on the sheer scale of available audience advertisers have the potential to reach. In economic terms, their available supply of potential audience increases the demand by advertisers.

Product Differentiation

Product differentiation refers to how products differ among sellers. Social media firms differ in terms of the types of content offered on their sites, but what really makes social media unique in comparison to other forms of media is that it is largely consumer-driven. Users review and post content that is of interest to them and members of their networks. This enables social media to create market trends and awareness of news and other events quickly. We often hear terms like "buzz" and "viral" used to describe how content becomes widespread via social media. This is particularly useful to those engaged in marketing, advertising, and public relations, as detailed by Miller in Chapter 5 in this volume. Further, social media has become just as critical a tool in political communication and elections in promoting candidates and their positions to voters.

The social media industries are known for creating platforms that appeal to users in different ways. Early in their development, the social media industries are not known for creating specific content products that consumers access as with traditional media like broadcasting and print. Yet, we have seen traditional media embrace social media, allowing users to "share" content by reposting, linking, tweeting, and other tools.

Barriers to Entry

Barriers to entry are obstacles new sellers must overcome in order to enter a market. Often barriers to entry consist of capital requirements (funding) and/or regulatory hurdles. The social media industries have very low barriers to entry in regards to both of these areas. While it does cost money to develop websites and mobile applications for a new social media startup, these are low in comparison to other forms of media. No significant regulatory barriers exist as well (at least in the United States), as no permits or licenses are required from the government. Firms must adhere to existing laws and regulations involving any business activity, but there are no unique requirements for social media firms.

The lack of significant barriers to entry makes it possible for even the smallest size entity to set up social media accounts/profiles quickly and easily. This is especially valuable for new startups, as social media provides opportunities for marketing and branding without incurring significant costs. It is one reason why there are so many social media platforms in existence early in the 21st Century. While it is easy to enter the market, a new startup must still achieve market share and interest among consumers in order to survive.

Cost Structures

Traditionally, cost structures refer to the combination of fixed and variable costs found in an industry, and how those costs differ among firms. With low capital requirements for starting social media firms, cost structures are lower than those found in traditional media, which tend to be quite high. Social media firms have fixed and variable costs. The fixed costs include their headquarters for operations, servers and other hardware, utilities, etc. As a social media company expands, it typically means additional variable costs including salaries for engineers, programmers, marketing personnel, and expenses related to branding and marketing and other areas.

Vertical and Horizontal Integration

Vertical and horizontal integration also help in understanding the level of concentration in an industry. In vertical integration, one considers how the company controls different aspects of production and distribution within a market, while horizontal consideration looks at activities across markets.

In analyzing the social media industries, there are some examples of vertical integration found among some of the firms. Google's YouTube is part of an integrated set of useful sites that Google markets as a group. Facebook has made several acquisitions, including the 2012 purchase of Instagram to add a photo-sharing tool to its social networking site. At this early stage, there is not a widespread practice of vertical integration across the social media industries.

Regarding horizontal integration, there are limited examples. Facebook started as a site only for college students but has since expanded both domestically and globally. LinkedIn has done a good job in creating markets for both individuals and businesses, and offers basic services and premium services for subscriptions. Zynga has successfully introduced several popular games appealing to different demographic groups. News Corporation, owner of the Fox networks, acquired Myspace to add social media to its holdings across media industries only to sell the entity years later for a huge loss.

While there are limited examples of vertical and horizontal integration in the social media industries at this early stage, future growth and development should trigger more action as firms begin to consolidate to achieve scale and economic efficiencies. We can also expect mergers and acquisitions to occur among social media firms, where some will be buyers and others sellers.

Market Conduct in the Social Media Industries

In analyzing market conduct, we consider the various behaviors, practices, and policies exhibited by the sellers and buyers in a market. We try to understand how these behaviors may be coordinated among the firms in a particular type of structure. Traditionally, market conduct takes in to account the following variables:

- pricing policies;
- product strategy;
- research and innovation;
- plant or capital investment;
- legal tactics.

Conduct can be difficult to assess, especially with companies that are privately held or relatively new startups. As seen in the bulleted list, many of these items would be treated as proprietary in nature; not many firms, for example, are likely to detail their strategy and research/development efforts until ready to launch. Therefore, some of the analysis in this section will be more conjectural in nature.

Pricing Policies

Pricing policies among social media firms appear limited to two primary areas. The first being the market for different types of advertising; the other would be subscription-based pricing, for those firms offering some type of premium service. Prices for advertising follow demand tendencies, in that higher demand will allow social media firms to charge a higher price for advertising; lower prices result when demand is weak.

In terms of advertising, some social media sites offer premium services on a subscription-based plan to consumers or businesses. One of the more successful has been LinkedIn, which offers premium tiers for a monthly fee that enables expanded features and unlimited search capabilities. Going forward, we can expect to see more social media firms offer different types of subscription plans that enable a higher level of functionality and features.

Product Strategy

Strategy can be considered from two main perspectives. One way is the strategy implemented by the actual social media firm (e.g., Facebook, LinkedIn, etc.); another by how firms use social media to enhance their branding and marketing. In keeping with the overall theme of this chapter, our focus is on the former, not the latter.

In the rapidly evolving social media industries strategy seems to change overnight. Strategy involves many considerations for social media firms, and like any business operating for profit, is trying to position their products and services to gain a competitive position in the market. In the social media industries, we have observed that the first-mover advantage strategy is not always successful. While Myspace was an early leader in social networking, Facebook was able to overtake Myspace in a relatively short time span to become the largest SNS in the world, forcing Myspace to redefine itself on more than one occasion to remain competitive.

Social media strategy is also tied to the development of mobile media. Social media's popularity in all of its various markets has been enabled by the growth of smart phones and tablets, and most sites/applications are designed for use in a mobile environment. Twitter, Groupon, Foursquare, and other sites are perfect for a mobile environment, and add to their utility. Social media firms encourage users to "like" and "check in" when visiting retail establishments and restaurants to take advantage of digital coupons and other offers for consumers.

Strategy considerations also take into account opportunities to grow market share among consumers. In this sense, we continue to see an expansion of social media platforms targeting every imaginable hobby, interest, and vocation. Numerous sites offer multiple language options to expand global reach. Strategy is an ongoing consideration for social media firms, and companies must move quickly to follow new patterns and trends.

Research and Innovation

Research and innovation are critical in any technology-driven industry. In the social media industries, internal research by firms has led to many improvements in developing social media applications and sites. At its core, research and innovation efforts are designed to help firms increase their market potential.

Companies are understandably secretive about their internal research and development efforts. Most companies will not detail new projects under consideration, nor offer any specifics as to how much funding and support is spent each year on research and innovation efforts.

Plant/Capital Investment

While social media sites and applications are accessed through the Internet, the firms still have a physical location that houses employees, programmers, software engineers and other professions. Social media firms also must invest a lot of resources in maintaining a base of servers and backup centers, along with the latest in security tools to limit hacking and other attacks.

Several of the larger social media firms have moved to raise capital through both private equity firms by offering a minority stake in a company, and for a select few, engaging in an initial public offering (IPO) to sell stock to the public. LinkedIn was one of the largest firms to launch an IPO in 2011, followed by several other firms including Groupon, Zynga, and Facebook. IPOs have the potential to raise billions in new capital for growth and expansion, but force companies to operate to meet the demands of shareholders. Going forward, we can expect more social media firms to enter the IPO market.

Legal Tactics

Legal tactics refers to the complete range of legal actions a firm may use in a particular market, and the social media industries are no exception. Many people were surprised that the 2010 hit movie *The Social Network* about the development of Facebook concentrated on the legal battles associated with who came up with the original idea for the SNS. A quick search with a social media firm name and the word "lawsuit" will detail what litigation is currently in focus.

Litigation can cover many different topics, but there are probably more lawsuits related to intellectual property than any other area. Intellectual property issues have taken on new meaning in the digital age, and companies may be forced into litigation to protect their IP property, especially ideas and creations. Concerns over patents and trademarks are other areas that are ripe for litigation among social media firms.

Market Performance in the Social Media Industries

In analyzing market performance, we try to determine if the firms are successful in meeting their goals based on different criteria. Market performance can also be considered from a societal perspective by regulators on the ability of the market as a whole to promote competition. Market performance considers three variables:

* efficiency;
* equity;
* progress.

Efficiency

Efficiency as a performance variable is understood as the efforts of a company to maximize wealth. Economists examine efficiency from two perspectives: (1) how efficient the firm is at using its resources to maximize output; and (2) how efficient the firm is in allocating resources to function at maximum capacity. As mentioned previously, social media firms operate across digital platforms that have low cost structures, and the actual "products" produced in the form of applications (which are intangible) have a near zero marginal cost basis rather than a traditional maker of a product that entails a "per unit" cost. Thus, there is a high degree of technical efficiency.

In terms of allocative efficiency, because the social media industries operate in a world where fixed and variable costs are much lower than other types of media industries, the firms are in a stronger position to allocate resources easily. Once a site or application is developed, the companies must provide updates and fixes on a regular basis, which requires additional programming and testing. As new formats for smart phones and tablets have been introduced, developers had to create new versions to work across different brands.

Regarding efficiency, the social media firms operate with a great deal of efficiency which is helpful in maximizing performance. But one must understand that sites and applications can take months and years of development and refinement; this means many startups operate at a loss for some time before realizing profits. At this early examination of the social media industries, only a handful of firms (e.g., LinkedIn, Facebook, Twitter) are profitable, yet the long-term outlook is for greater profitability, provided monetization efforts are realized in the coming years.

Equity

In examining the equity in a market, one considers how the wealth is distributed among both producers and consumers. Ideally, a market economy should provide a good distribution of equity so no single firm realizes a dominant position. However, history tells us that both monopolistic and oligopoly markets are more likely to have situations where equity is concentrated among a small set of firms.

This is of course the situation in the social media firms. The leading producers are in very strong positions across many sub-markets. That is not to say that competitive positions will not change over time; simply that this first look at social media from an industry perspective finds that many of the well-known sites (Facebook, LinkedIn, YouTube, Twitter, Wikipedia, Groupon, etc.) do "capture" both the bulk of the revenue via advertising and have the greatest concentration of users. However, this inequality in the market is not something that has yet captured the interest or attention of policymakers. Concentration in the social media industries is not a pressing concern when compared to issues like the economy, health care, and terrorism. Further, it is unlikely that policymakers would intervene in the social media industries since the industry is perceived by many as simply providing entertainment and information tools for consumers.

It is from the consumer side where the picture is much more competitive and illustrates a better equity distribution among firms. Most social media applications and sites are free to the user, so there is no investment other than time to access a site. Consumers sample different social media tools, and gravitate towards those that provide the most to the user in terms of utility and value. Later chapters in this volume look at the consumer demand for social media by considering use among older adults (Valentine, Chapter 10), Latinos (Chapter 11) and African and Asian Americans (Chapter 12).

Progress

Progress is normally thought of as the ability of the firms in a market to collectively increase output over time. Such action would indicate growth in a market, and if firms are efficient in allocating resources and there is a good distribution of equity, progress should follow naturally.

Output among social media firms must be measured differently; at best we can consider trends over time like the number of subscribers for a particular site or application, the time people spend with the actual sites, the growth of advertising or other digital revenues among the firms, and the global reach of the site or application. While these are simplistic, they offer two data points for both the consumer side and the producer side to gauge trends in progress.

Analysis of the Findings

By following the industrial organization model of an industry, and breaking it down into its specific structure–conduct–performance criteria, we now have a comprehensive way to look at social media as a functioning set of industries. These findings are summarized in Table 1.2 by presenting an overall analysis of the emerging social media industries. As discussed in this chapter, the social media industries represent a collection of different markets of activity. Rather than look at each sub-market, this analysis considers the social media industries as a whole.

TABLE 1.2 Review of the social media industries using the IO/SCP model

IO/SCP variable	Preliminary findings
Market structure Number of sellers	Organized around different sub-markets; most offer a dual product to consumers/advertisers
Product differentiation	Products consist of sites/applications and their differences in appeal to users
Barriers to entry	No significant capital or regulatory barriers identified
Cost structures	Generally lower than other forms of media
Vertical/horizontal integration	Limited to larger firms; evidence of horizontal integration exists in a few sectors
Market conduct Pricing policies	Limited to advertising and subscription products
Product strategy	Heavily tied to mobile development; firms must respond quickly to market changes
Research and innovation	Proprietary in nature; designed to improve market share/revenues
Plant or capital investment	Capital requirements less than many other industries; larger firms pursuing IPO status
Legal tactics	Usually concerned with protection of intellectual property, hacking and privacy issues
Market performance Efficiency	Firms operating with high degree of efficiency but many still yet to be profitable
Equity	More competitive in regards to consumer demand; some inequality exists among the larger firms
Progress	Most firms showing growth in terms of both consumer demand and revenue/reach metrics; still very early in development

The summary analysis provided in Table 1.2 gives an overall picture of the emerging social media industries from an industrial organization perspective. This is presented with caution, in that social media is a rapidly evolving industry, and observations made at this early point in time may not hold for the long haul. Still, we can draw several insights from this analysis in comparison to other communication and media industries:

1   In terms of market structure, the social media industries are evolving along the lines of a hybrid structure, with the leaders in the sub-markets forming an oligopoly model and other smaller competitors striving for market share in a monopolistic competitive model. Most sub-markets follow a dual product market in that their services are offered to both consumers and advertisers.

2   Social media differs in that it offers lower barriers to entry and cost structures than traditional types of media and communication industries. The cost structures are also significantly lower in the social media industries, another clear advantage for startups and entrepreneurs.

3   Social media industries are heavily dependent on advertising, and must work to develop new revenue streams. Subscriptions and premium services have been introduced by some players, but the practice is not widespread. The question most asked among industry analysts is how to monetize the large consumer base. From an industry perspective, this is one of social media's greatest challenges.

4   Social media is naturally tied to mobile media, and as the penetration of smart phones and tablets continues to rise, more users will access social media away from home. This raises challengers for developers in creating applications and sites that function well in a mobile environment.

5   The social media industries are efficient in allocating resources in this early stage of development, but are a long way from reaching their full economic potential. We can expect to see social media firms continue to struggle with profitability as they seek to identify new revenue streams and methods to increase market share.

6   A huge advantage for the nascent social media industries is the social impact they have established in such a short period of time. Social media has become a new communications tool for millions of consumers; every business has embraced social media along with politics, education, and every other field. Social media has in a short amount of time developed a great deal of social capital. Firms involved in social media must respect this important relationship the industries have with their user base.

7   Privacy is a huge issue with social media, and the inability to address continuing privacy issues and concerns could limit the long-term performance of the market. Data mining of users and tracking their online sessions is a common practice among social media firms; how this data is ultimately utilized is a societal concern, and could lead to regulatory action in some countries.

8 Consumer tastes and preferences will continue to guide the development of the social media industries. While other businesses and industries utilize social media, it is the demand driven by consumers that has enabled the rapid growth to occur. The social media industries will need ongoing and varied research to maintain awareness of audience trends, and be proactive in continuing to meet the needs of consumers.

Conclusion

The social media industries have had a remarkable impact in a very short period of existence. Social media is innovative, interesting, and exciting to observe as a new yet disruptive communications industry (Downes, 2009). This initial analysis of the social media industries reveals a number of unique characteristics, but also some similarities to the traditional media industries.

Certainly there will be more evolution and change across social media as the industries move through their life cycle. Continuing to utilize a framework like the industrial organization model can help identify how the industries are evolving over time. Scholars will need to continue to monitor the development of the social media industries, and document how the structure, conduct and performance of the various sub-markets expand and contract.

References

Albarran, A. B. (2002). *Media economics: Understanding markets, industries and concepts* (2nd ed.). Blackwell, IO: Iowa State University Press.

Albarran, A. B. (2010a). *The media economy.* New York: Taylor & Francis.

Albarran, A. B. (2010b). *The transformation of the media and communication industries.* Pamplona, Spain: EUSNA.

Bain, J. S. (1956). *Barriers to new competition.* Cambridge, MA: Harvard University Press.

boyd, d. m., & Ellison, N. B. (2008). Social network sites: Definition, history, and scholarship. *Journal of Computer-Mediated Communication, 13*(1), 210–230.

Chan-Olmsted, S. M. (2005). *Competitive strategy for media firms.* New York: Taylor & Francis.

Downes, L. (2009). *The laws of disruption: Harnessing the new forces that govern life and business in the digital age.* New York: Basic Books.

Ellison, N. B., Steinfield, C., & Lampe, C. (2007). The benefits of Facebook "friends:" Social capital and college students' use of online social network sites. *Journal of Computer-Mediated Communication, 12*(4), 1143–1168.

Golder, S., & Huberman, B. A. (2006). Usage patterns of collaborative tagging systems. *Journal of Information Science, 32*(2), 198–208.

Gomery, D. (1989). Media economics: Terms of analysis. *Critical Studies in Mass Communication, 6*, 43–60.

Hargittai, E. (2007). Whose space? Differences among users and non-users of social network sites. *Journal of Computer-Mediated Communication, 13*(1), article 14. Retrieved from: http://jcmc.indiana.edu/vol13/issue1/hargittai.html (accessed October 18, 2009).

Li, C., & Bernoff, J. (2008). *Groundswell: Winning in a world transformed by social technologies*. Boston, MA: Harvard Business Press.

Pempek, T. A., Yermolayeva, Y. A., & Calvert, S. L. (2009). College students' social networking experiences on Facebook. *Journal of Applied Developmental Psychology*, *30*(3), 227–238.

Picard. R. G. (1989). *Media economics*. Thousand Oaks, CA: Sage.

Picard, R. G. (2006). Historical trends and patterns in media economics. In A. B., Albarran, S. M. Chan-Olmsted, & M. O. Wirth (Eds.), *Handbook of media management and economics* (pp. 23–36). Mahwah, NJ: Lawrence Erlbaum.

Scherer, F. M., & Ross, D. (1990). *Industrial market structure and economic performance* (3rd ed.). Boston, MA: Houghton Mifflin.

Wirth, M. O., & Block, H. (1995). Industrial organization theory and media industry analysis. *Journal of Media Economics*, *8*(2), 15–26.

2

A HISTORY OF THE SOCIAL MEDIA INDUSTRIES

David H. Goff

Introduction

In summarizing the key 21st-Century developments in the media industries, McKelvie and Picard (2008) observed, "The media space was previously controlled by media firms; however, it is today increasingly controlled by consumers. It is no longer a supply market but has become a demand market" (p. 1). Not only is abundant media content now consumed wherever and whenever the consumer desires, consumers increasingly generate media content as they utilize the fastest growing segment of online media, social media. This chapter reviews the history and development of social media and their role in the changing media landscape. It covers the factors that led to the emergence of social media and elaborates the distinct characteristics of this media form. Following an overview of the factors leading to the development of social media websites the chapter examines the development of blogs and major social media websites: Twitter, Wikipedia, YouTube, MySpace, LinkedIn, and the largest social media firm, Facebook. Subsequent chapters extend the analysis of social media firms by addressing their business models and the significant roles that they play in news content and in marketing communication.

The Evolution of Media Forms

In the long history of human communication the era of mass media that began with the early 19th-Century development of the steam-powered rotary press has been relatively brief, and some believe that with the early 21st-Century proliferation of social media, the era is ending (The people formerly known as the audience, 2011). The powered press led to a newspaper industry that shaped the parameters of mass media industries: one-way communication from a limited number of specialized organizations to the general public through a unique channel. The addition of the electronic media industries of radio and television in the 20th Century extended this paradigm. Globally, media industries evolved under varying degrees of government control. Both public/government and private (individual and corporate) ownership models developed and media operated both commercially and non-commercially. The business model relied upon the creation of a supply of content by media firms for audience consumption and subsidized through audience subscriptions and/or advertising. Of these revenue streams, advertising generally contributed the largest share as marketers took advantage of the media's ability to control the delivery of messages to large audiences.

In the final decades of the 20th Century, media industries and their audiences were undergoing significant changes resulting from the combined forces of economics, politics, globalization, and technology. The historic mass media of the Industrial Age were increasingly characterized as "old media," or "legacy media" in contrast to the "new media" forms enabled by the shift from analog to digital technologies that led to the convergence of media, telecommunications, and computing industries. The epicenter of these developments has been the Internet and since the mid-1990s the World Wide Web. Today the Internet is accessed from an expanding list of fixed and mobile devices by over two billion people. By November 2011, the percentage of the world's online population stood at 34.7 (ITU, 2011). The Internet is a major component of an expanding mix of media that together serve large and small audiences that are increasingly diverse, fragmented, and active. And as noted above, social media are the fastest growing segment of online media and their influence is profound.

Social Media: Enabling Technologies and Characteristics

Like the print and electronic media that preceded them, social media are communication channels. More precisely,

> Social media is a set of technologies and channels targeted at forming and enabling a potentially massive community of participants to productively collaborate. IT tools to support collaboration have existed for decades. But social media technologies, such as social networking, wikis and blogs, enable collaboration on a much grander scale and support tapping the power of the collective in ways previously unachievable.
>
> *(Bradley, 2010, para. 2)*

Social media derive from a business model employed to gain advantage from user-generated content, content that is created by and with other Web users. They utilize free and easy-to-use technologies and approaches to the Internet often labeled "Web 2.0." Tim O'Reilly, of California-based O'Reilly Media, is widely credited with the term and describes the concept as "the network as platform, spanning all connected devices" and "delivering software as a continually-updated service that gets better the more people use it, . . . through an 'architecture of participation,'" (2007, p. 17). Initially, Adobe Flash provided interactivity and enabled users to add media content to websites. RSS (Really Simple Syndication) facilitated receiving and sharing frequently updated web content and Asynchronous Java Script and XML (so-called AJAX technologies) enabled immediate updating of page elements without the need to reload the entire webpage. Social media users usually need no knowledge of how these technologies work because they are incorporated into social media websites.

Levinson (2009) characterizes social media as part of "new new media" and notes their shared characteristics. First, consumers are also producers who are generally not motivated by receiving compensation for generating content. Content can take any form (text or audiovisual) and is typically available to consume and redistribute free of charge. These media forms may compete for attention with each other and with older media forms but at the same time they are synergistically "mutually catalytic" (p. 56) as the media forms actively promote the sharing of the consumer-generated content. Worldwide, over 200 social media websites exist, serving a wide range of purposes and new ones are created almost daily. Hogan and Quan-Haase (2010) have noted that that all media have social elements and that with respect to social media, "the boundaries of this term are not straightforward" (p. 310). Efforts to classify social media utilize function-related labels that stem from not only their creators' intentions but also the fact that "they coevolve with their user base" (p. 310). Table 2.1 lists the major categories of social media and major websites within each (Kaplan & Haenlein, 2010; Mangold & Faulds, 2009). The history of the websites listed in boldface are discussed in more detail later in the chapter. It is important to note that individual social media often incorporate multiple functional elements. For example, social networking sites are likely to provide email capability, chat, and the ability to blog and post media/ creative content. In addition, many social media users utilize multiple forms of social media.

Development of Social Media Forms: An Overview

The Pew Research Center's Internet and American Life Project has been examining the Internet's impacts on society since 1999 and began reporting on social media in 2005. A fall 2009 Pew survey reported that 79% of American adults used the Internet, and of these, 59% reported use of at least one social networking site. Among Internet users, Facebook was used by 92%, Myspace by 29%, LinkedIn by 18% and Twitter by 6% (Hampton, Goulet, Rainie, & Purcell, 2011). In terms of the history of social media, both blogs and social networking sites were the first types to emerge and together account for roughly 25% of all Internet use (Nielsen, 2011). Pew generally does not rank social media websites. Available rankings usually reflect a website's registered users and/or website traffic. Just as the population of social media websites changes constantly, the data on the rankings of all social media websites is highly variable due to both change in the population of the websites and the variety of methodologies employed to gather the data. Any

TABLE 2.1 Social media: major categories and brands

Major categories	Major brands, December 2011	Launched	URL
Blogs	The Daily Post at WordPress.com	2011	dailypost.wordpress.com/
	Engadget	March, 2004	www.engadget.com/
Microblogging Sites	**Twitter**	July, 2006	twitter.com/
	Tumblr	2007	www.tumblr.com/
Social networking sites	**Facebook**	February, 2004	www.facebook.com/
	Myspace	August, 2003	www.myspace.com/
	Google+	June, 2011	plus.google.com
	Badoo	November, 2006	badoo.com/
	Orkut	January, 2004	www.orkut.com/
	Hi5	2005	hi5.com
Collaborative websites	**Wikipedia**	2001	www.wikipedia.org/
Content Communities/Creative works Sharing sites	**YouTube**	February, 2005	www.youtube.com/
	Flickr	2004	www.flickr.com/
Business Networking sites	**LinkedIn**	May, 2003	http://www.flickr.com/
	Ryze	2001	http://www.ryze.com/
Social News and Bookmarking Sites	Digg	November, 2004	http://digg.com/
	del.icio.us	2003	http://delicious.com/
	Reddit	October, 2006	http://www.reddit.com/
Social gaming and virtual worlds sites	Second Life	June, 2003	http://secondlife.com/

Sources: Mangold & Faulds (2009); Kaplan & Haenlein (2010). (Data on blogs is found at www.blogpulse.com and technorati.com. General social media data can be found at www.ebizmba.com, www.compete.com, www.quantcast.com, and www.alexa.com.)

published table of social media rankings will have a short shelf life. However, several websites provide constantly updated data. Examples are eBizMBA, Compete, Quantcast, Alexa Internet, and Technorati.

Blogs

Blogs, originally called "web logs," arguably predate the first social networking site and there are several claimants for the first blog. Bloggers create and post content about topics that interest them and the content can take many forms including diary-like text and commentary, as well as multimedia content for others to consume. Consumers are often other bloggers and are able to post responses on the blog sites of others and read the responses posted by all. Blog entries are usually displayed in reverse chronological order and bloggers typically include lists of links to the blogs that they follow and other websites.

The concept of the blog evolved from online message boards, newsgroups, and bulletin boards that emerged as early as the 1970s and the identity of the creator of the first blog is a subject of endless debate. Nonetheless, the term "weblog" was coined in December 1997 by Jorn Barger who used it to describe his website, Robot Wisdom, in which he posted a daily log of the "articles about politics, culture, books and technology that he found interesting" (McCullagh & Broache, 2007, p. 1). The shorter label, "blog" emerged in 1999 after Barger began to substitute the phrase "we blog" for the word, "weblog." "Blog" became the preferred label and the word was first recorded in the Merriam Webster dictionary that same year. The first known census of weblogs (1999) listed only 23 but by the fall of 2000 they numbered in the thousands (Blood, 2000).

The online blogging directory and search engine Technorati (Technorati.com) began tracking the growth of the "blogosphere" in November 2002 when the number of blogs was between one and two thousand. By October 2004 the number had swelled to over 4 million and a new blog was being created at a rate of one every 7.4 seconds (Sifry, 2004). Early blogs conveyed the thoughts of their creators along with links to other web content of interest to the blogger (Boyer, 2001). While many others could read early blogs, actually creating one required some knowledge of HTML, the language of webpage creation, until the appearance of the online blog-building utility Blogger in 1999. Other free blog publishing tools quickly emerged, and the number of blogs and their user-generated content exploded as noted above (Blood, 2000). Blogger was acquired by Google in 2003 and remains one of the top five web publishing content management systems. WordPress, established in 2003, is the largest with a market share for content management systems of more than 50%. Drupal, Joomla, vBulletin, and Blogger rank second through fifth with market shares below 10% (W3Techs, 2011).

Microblogs: Twitter

Twitter (twitter.com) is a free microblogging service founded in March 2006 by Jack Dorsey, Evan Williams, and Biz Stone, three members of Odeo, a struggling podcasting business owned by Obvious Corp., a San Francisco firm (Twitter, n.d.). While traditional blog posts can be any length, microblogging involves sending and receiving short text messages shared with others through Short Message Service protocol (SMS; also called text messaging) or other online forms of communication. SMS messages conform to a standard length limit of 160 characters and the designers decided to limit Twitter messages, or "tweets" to 140 characters in order to leave space for the user's identification. Twitter operates on any device that accesses the Internet and is ideal for mobile devices like smart phones and tablets.

In its first year, many were skeptical of Twitter's value. The initial concept for Twitter encouraged users to compose and send a message that answered the question, "What are you doing?" Technology pundits mocked the service for the perceived banality of its short tweets and predicted its hasty demise. That view began to change when Twitter staged an effective demonstration at the 2007 South by Southwest Music, Film, and Interactive Festival in Austin, Texas (Green, 2007). As Twitter grew, it attracted notice in 2008 and 2009 for reporting breaking news before traditional media outlets (Arceneaux & Weiss, 2010). By 2011, Twitter was the number three social network or blog brand with more than 23.5 million unique visitors per month (Nielsen's Tops, 2011).

The Pew Internet & American Life Project (Hampton, et al., 2011) noted Twitter was used by 13% of the social networking community and that one-third of Twitter users used the SNS daily. A substantial percentage (34%) was between the ages of 23 and 35 with 60% younger than age 36. At the same time nearly one-fourth of Twitter users were between the ages of 36 and 49. With the exception of LinkedIn, the users of major social networking sites were women (64% in the case of Twitter) and predominantly White. In terms of education, 39% of Twitter users had either a trade school education or some college while 21% held a bachelor's degree and 18% had attended graduate school.

Twitter users first create a profile page that includes a photo, the user's location, website or blog home page address and a short biographical sketch. A link is provided that enables tweets to be posted to the user's Facebook page. Users can also link their Twitter accounts to their mobile phones and a host of third party software applications are available to facilitate linking Twitter accounts to other websites. As with all successful social networking sites, Twitter adds new tools and features regularly (Twitter basics, n.d.). For example, Twitter enables users to post web addresses as part of their tweets and will automatically shorten lengthy URLs to 14 characters. While Twitter does not host video clips, it enables the posting of clips from sites like YouTube and Vimeo. A "Twitter basics" page provides access to information on Twitter's basic and advanced functions and tools. While Twitter allows a private message to be sent to another user (called a DM or direct message), most tweets can be read by anyone with access to Twitter. This makes Twitter especially valuable for politicians, marketers, and media as well as many other types of organizations that thrive on promotion or publicity.

Twitter users can reply to tweets or mention them in tweets to others. Users also forward or "retweet" (abbreviated, RT) interesting tweets to others and are often encouraged to do so by individuals and organizations intent on publicity. Twitter enables users to find and follow the tweets of others and to also search for tweets related to key words or topics. Twitter users developed the convention of using the # (hashtag) symbol to identify a searchable keyword. For example, a tweet about an Academy Award nomination might include #Oscars appearing as a hyperlink that leads to all tweets containing the same hashtag. A core value of Twitter is the ability to find and follow the tweets of friends and other individuals and organizations with its search function.

A consistent issue for social media firms is that of monetization, the development of revenue sources. Investments are a key resource. Some social network sites, like Myspace and YouTube, have been acquired by larger corporations that are publicly traded while others issue their own IPOs (initial public offerings) and raise revenue through the sale of stock. Among social network sites, LinkedIn has done this and Facebook went public in 2012. Twitter has been a privately owned enterprise from the outset and discloses little about its finances. In 2009, the online technology information directory CrunchBase published a list totaling $1.6 billion in venture capital investments in Twitter since 2007 (Twitter, n.d.). The data had not been released by Twitter but rather it had been acquired by an Internet hacker and subsequently provided to CrunchBase (Miller & Stone, 2009). Other sources of revenue come from operations (usually from advertising and/or the provision of premium services).

For most of its first three years, Twitter operated on investment income while it concentrated on building the service, improving functionality, and adding users. The firm derived some income from licensing its stream of tweets to Google, Yahoo, and Microsoft. Then, in April 2010, Twitter announced it would initiate advertising in the form of Promoted Tweets that would appear when a user includes a designated keyword in a Twitter search (Miller, 2010; Tartakoff, 2010). The program has expanded with the addition of Promoted Trends and Promoted Accounts. Twitter provides a Trending Topics list function for its users and the paid Promoted Trends appear at the top of the list. Users who click on a Promoted Trend see all related tweets and can add their own comments. Twitter also provides a Who to Follow feature accessible by first clicking on the #Discover link on the toolbar at the top of the user's homepage. An algorithm-generated list of prospective Twitter accounts based on a user's Twitter activity is provided. The Twitter accounts of advertisers who pay for Promoted Accounts appear at the top of the window and are clearly labeled as "promoted" with a yellow icon (What are promoted accounts?, n.d.). Finally, the growing political significance of Twitter has caused the company to establish a separate promotional category for promoted

Tweets, Trends, or Accounts of a political advertiser. Political ads are designated with a purple icon (What are political ads?, n.d.).

Limited information is available about the cost of advertising on Twitter and the revenue generated. In December 2011, a story appeared in several online sources reporting that an email from Twitter's sales department had revealed then-current advertising charges. Promoted Tweets were priced on a cost-per-engagement (CPE) basis for "clicks, favorites, retweets and '@Replies.'" at $0.75 to $2.50. Promoted Accounts ads were priced according to a cost-per-follower (CPF) between $2.50 and $4 (Trewe, 2011, para. 2). Prospective advertisers were advised in the memo that they must have an established Twitter presence, and must commit to spending $15,000 to $25,000 in the first three months. The program was described as operating at the beta test level and at the time was reaching about 25% of Twitter users (Heine, 2011).

Wikipedia

Wikipedia (www.wikipedia.org) was created in 2001 by Jimmy Wales and Larry Sanger and is operated by the nonprofit Wikimedia Foundation. Wikipedia is an international Internet encyclopedia that is the product of the collaboration of an online community of tens of thousands of volunteer contributors from around the world. Traditional published encyclopedias are created and edited by content authorities, but anyone can add or edit entries in Wikipedia. In this way Wikipedia exemplifies the idea of user collaboration that is at the heart of the Web 2.0 concept and social media forms. In 2000, Wales and Sanger failed in an attempt to develop a more traditional, expert-based online encyclopedia, Nupedia, because the process of developing each entry was too long: two completed entries in six months. In contrast, the volunteer-based Wikipedia offered over 20,000 entries at the end of its first year (Fletcher, 2009). At the start of 2012, Wikipedia offered over 20 million entries of articles in 283 languages and was supported by over 100,000 regular contributors (Wikipedia, n.d.). Data on the English language version reported more than 3.8 million articles. Wikipedia accepts no advertising and instead relies on foundation support and user donations to the Wikimedia Foundation raising $20 million in 2011 alone (Walsh, 2012). Wikipedia is consistently ranked among the ten most visited websites in the U.S. and worldwide.

Wikipedia operates under a set of rules that have been modified over its eleven-year history to confront challenges to the website's integrity and its information's reliability. The website directs potential contributors to Wikipedia's own style manual and provides information on basic principles (e.g., verifiable accuracy, verification of information through citation of reliable sources, impartiality, adherence to copyright and other laws, and child protection) as well as guidelines related to offensive material, etiquette in online collaboration, and the avoidance of "gaming the system" or otherwise acting in bad faith (e.g., vandalizing a page) (Wikipedia Guidelines, n.d.).

Despite the rules and guidelines established by Wikipedia, concerns about the reliability of its contents persist. It has been common practice in academic settings for educators, librarians, and others to caution learners against relying on Wikipedia entries as source material. In order to evaluate these concerns, Fallis (2008) investigated the epistemic consequences or contributions to knowledge of Wikipedia use and his work lists and evaluates the primary criticisms of Wikipedia, including first and foremost, its accuracy (and honesty), and the thoroughness, currency, and comprehensibility of its entries. Fallis notes inaccurate information can be reported through error or design and that there have been instances of inaccurate information appearing in Wikipedia for months before being corrected by administrators or other registered users.

Another concern with Wikipedia stems from the fact that content creators work anonymously. This can obscure readers' ability to judge contributors' potential for bias and conflicts of interests. The credibility of contributors and their work can be revealed by the quality of their writing and documentation of source material, but subsequent edits can conceal the questionable quality of the work of the initial contributor. Inaccuracy can remain but not be as evident. Removal of important and correct information can be especially problematic as it may not be noticed without a close reading of the page's history. Despite these concerns, Fallis concludes that information in Wikipedia, while not perfect, compares favorably with information in more traditional encyclopedias and with information that people would be likely to locate online if Wikipedia did not exist.

YouTube

YouTube (www.youtube.com) is a video-sharing website created in early 2005 and officially launched in December of that year by Steve Chen, Chad Hurley, and Jawed Karim (Cloud, 2006). Chen, Hurley, and Karim are members of the so-called "PayPal Mafia," a group of about 20 former associates of online payments service PayPal before it was acquired in 2002 by eBay. Members of this group have been key figures in the establishment and success of a large number of social media (O'Brien, 2007).

YouTube consistently ranks among the ten most visited websites, thereby increasing the dominance of parent corporation, Google, Inc., the most visited website in the world. YouTube demonstrated several key characteristics of social media forms from the outset. It was designed to be advertiser-supported, built to provide user-generated content, and it did not require sophisticated technical knowledge to participate. Within two months of its first posted video in 2005, YouTube had achieved 13.9 million views. Further, the young membership of the then-popular social networking site Myspace had embraced YouTube and were actively posting clips and linking them to their Myspace pages. This, along with technical enhancements, enabled users to include YouTube videos in other websites and create links between videos accelerated the growth of YouTube (Cloud, 2006; Grossman, 2012).

YouTube faced numerous challenges in its early period of operation. First, the expense of bandwidth and expanding both server capacity and staffing to accommodate the exponential growth of the site's video content would require not only increased advertising revenue but also substantial investor support. YouTube picked up $1.5 million in financial support from hedge fund Sequoia Capital in its first year (Cloud, 2006; Helft, 2006; Sorkin & Peters, 2006). Its rapid growth was certainly noticed by advertisers and YouTube responded with a program that enabled advertisers to create and post their own promotional web videos.

YouTube monitored posted videos and routinely removed content that it deemed inappropriate but the issue of copyright would prove to be a greater challenge as YouTube fans posted music videos and clips from television shows and movies popular with younger viewers (The trouble with YouTube, 2006; Seabrook, 2012). YouTube also followed a policy of removing copyrighted material not as a matter of course, but rather if the copyright owner asked for it to be removed. In mid-2006 YouTube was growing at the rate of 65 million new video clips posted each day and copyright concerns were growing. YouTube introduced Content ID, a technology that facilitated identifying content uploaded without copyright permission and alerted its owners. Notified copyright owners could then order that the content be removed, link their own ads to it (sharing revenue with YouTube), or do nothing. NBC signed on in June and shortly thereafter Warner Music agreed to post its entire collection of music videos in exchange for a negotiated percentage from the YouTube-placed ads that appeared with the videos. This would not only allow YouTube users access to the music videos for viewing but also to use the music in soundtracks of their own video creations (YouTube model is compromise over copyrights, 2006; Seabrook, 2012). Within a few years Content ID was responsible for more than 30% of YouTube revenue (Seabrook, 2012).

Despite its challenges, the growth of YouTube was enticing to larger firms like Microsoft, Yahoo, News Corp., and Viacom, and YouTube became a target for acquisition. However, it was web giant Google, Inc. that reached an agreement to purchase YouTube on October 6, 2006, for $1.65 billion in stock. By this time YouTube videos were being viewed at a rate of 100 million per day (Ovide, 2011). Having the financial and legal resources of Google behind YouTube promised a brighter future as it faced growth and copyright challenges. On the same day the Google deal was signed, YouTube also reached deals that would enable it to carry CBS programming as an experimental "brand channel" as well as music videos from Universal Music Group and Sony BMG Music Entertainment (Collins, 2006; Sorkin & Peters, 2006; Wood, 2006).

Earlier predictions of copyright litigation involving YouTube became reality in early 2007. In February, Viacom (owner of MTV, BET, VH-1, Comedy Central and Nickelodeon) demanded YouTube remove more than 100,000 Viacom-produced video clips and YouTube complied promptly (Lombardi, 2007). However, in March, Viacom sued YouTube and Google alleging willful copyright infringement. Viacom cited YouTube's postings of 160,000 Viacom-owned video clips that had been viewed more than 1.5 billion times and the lawsuit sought both a permanent injunction and more than $1 billion in damages. However, in an October 2010 decision the New York Federal District Court ruled the 1998 Digital Millennium Copyright Act protected websites from copyright infringement claims even if the websites knew that copyright infringement was taking place on their sites. Instead, such websites are only required to address infringed material that has been specifically identified by its copyright holder. While the ruling was seen as a significant victory for YouTube, Viacom appealed. In October 2011 Viacom's attorneys went before the 2nd U.S. Circuit Court of Appeals in New York to have the 2010 lower court decision overturned (Neumeister, 2011). A decision is pending.

As the Viacom copyright litigation progressed, YouTube achieved a number of significant milestones. Advertising on YouTube took the form of banner ads on its homepage and smaller ads adjacent to thumbnails promoting other video clips. In 2007 YouTube began superimposing pop-up banner ads over the lower portion of actual videos. The next year YouTube introduced pre-roll ads: running an ad just before the desired video clip begins, a common technique on websites that feature video content (Ovide, 2011). Also in 2007 YouTube began a Partner Program. Partners are individuals (often would-be celebrities), groups, and other online media entrepreneurs who create and supply content for channels. Partners derive income from ads placed on their channels (Seabrook, 2012).

The political role of YouTube evolved substantially between 2006 and the 2008 Presidential election and the website developed into a key information source. In an April 2007 announcement YouTube stated it would syndicate political content to a sister site, CitizenTube, a news and politics blog that provides the added dimension of comments on both video posts and the posts of fellow bloggers. Seven presidential candidates announced candidacies on YouTube and soon campaigns for state and local elections appeared. "YouTube has, in some very real ways, become the 21st century town hall for political discussion" (Welcome to (the new) CitizenTube!, 2008, para. 3). In advance of the 2008 Presidential election YouTube partnered with CNN in both Democratic and Republican primary debates that began in 2007. Citizens submitted questions for the candidates as YouTube videos and the debates were streamed live on YouTube. News clips from media sources have been a staple of YouTube from the beginning. Candidates, governments, as well as political parties and groups have learned to use YouTube and other websites to deliver targeted messages directly to voters, bypassing traditional media in their original form while at the same time becoming part of the source material for regular news reporting.

In 2009, YouTube introduced Auto-Share, an important tool for promoting newly posted video content. When a YouTube partner posts a clip, the Auto-Share option on the upload page enables instant notifications to the Partner's contacts via webmail and social media like Facebook or Twitter (Seabrook, 2012).

YouTube began a transformation in 2010 designed to increase its revenue and transition to profitability. The homepage was redesigned to make it less cluttered by replacing the familiar grid of video frame thumbnails with a banner ad at the top, a prominent center column of current popular video clips, a column of channel buttons on the left, and a column of recommended videos on the right (Grossman, 2012). A streaming movie service was added in 2010 following the success of Netflix, but in addition to first-mover advantage in the field Netflix had access to more content and offered a monthly flat rate while YouTube charged by the video. YouTube's solution to this issue has been the pursuit of professionally created original content.

YouTube reached 1 trillion unique visitors in December 2011 and its other statistics were equally staggering: an average of 48 hours of new video uploaded every minute and more than 3 billion page views per day. However, YouTube fans averaged only 15 minutes on the site per day and that would have to increase in order to attract more revenue (Seabrook, 2012; Tsukayama, 2012). In the keynote address to the 2012 Consumer Electronics Show in Las Vegas, Google's Vice President of TV and Entertainment Robert Kyncl predicted that over 75% of the next decade's television channels will emerge online (Tsukayama, 2012). His reasoning appears to be sound. In a January 2012 interview Kyncl reviewed the decades-long expansion of channels and resulting audience fragmentation of television and noted that small audiences are deadly for broadcast and cable television but normal and potentially even profitable for online content. Opportunity exists online. Advertisers spend $60 billion annually on television, but only 5% of this amount supports online television. Further, in addition to the continued growth of smart phone and tablet devices, households are rapidly acquiring both Wi-Fi-enabled digital televisions and other devices that stream video to the home screen (Seabrook, 2012). Arizona-based research firm NPD In-Stat predicts that between 2011 and 2016 the installed base of networked devices capable of delivering video content will increase more than 500% to 1.34 billion units (Installed base of connected devices to reach 1.34 billion in 2016, 2012).

In 2011, YouTube announced it would invest $100 million of development money in new channels. Channel creators, who would own the content they produce, would agree to provide a minimum amount of programming while YouTube sells advertising and enjoys exclusive rights to carry the content for one year. Development funds received from YouTube would be considered an advance on advertising revenue. In October 2011, over 100 YouTube Original Channels were announced along with plans for most to debut by 2012 (Seabrook, 2012). Channels represent an enormous range of interests from established sources (e.g., The Onion, *The Wall Street Journal*, and Slate), and new ventures (e.g., Deep Sky Videos, New Animators, and Digs) (More great content creators coming to YouTube, 2012).

Social Networking Sites

Social networking sites (SNSs) are the most popular, widely used, and recognizable social media. They are

> web-based services that allow individuals to (1) construct a public or semi-public profile within a bounded system, (2) articulate a list of other users (friends) with whom they share a connection, and (3) view and traverse their list of connections and those made by others in the system.
>
> *(boyd & Ellison, 2008, p. 211)*

Key features of social network sites are profiles that list a user's friends and the absence of a predetermined structure that allows structure to emerge through the interaction and collaboration of the site's users (boyd & Ellison, 2008; McAfee, 2009).

boyd and Ellison (2008) have documented the history of social media and social network sites from 1997 to 2006. Beer lauded the authors' work, noting that

> perhaps most credit should be given for their attempts to construct a history of SNS, the resulting timeline is highly usable and highlights just how quickly these things are moving into everyday life (and even falling out again in the case of Friendster).
>
> *(2008, p. 210)*

The first website that displayed the characteristic features of an SNS was SixDegrees.com, launched in 1997. This site incorporated user profiles and its members began by listing email address of ten friends (contacts) that represented the user's first degree. Boyd and Ellison note earlier sites (e.g., dating and community websites) had incorporated user profiles, and lists of friends were common to instant messaging sites but the lists were not displayed to others. In SixDegrees, friends of the initial "first degree" who agreed to join listed 10 more friends and this process was replicated through four more levels (the sixth degree). SixDegrees provided email, online bulletin boards, and messaging services (Bedell, 1998). Although SixDegrees attracted millions of users, it never developed a sustainable business model and ended in 2000 (boyd & Ellison, 2008).

The timeline of SNS launch dates provided by boyd and Ellison shows that the pace of creation of new social network sites increased dramatically after 2002 and that the most successful and prominent SNS sites were established after 2003. However, between 1999 and the end of 2002 a small but steadily growing number of social network sites were launched and all but one still exist in some form. Ten of these were included in the boyd and Ellison timeline as true social network sites. Like SixDegrees, these sites demonstrated the potential of social networking and as early entrants helped to shape this media segment. The ten expanded the diversity of social network users by demonstrating the potential for SNSs to attract users based on more than acquaintanceship as they were built around shared language, nationality, ethnic heritage, interests, and professional associations. Their evolution is illustrative of the impacts of both competition from newer social media and acquisition by other media firms.

Early Social Networking Sites

LiveJournal (1999), a platform for blogs and user journals, began as a "college project" shared among friends but its user base expanded rapidly. LiveJournal is based in San Francisco but has been owned by SUP, a Russian Internet firm, since 2007 (LiveJournal, Inc., 2011). Several social network sites geared toward specific segments of the population also emerged during this period. AsianAvenue (oriented toward Asian Americans and Asians living in the U.S.) and BlackPlanet (Black Americans) were established in 1999. The next year MiGente (Latino Americans) and LunarStorm (Swedish teens) were launched. LunarStorm was extremely popular with Swedish teens for a time but its popularity waned as new social network sites emerged and the site was closed in 2010 (LunarStorm, 2011). AsianAvenue, BlackPlanet, and MiGente are all owned by the New York-based firm Community Connect Inc., a subsidiary of Radio One Inc. (Community Connect Inc., n.d.). Cyworld, established in South Korea in 1999 and currently owned by the nation's dominant telecom provider, SK Telecom, evolved to become that country's most popular social networking site. In November 2011, Cyworld launched Global Cyworld in an effort to overcome problems that had thwarted earlier attempts to penetrate the North American, Japanese, and European markets (Tebay, 2011). Fotolog, established in 2002, facilitates sharing of online photoblogs or photo diaries. Like other early social networking sites, Fotolog was created to connect its creators and about 200 of their friends (About Fotolog, n.d.). By August 2007, Fotolog had attracted 10 million users and was acquired by the Hi-Media Group based in France for $90 million (Frommer, 2007). Skyblog (now Skyrock) was established in France in 2002 as a blogging website. However, the site was rebranded in 2007 as Skyrock, a more full-featured social network site in order to link the site's identity with that of Skyrock radio, France's most popular radio station for the under-25 market. In April 2011, Skyrock (the website) hosted 33.5 million blogs while Skyrock Radio reached 4 million listeners per day (Chrisafis, 2011). The early social network site Ryze (2001) was oriented toward the business community, particularly that of the San Francisco area where many social network sites would emerge (boyd & Ellison, 2008). Ryze still operates but does not attract many users having been eclipsed by other business-oriented SNSs, particularly LinkedIn (Hansell, 2006a).

The history of Friendster, launched in 2002, is a cautionary tale that serves as a particularly interesting transition from the early period of social network sites to the more significant firms that emerged after 2002. Friendster's developer, Jonathan

Abrams, employed the now-familiar concepts of user profiles and friends and early users were interested in dating and other social contacts. Established in California's Silicon Valley, Friendster rapidly attracted both media attention and a burgeoning user base that grew to 3 million in the first six months of operation. Developing online giant Google offered $30 million for Friendster in 2003 but Abrams declined and recruited other investors. However, Friendster's ability to innovate could not keep pace with its growth and new competitors, particularly Myspace, added features that Friendster lacked. In addition, Friendster's fast growth overtaxed its technological infrastructure and as Friendster users soon learned that Myspace pages loaded ten times faster than Friendster pages, they moved to the newer social network (Sellers, 2006). Friendster's board replaced Abrams as CEO in 2004 and the position turned over two more times by the end of 2005. Friendster never regained the traction enjoyed in its early days (Rivlin, 2006; Chafkin, 2007). Friendster was acquired in 2009 by a Malaysian firm and since 2011 has functioned as a social gaming site and the user data from Friendster's social networking years was deleted (Friendster, n.d.).

The Development of Major Social Networking Firms

Myspace

The creation of Myspace (www.Myspace.com) in 2003 has been attributed to Friendster's enormous early popularity and success (Hansell, 2006a; Sellers, 2006). Like Friendster, Myspace also achieved rapid success that contributed to the decline of Friendster. Ironically, the initial appeal of Myspace also proved to be short-lived for reasons that parallel Friendster's difficulties (Gillette, 2011). Myspace was established by Chris DeWolfe and Tom Anderson, whose firm Response Base, an online marketing business was acquired in 2002 by eUniverse. Anderson was already familiar with earlier social networking sites like AsianAvenue, BlackPlanet, and MiGente. Further, Anderson, DeWolfe, and others at eUniverse were early members of Friendster and began to see potential for other approaches.

Anderson and DeWolfe recruited local bands seeking publicity as well as other creative types including "artists" whose appeal often included scanty attire. Percival (2009) reports eUniverse ran a contest among employees to see who could sign up the most members for MySpace and that the firm also recruited via an email campaign directed to members of its other company-owned websites. Gillette (2011) asserts that through an oversight in planning, "developers realized that they had accidentally permitted users to insert Web markup code, allowing them to play around with the background colors and personalize their pages" (para. 18). Rosenbush (2005) credits the early success of Myspace in part to this oversight as it added user-controlled openness that allowed customization of pages by individuals and groups, noting that "results can be sophomoric or salacious, but they're riveting in the same way reality-TV is" (para. 10).

By June 2005, Myspace achieved 14 million unique monthly visitors while Friendster's popularity peaked. The site was incredibly popular with 16–34-year-olds and attracting advertising from firms like Target and Proctor and Gamble. Record companies launched new albums on Myspace. More established Internet firms like Microsoft, America Online, and Yahoo! saw the success of Myspace and were evaluating the addition of social networking to extending the array of services provided by these web portals (Rosenbush, 2005). In July 2005, the international media conglomerate News Corp. purchased Myspace for $580 million (Jackson, 2011). News Corp. also acquired other web entertainment sites for approximately $720 million more with the intention of building its own online portal. While Anderson and DeWolfe continued to run Myspace, News Corp established the Fox Interactive Media division (FIM) under Fox executive Ross Levinsohn to run it. Myspace became the centerpiece of FIM and instead of branding the venture with the well-known Fox name, News Corp. CEO Rupert Murdoch announced that the youth-oriented portal would be built around the Myspace brand with video downloads, improved instant-messaging, international sites in a dozen countries, and VoIP phone service as enhancements (Angwin, 2006; Gillette, 2011). Some analysts suggested Murdoch also envisioned building the strong following of Myspace among music enthusiasts into a competitor to MTV (Sellers, 2006; Jackson, 2011). However, Murdoch's plans would require several challenges to be surmounted.

Myspace exemplified the social network characteristic of user-generated content. It was "home to 2.2 million bands, 8,000 comedians, thousands of film-makers, and millions of attention-starved wannabes" (Sellers, 2006, para. 5). Members enjoyed customizing their Myspace pages with music videos and with forms of self-expression including sometimes provocative pictures of themselves along with their art; poetry, blog posts, and other writing (usually about them-selves); video clips, music, and links to their favorite websites. As much as members enjoyed creating and maintaining their own pages, it was common for teens to spend two or more hours per day visiting other Myspace pages, and sending instant messages and short announcements called "bulletins" to their friends. In the words of one Fox executive, Myspace was "a site programmed by its users" (Hansell, 2006b, para. 30). Young members frequently described the Myspace experience as addictive (Kornblum, 2006). Other observers were more critical, calling the often risqué online destination "a den of youthful excess and, potentially, as a lure for sexual predators," labels that might deter many advertisers (Hansell, 2006b, para. 10). State attorneys general began investigations into the safety of Myspace for young consumers and in the wake of this negative publicity Myspace agreed to a series of safety agreements with the states (Gillette, 2011).

In addition to dealing with the reputation of tawdry content, FIM would also have to raise the advertising rates charged by Myspace as it increased the volume of advertising content through the integration of MySpace with other News Corp. properties and expanded the number of advertisers. Further, it would have to take these steps without alienating a loyal Myspace user base by over-commercializing the site (Hansell, 2006). Levinsohn wanted to expand the role of an innovation started by DeWolfe wherein advertisers could join the online community with their own profile pages, thereby allowing other members to interact with them like any other friends. Hansell (2006a) cites as an example how Wendy's Old Fashioned Hamburgers created an animated profile that was soon joined by nearly 100,000 friends. During the summer of 2006, FIM and Myspace negotiated a deal in which Google would pay $300 million per year for three years. Myspace made Google its search engine and agreed to a series of growing page view targets. Ad volume doubled but page clutter increased significantly (Hansell, 2006a).

In January 2006, Myspace had 47.3 million (mostly young) members and was growing at a rate of five million per month. Already attracting more traffic than Google, in August 2006 Myspace was second in page views behind Yahoo and captured 82% of the traffic of existing SNSs (Sellers, 2006). New features were added including classifieds, security and privacy tools, and even virtual karaoke with most enhancements created in-house rather than by third party interests. However, in an effort to bring Myspace to life quickly, in 2003, developers built the site on the easy-to-use but unsophisticated ColdFusion programming language. Glitches and bugs in Myspace technologies multiplied and the need to upgrade Myspace to a newer and more robust language became clear (Gillette, 2011).

As Myspace encountered the headwinds of legal and public scrutiny of its content, safety practices, and technological shortcomings during 2006, Twitter emerged and Facebook became open to everyone. Just as Myspace had learned from the problems encountered by Friendster, Facebook learned from Myspace and created a safer-appearing online home. Gillette (2011) asserts News Corp.'s CEO Rupert Murdoch increasingly directed his attention to new ventures including acquiring the *Wall Street Journal*, a deal finalized in 2007. Myspace traffic peaked in December 2008 in the U.S. (Gillette, 2011). By the start of 2011, Myspace membership was 63 million while Facebook exceeded 500 million (Jackson, 2011). In April 2009, founders DeWolfe and Anderson were replaced and staff was reduced dramatically (Gillette, 2011).

By May 2011, Myspace traffic had dropped to 34.8 million unique visitors per month and ad revenue was less than half of the 2009 peak ($470 million). In February 2011, News Corp. announced it would sell Myspace and its asking price was around $100 million. In June, a deal was reached with online advertising company Specific Media for $35 million in cash and a 5% stake in Specific Media (Fixmer, 2011). Specific Media characterizes Myspace as a "social entertainment destination" (www.myspace.com). Ironically, the homepage contains a link for connecting to Myspace via Facebook.

LinkedIn

LinkedIn is the dominant online social network focused on business interests and the professional community. LinkedIn's focus on networking among business and professional users sets it apart from more general social networks like Myspace and Facebook. LinkedIn was created in 2002 by noted social media entrepreneur Reid Hoffman who, along with 10 associates, launched the service as LinkedIn Ltd. in May, 2003. In early 2012 LinkedIn counted more than 150 million members worldwide, and operated in 16 languages. The company is headquartered in Mountain View, California, and operates in five other U.S. cities and 16 major business centers outside the U.S. (About Us, n.d.). LinkedIn's "members are able to create, manage and share their professional identity online, build and engage with their professional network, access shared knowledge and insights, and find business opportunities, enabling them to be more productive and successful" (What does LinkedIn do? n.d., para 1).

Like the founders of YouTube, Hoffman is a member of the "PayPal Mafia" and attributes his vision for LinkedIn from lessons learned during his time with the online payments service. Hoffman realized that PayPal's success depended substantially upon knowledge acquired from professionals in such diverse fields as finance, computer science, e-commerce, and regulation (Lee, 2009). "I realized that everyone will have their professional identity online so they can be discoverable for the things that will be important to them," he remembers, waving his hand as he sits back in his chair. "The obvious one is jobs, but it's not just jobs. It's also clients and services. It's people looking to trade tips on how you do, say, debt financing in the new capital markets" (Hempel, 2010, para. 16). Hoffman and his colleagues sought to build a network whose value would lie within the knowledge and experience of connected professionals, focusing first on network growth in 2003 and then adding job listings, enhanced search and communication functions (offered as subscription-based services), and advertising in 2005 (Lee, 2009).

Initially LinkedIn user profiles contained basic information about the member's academic and professional credentials and professional experience. It functioned as a type of online résumé and in many respects it still does. However, as early users of other social media quickly acquired the practice of updating personal information, links, and other posts on their Myspace and Facebook pages, it made sense to offer ways to update and enhance LinkedIn profiles making them more interesting with professionally appropriate information and, more valuable, with an expanding array of methods for connecting with others. The 2003 version of the homepage provided buttons that enabled users to find people (clients, partners, sales leads, and customers), jobs and reputable job prospects, and services (recommended by others). A hyperlink at the bottom of the page enabled access to a growing number of groups based on members' common interests and shared experiences. The slogan, "Relationships Matter" was added to the homepage in 2006 as LinkedIn continued to emphasize the value of members' knowledge and encouraged members to use LinkedIn to reconnect with former colleagues, gain advantage in finding the ideal job or job prospects, and find the people who could help the member achieve his or her goals. At the same time members were reminded that LinkedIn was a valuable tool in controlling their professional identity online, a consideration that people might overlook in their representation in other social media (Smarty, A., n.d.).

The contemporary version of a profile page presents a comprehensive picture of the member's professional life. A subset of this information appears in a grey box at the top of the profile and a customizable list of other categories continues below the box. The box features the member's name prominently along with his or her picture and a heading below the member's name. The box also contains a summary listing current and past positions held, education, brief statements of recommendations solicited from present or former associates, the number of LinkedIn connections of the member, and the member's Twitter account and other websites. While the information is fixed and brief, standard categories enable the same information to be presented in an expanded format and categories can be rearranged or even removed. Further, an "Add Sections" link allows users to list additional categories. Beyond expanded versions of information from the grey box, categories include interests, groups, limited personal information, a list of the types of contacts the member would like to receive from others, a selection of applications ("apps") that enable further customization of the profile, and a list of skills and expertise. Perhaps the most significant category option is the "Summary" that appears just below the grey information box. Beyond the categorized information of the profile, the summary should present the member to the larger LinkedIn community in a manner that highlights both accomplishment and potential.

Clearly LinkedIn is configured to serve as a powerful tool in finding a job. Members are encouraged to build their personal networks by establishing connections with present and former associates, business contacts, members of groups, and members with similar interests and expertise. These members become first degree connections and their contacts are potential second degree connections. Connections can be queried for leads on jobs and members can use LinkedIn's Job search tool to identify posted openings and at the same time research the prospective employer and the networked professionals who already work there. LinkedIn's Answers tool enables members to pose questions for others in the network to answer. This process enables members who pose questions to tap into the knowledge of others when problem solving. At the same time answering questions posed by others helps establish a member's expertise in way that can lead to an employment inquiry from a firm.

LinkedIn became a publicly traded company with an initial public offering on May 19, 2011 (Mui, 2011). For 2011, revenue was $522 million, more than doubling the 2010 figure. LinkedIn has three revenue streams. LinkedIn Hiring Solutions, a suite of recruiting tools that seeks to identify and reach both active and passive job prospects, is used by more than 9,000 organizations and generates half of LinkedIn's revenue. LinkedIn Marketing Solutions is the company's advertising unit and generates roughly 30% of annual revenue. Finally, LinkedIn Premium Subscriptions revenues contribute about 20% of revenue (About Us, n.d.; Mui, 2011).

Facebook

Facebook (www.facebook.com) has grown to become the world's largest social networking site with over 900 million active monthly users. An October 2011 report from the digital marketing research firm comScore reported that one of every seven minutes spent online was devoted to Facebook (It's a social world, 2011). On February 1, 2012, Facebook filed documents with the U.S. Securities and Exchange Commission (SEC) outlining a much anticipated initial public offering (IPO) in the company, which was completed in May 2012. The documents provide details of Facebook's finances that had previously been the subject of speculative estimates. These included a report of prior year profit of $1 billion from $3.7 billion in revenue (Facebook, Inc., 2012; The value of friendship, 2012). Facebook revenue comes from advertising and payments for virtual and digital goods.

Evans (n.d.) noted that non-advertising revenue had increased 247% between late 2010 and late 2011 and generated approximately 15% of Facebook's 2011 revenue. Most of this revenue is associated with spending on games developed by the firm, Zynga. A popular Zynga game is "Farmville" in which players start with credits that enable them to establish a farm from scratch. Naturally, a farm needs livestock, seeds to plant, and farm implements, so the game entails start-up costs. To succeed, players must generate additional credits through the success of their operations or buy them in the form of Facebook Credits. Facebook intends to extend the use of its credits system to other types of purchases. Evans likens Facebook credits to a foreign currency, noting Facebook's membership would comprise the third largest country in the world if it were one nation. Just as in the real world, currencies can be converted, Facebook Credits can be converted to a currency like the U.S. Dollar. Evans notes that when Facebook Credits are used for products, Facebook intends to keep 30% of the dollar value of the sale.

The establishment of Facebook has been the subject of innumerable articles, several books, and at least one 2010 feature film (*The Social Network*). The now familiar storyline begins with the work of Harvard University undergraduate Mark Zuckerberg to create an online directory, initially called Thefacebook, in February 2004. Thefacebook functioned as an early social networking site that enabled Harvard students to create and share online profiles. However, three other students accused Zuckerberg of stealing their idea for a website and the dispute led to litigation that was not settled until 2008 (Swartz, 2011). Thefacebook expanded to cover several other universities in 2004 and in that same year Zuckerberg and three colleagues incorporated and moved operations to Palo Alto, California. The firm's name was changed to Facebook in August 2005 and received a $500,000 infusion of investment backing from former PayPal executives (Facebook, n.d.). Facebook expanded to high schools in 2005 and finally to anyone over the age of 13 in September 2006.

Following what has become common practice in the use of social networking sites, Facebook users create an account that presents the user's profile, covering age, sex, relationship status, interests, political and religious views, education, employment, and favorites (bands, movies, TV shows, books, and activities). In order to expand the network of Facebook friends, new members are asked to join a network of Facebook users in their area and encouraged to establish connections instantly to, for example, all Facebook users who work for the same organization (or who listed the same high school or college affiliation). For most personal information Facebook users can control who has access to it (friends, friends of friends, the user's whole network, or no one).

By the end of 2006, Facebook had 12 million registered users (Timeline, n.d.). In the early stages of a social networking site's development rapid growth is accompanied by rising costs and a firm must secure its financial future. Facebook received major investments of $12.7 million in 2006 and $27.5 million in 2007. In addition, Microsoft became a major investor in 2007, having first signed a deal in 2006 whereby Microsoft gained exclusive rights to provide banner advertising on Facebook in the U.S. The deal was expanded to international advertising in 2007 as part of a $240 million equity investment in Facebook by Microsoft (Microsoft and Facebook, 2006; Facebook and Microsoft, 2007). Following the 2005 acquisition of Myspace by News Corp. speculation arose that Facebook would also be acquired by an established firm. However, Zuckerberg rejected a $750 million bid from Viacom and a $900 million offer from Yahoo (Hansell, 2006a; Rosenbush, 2006). Additional investments in subsequent years combined with the development of revenue from operations enabled Facebook to remain independent. Through January 2011, Facebook has received investments totaling $2.24 billion (Facebook, n.d.).

Facebook has made extensive use of a tool called the application programming interface (API). An API provides an interface between the software of two entities. As a common example, when you make an online purchase with a credit card, the vendor verifies your credit card information and status through an API. Facebook officially launched the Facebook Profile on May 24, 2007. The tool enabled third party developers to create applications inside Facebook's network. For example, developers were able to display their own advertising and provide services (like games) that will generate revenues shared with Facebook. At the launch event, Facebook announced that 70 firms including Microsoft, Amazon, and *The Washington Post* were developing applications (Arrington, 2007). The Facebook Profile is the foundation upon which Facebook's revenue from operations is based. Other 2007 revenue-oriented developments included the Platform for

Mobile, classified advertising (Marketplace), and a self-service advertising platform (Timeline, n.d.).

Facebook's value to other members, advertisers, and application developers resides in the information about themselves disclosed by its nearly one billion users and the privacy of information Facebook holds from its users has been a consistent issue for the firm. A 2006 innovation, News Feed, was not well received by the growing Facebook community but Facebook responded quickly and averted an escalating problem. News Feed automatically sent notice of Facebook page updates (e.g., new friends, new posted material) to a member's entire network of friends. Users with many friends were suddenly overwhelmed by these updates. More importantly, some users protested that the practice compromised their privacy despite the fact that News Feed only disseminated information already posted to members' Facebook pages. Zuckerberg intervened and Facebook quickly provided a privacy feature but otherwise left News Feed intact. Relatively few people opted out and News Feed contributed to even more rapid growth of Facebook's online community (Thompson, 2008). In November 2007, a more serious problem developed when Facebook launched Beacon, a tool that notified members via the News Feed about their friends' purchases and other online activity connected to selected web-based firms. Along with these notifications Beacon displayed relevant ads adjacent to the News Feed updates in an online form of word-of-mouth advertising (Story & Stone, 2007). Users were able to decline tracking but only on a site-by-site basis rather than across the board. The practice led to a class action lawsuit filed in 2008 over the issue of revealing users' personal information to gain advertising revenue and the program was ended in 2009 with a settlement in which Facebook provided $9.5 million to establish an online privacy, safety, and security foundation (Ortutay, 2009).

A 2008 Facebook innovation, Facebook Connect, enabled members to log into third party websites "using their Facebook identification and see their friends' activities on those sites" (Stone, 2008, para. 2). In 2010, Facebook announced plans to replace Facebook Connect with the concept of the "Open Graph" in its continuing effort to make the web more social through increased connections. A key feature of the concept is the "Like" button introduced in April 2010. A "Like" link was added below each Facebook post (and comments on posts) that appeared in a member's News Feed and a "Like" button was added to most Facebook ads. Third party organizations were also able to install "Like" buttons. Clicking a "Like" button on a member's post, an ad, or a story in a newspaper's website notified the member's friends that the member had just "liked" something. Members could see what their friends liked online (and follow their lead) and also how many of their friends liked the same thing. At the same time Facebook possessed the ability to track its members' visits to websites that contained a "Like" link even if the member did not click on it. Nonetheless, within a year 350,000 sites had installed "Like" buttons (Gelles, 2010).

Shortly before its February 1, 2012 filing of pre-IPO documents with the SEC, Facebook settled a set of charges with the Federal Trade Commission stemming from seven specific alleged failures to abide by its stated privacy policies (Facebook settles, 2011). The FTC concluded that Facebook had misrepresented facts concerning sharing of members' data with third-party firms, especially for advertising purposes. The settlement "bars Facebook from making any further deceptive privacy claims, requires that the company get consumers' approval before it changes the way it shares their data, and requires that it obtain periodic assessments of its privacy practices by independent, third-party auditors for the next 20 years" (Facebook settles, 2011, para. 5). Facebook has agreed to follow the law and faces financial penalties if it does not.

An analysis of the relationship between the settlement with the FTC and the announced plan for an initial public offering of Facebook stock (Sengupta, 2012) observed that "Facebook's greatest achievement is also the source of its greatest challenge" (para. 7). On the one hand, Facebook has been successful in getting its members to reveal tremendous amounts of data about themselves and thereby transform the ability of advertisers to target them with messages. At the same time Facebook's privacy practices will be subject to FTC scrutiny for the next 20 years, European regulators are focusing increasing attention on the same issues, and some privacy-related lawsuits are proceeding. Kang (2012) notes the FTC settlement and increased government scrutiny of online privacy practices may benefit Facebook and other large SNS by discouraging new competitors from entering the market.

In late 2011, Facebook announced a major change that will be considered in light of escalating privacy concerns. Facebook Timeline is a feature that will convert a member's Facebook history into a biographical timeline with the most recent material at the top. Facebook started rolling out Timeline to all users in early 2012 and the change is not optional. Users will be encouraged to remove or hide content from the timeline during the first seven days following its creation. Initial concerns have been raised regarding the fact that the existing presentation of a member on Facebook focuses on recent events and activities. Members who started with Facebook in high school or college have matured and may have even forgotten about photos and other content from the past that might embarrass them now. Timeline will make all of this more easily accessible to current friends and colleagues. On February 29, 2012, Facebook announced that it would be converting the Facebook accounts of its business members to Timeline as well (Bond, 2011; Moscaritolo, 2012).

The size of Facebook and its integration with other organizations, combined with the increasing sophistication of its ability to target advertising, bode well for its future. The February 1, 2012 SEC filing details a comprehensive list of potential risks or obstacles to success in the future. Certainly increased scrutiny by governments and regulations, combined with expected continued litigation, are causes for concern. Facebook, having grown so rapidly, faces a flattening growth curve so revenue growth will require new approaches to advertising and the expansion of revenue from payments. Changes in advertising and other practices can anger or alienate members causing them to lose interest or even leave Facebook (new competitors are always a possibility). Facebook users increasingly access the network from mobile devices and the planned expansion of the Facebook Timeline to business members' accounts may inundate mobiles with frequent ads from every entity that they have ever "liked."

Conclusion

The chief difficulty experienced in writing this chapter is the fact that social media firms are quite young. Historical records are fragmentary as a great deal of important information is proprietary and will likely not be available to the public for many more years. Nonetheless, the histories of social media firms, to date, reveal several common themes. First, social networking websites have become highly integrated as content is shared across multiple platforms and audiences (members) are increasingly interconnected. This practice stands in stark contrast to practices of legacy media that maintained tight control over access to their content and audiences. Even in the Internet era, early online media sought to hold web users within so-called "walled gardens."

Second, the migration of social media content to mobile devices will accelerate as mobile devices (smart phones and tablets) become the web platform of choice. Third, as social media firms become more sophisticated in their efforts to gather user data and develop algorithms to precisely target ads, it will be increasingly difficult for consumers to guard their online privacy. At the same time the privacy issues already raised with respect to Facebook have made it rather clear that governments and regulators are ill-prepared to deal with abuses of an increasingly social web. More litigation will ensue and regulators and lawmakers will be spurred to action both in the U.S. and in other countries. These actions have the potential to change the course of social media industries but in countries like the U.S., government regulation appears to be unpopular and characterized as "anti-business." Large and powerful companies like Facebook and Google have significant financial resources with which to counter legal and regulatory threats. Further, social media have become well-integrated into the political process and are likely to come to enjoy a privileged position with respect to politicians and political organizations.

The roll-out of social media over the past decade has been impressive and new variants will continue to emerge. The relatively short history of social media shows that some did succeed for a time and then declined and were forced to change their business models. While it may seem unlikely that a new firm can supplant the present-day giants covered in this chapter, the better lesson from history is that no firm or industry is immune from decline and change.

References

About Fotolog (n.d.). Retrieved January 27, 2012 from: Fotolog Inc. http://www.fotolog.com/a/info/aboutus.

About Ryze (n.d.). Retrieved January 27, 2012 from: Ryze Business Networking. http://www.ryze.com/faq.php.

About Us. (n.d.). LinkedIn Press Center. Retrieved February 19, 2012 from: http://press.linkedin.com/about.

Angwin, J. (2006, Jan. 10). News Corp.'s Murdoch details MySpace.com.; plan site to revamp messaging, add free video downloads in bid to rival yahoo, MSN. *The Wall Street Journal*, pp. B.2–B.2. Retrieved from: http://search.proquest.com/docview/39892 3899?accountid=14690.

Arceneaux, N., & Weiss, A. (2010). Seems stupid until you try it: Press coverage of Twitter, 2006–9. *New Media & Society*, *12*(8), 1262–1279. doi:10.1177/1461444809360773.

Arrington, M. (2007, May 24). Facebook launches Facebook platform; they are the anti-MySpace. *TechCrunch*. Retrieved from: http://techcrunch.com/2007/05/24/facebook-launches-facebook-platform-they-are-the-anti-myspace/.

Bedell, D. (1998, October 27). Meeting your new best friends: Six Degrees widens your contacts in exchange for sampling Web sites. *The Dallas Morning News*. Retrieved from: http://www.dougbedell.com/sixdegrees1.html.

Beer, D. (2008). Social network(ing) sites . . . revisiting the story so far: A response to danah boyd & Nicole Ellison. *Journal of Computer-Mediated Communication*, *13*(2), 526–529. doi:10.1111/j.1083-6101.2008.00408.x.

Blood, R. (2000, September 7). Weblogs: A history and perspective. *Rebecca's Pocket*. Retrieved from: http://www.rebeccablood.net/essays/weblog_history.html.

Bond, M. (2011, November 2). Facebook Timeline a new privacy test. *USA Today*. Retrieved from: http://www.usatoday.com/tech/news/internetprivacy/story/2011-11-02/facebook-timeline-privacy/51047658/1.

boyd, d. m., & Ellison, N. B. (2008). Social network sites: Definition, history, and scholarship. *Journal of Computer-Mediated Communication*, *13*(1), 210–230. doi: 10.1111/j.1083-6101.2007.00393.x.

Boyer, A. (2001, August 24). The history of blogging: 12 years of blogs. *BlogWorld*. http://www.blogworld.com/2011/08/24/the-history-of-blogging-12-years-of-blogs/.

Bradley, A. J. (2010, January 7). A new definition of social media. [weblog post]. Gartner Group. Retrieved from: http://blogs.gartner.com/anthony_bradley/2010/01/07/a-new-definition-of-social-media/.

Chafkin, M. (2007, June 1). How to kill a great idea! *Inc. com*. Retrieved from: http://www.inc.com/magazine/20070601/features-how-to-kill-a-great-idea.html.

Chrisafis, A. (15 April 2011). French radio station founder locks himself in office in shareholder row. *The Guardian*. Retrieved from: Guardian News and Media Limited: http://www.guardian.co.uk/world/2011/apr/15/pierre-bellanger-skyrock-locks-himself-office.

Cloud, J. (2006). The YouTube Gurus. *Time*, *168*(26), 66–74.

Collins, C. (2006, October 13). It's a YouTube world. *Christian Science Monitor*, pp. 11–16.

Community Connect Inc. (n.d.). Community Connect Inc. *Bloomberg Businessweek*. Retrieved, December 13, 2011 from: http://investing.businessweek.com/research/stocks/private/snapshot.asp?privcapId=115659.

Evans, D. S. (n.d.). What Facebook's IPO filing reveals about its payments business. PYMNTS.com. Retrieved March 1, 2012 from: http://pymnts.com/briefing-room/commerce-3-0/social-commerce/What-Facebook-s-IPO-Filing-Reveals-about-Its-Payments-Business/.

Facebook (n.d.). CrunchBase companies directory. Retrieved February 25, 2012 from: http://www.crunchbase.com/company/facebook#src23.

Facebook, Inc. (2012, February 1). Form S-1 Registration Statement. Retrieved from: http://www.sec.gov/Archives/edgar/data/1326801/000119312512034517/d287954ds 1.htm.

Facebook and Microsoft expand strategic alliance. (2007, October 24). Press Release: Microsoft News Center. Retrieved from: http://www.microsoft.com/Presspass/press/2007/oct07/10-24FacebookPR.mspx.

Facebook settles FTC charges that it deceived consumers by failing to keep privacy promises (2011, November 29). Federal Trade Commission [press release]. Retrieved from: http://www.ftc.gov/opa/2011/11/privacysettlement.shtm.

Fallis, D. (2008). Toward an epistemology of Wikipedia. *Journal of The American Society for Information Science & Technology*, *59*(10), 1662–1674.

A fistful of dollars. (2012). *The Economist*, *402*(8770), 11.

Fixmer, A. (2011, June 29). News Corp. calls quits on Myspace with Specific Media sale. *Bloomberg Businessweek*. Retrieved from: http://www.businessweek.com/news/2011-06-29/news-corp-calls-quits-on-myspace-with-specific-media-sale.html.

Fletcher, D. (2009, August 18). A brief history of Wikipedia. *Time*. Retrieved from: http://www.time.com/time/business/article/0,8599,1917002,00.html.

Friendster (n.d.). Database entry. Crunchbase. Retrieved January 28, 2012 from: http://www.crunchbase.com/company/friendster.

Frommer, D. (2007, August 27). Updated: Fotolog sells to French Hi-Media Group for $90 million. *Business Insider*. Retrieved from: http://articles.businessinsider.com/2007-08-27/tech/30008896_1_ad-network-media-million-in-total-funding.

Gelles, D. (2010, September 21). E-commerce takes instant liking to Facebook button. *Financial Times*. Retrieved from: http://www.ft.com/cms/s/2/1599be2e-c5a9-11df-ab48-00144feab49a.html?=dbk#axzz1nnUGGvaC.

Gillette, F. (2011, June 22). The rise and inglorious fall of Myspace. *Bloomberg Businessweek*. Retrieved from: http://www.businessweek.com/magazine/content/11_27/b4235053 917570.htm.

Green, H. (2007, April 11). Twitter: All trivia, all the time. *Bloomberg Businessweek*. Retrieved from: http://www.businessweek.com/magazine/content/07_14/b40280 52.htm.

Grossman, L. (2012). The beast with a billion eyes. *Time*, *179*(4), 38–43.

Hampton, K. N., Goulet, L.S., Rainie, L., & Purcell K. (2011, June 16). *Social networking sites and our lives*. Pew Research Center's Internet & American Life Project, Washington, DC. http://www.pewinternet.org/~/media//Files/Reports/2011/PIP%20-%20Social %20networking%20sites%20and%20our%20lives.pdf.

Hansell, S. (2006a, April 23). Making friends was easy. Big profit is tougher. *The New York Times*. Retrieved January 29, 2012 from: http://www.nytimes.com/2006/04/23/business/yourmoney/23myspace.html?pagewanted=all.

Hansell, S. (2006b, September 22). Yahoo woos a social networking site. *The New York Times*. Retrieved from: http://www.nytimes.com/2006/09/22/technology/22facebook.html.

Heine, C. (2011, December 6). Here's what a Twitter follower costs. *ClickZ*. Retrieved from: http://www.clickz.com/clickz/news/2130610/heres-twitter-follower-costs.

Helft, M. (2006, Oct. 12). San Francisco hedge fund invested in YouTube. *The New York Times*. Retrieved from: http://www.nytimes.com/2006/10/12/technology/12hedges.html.

Hempel, J. (2010). How LinkedIn will fire up your career. *Fortune, 161*(5), 74–82.

Hendler, J., & Golbeck, J. (2008). Metcalfe's law, web 2.0, and the semantic web. *Web Semantics: Science, Services and Agents on the World Wide Web, 6*(1), 14–20. doi:10. 1016/j.websem.2007.11.008.

Hogan, B., & Quan-Haase, A. (2010). Persistence and change in social media, *Bulletin of Science, Technology, and Society, 30*(5), 309–315. doi: 10.1177/0270467610380012.

Installed base of connected devices to reach 1.34 billion in 2016. (2012, January 25). *In-Stat Market Alert*. Retrieved February 13, 2012 from: http://www.instat.com/newmk. asp?ID=3331&SourceID=00000498000000000000.

It's a social world: Top 10 need-to-knows about social networking and where it's headed. (2011, December 21). comScore, Inc. [whitepaper]. Retrieved from: http://www.com score.com/Press_Events/Presentations_Whitepapers/2011/it_is_a_social_world_top_ 10_need-to-knows_about_social_networking.

ITU. (2011). Key ICT indicators for the ITU/BDT regions (totals and penetration rates). *International Telecommunication Union*. Retrieved May 1, 2012 from: http://www.itu.int/ ITU-D/ict/statistics/at_glance/KeyTelecom.html.

Jackson, N. (2011, June 29). As Myspace sells for $35 million, a history of the network's valuation. Retrieved from: http://www.theatlantic.com/technology/archive/2011/06/ as-myspace-sells-for-35-million-a-history-of-the-networks-valuation/241224/.

Kang, C. (2012, January 30). FTC settlement gives Facebook leverage over competitors. *The Washington Post*. Retrieved from: http://www.washingtonpost.com/business/ technology/ftc-settlement-gives-facebook-leverage-over-competitors/2012/01/30/g IQA9JnfdQ_story.html.

Kaplan, A.M., & Haenlein, M. (2010). Users of the world unite! The challenges and opportunities of social media. *Business Horizons, 53*, 59–68.

Kornblum, J. (2006, January 8). Teens hang out at MySpace. *USA Today*. Retrieved from: http://www.usatoday.com/tech/news/2006-01-08-myspace-teens_x.htm#.

Lee, E. (2009, June 2). LinkedIn's startup story: Connecting the business world. *CNN Money*. Retrieved from: http://money.cnn.com/2009/06/02/smallbusiness/linkedin_ startup_story.smb/.

Levinson, P. (2009). *New new media*. Boston, MA: Allyn & Bacon.

LiveJournal, Inc. (2011). About us: The LiveJournal story. Retrieved from: http://www. livejournalinc.com/aboutus.phphttp://www.livejournalinc.com/aboutus.php.

Lombardi, C. (2007, February 2). Viacom to YouTube: Take down pirated clips. *CNET News*. Retrieved from: http://news.cnet.com/2100-1026_3-6155771.html.

LunarStorm. (2011, October 22). *Wikipedia, the free Encyclopedia*. Retrieved January 23, 2012 from: http://en.wikipedia.org/w/index.php?title=LunarStorm&oldid=45682 4666.

Mangold, W.G., & Faulds, D.J. (2009). Social media: The new hybrid element of the promotion mix. *Business Horizons, 52*, 357–365.

McAfee, A. (2009) Enterprise 2.0: New collaborative tools for your organization's toughest challenges. *Harvard Business Press*. Retrieved from: http://hbr.org/2009/12/enterprise-20-how-a-connected-workforce-innovates/ar/1.

McCullagh, D., & Broache, A. (2007, March 20). Blogs turn 10—who's the father? *CNET News*. http://news.cnet.com/2100-1025_3-6168681.html.

McKelvie, A., & Picard, R. (2008). The growth and development of new and young media firms. *Journal of Media Business Studies, 5*(1), 1–8.

Microsoft and Facebook team up for advertising syndication. (2006, August 22). Microsoft News Center [Press Release]. Retrieved from: http://www.microsoft.com/presspass/ press/2006/aug06/08-22MSFacebookPR.mspx.

Miller, C. C. (2010, April 12). Twitter unveils plans to draw money from ads. *The New York Times*. Retrieved from: http://www.nytimes.com/2010/04/13/technology/internet/13twitter.html.

Miller, C. C., & Stone, B. (2009, July 15). Hacker exposes private Twitter documents. Bits. *The New York Times*. Retrieved from: http://bits.blogs.nytimes.com/2009/07/15/hacker-exposes-private-twitter-documents/?hpw.

More great content creators coming to YouTube. (n.d.). YouTube, L. L. C. Retrieved February 13, 2012 from: http://www.youtube.com/creators/original-channels.html.

Moscaritolo, A. (2012, February 29). Facebook Timeline rolling out to business pages. *PC Magazine*. Retrieved from: http://www.pcmag.com/article2/0,2817,2400969,00.asp-x.

Mui, Y. Q. (2011, May 19). LinkedIn IPO shatters expectations. *The Washington Post*. Retrieved from: http://www.washingtonpost.com/business/economy/linkedin-ipo-shatters-expectations/2011/05/19/AF3SJR7G_story.html.

Neumeister, L. (2011, October 18). Viacom: scrap YouTube copyright ruling. *USA Today*. Retrieved from: http://www.usatoday.com/tech/news/story/2011-10-18/viacom-google-youtube-lawsuit/50817760/1.

Nielsen. (2011). *State of the media: The social media report*, Q3 2011. http://nielsen.com/us/en/insights/reports-downloads/2011/social-media-report-q3.html.

Nielsen's Tops of 2011: Digital. (2011, December 28). Nielsenwire. Retrieved from: http://blog.nielsen.com/nielsenwire/online_mobile/nielsens-tops-of-2011-digital/.

O'Brien, J. M. (2007). The PayPal mafia. *Fortune*, *156*(11), 96–106.

O'Reilly, T. (2007). What is Web 2.0?: Design patterns and business models for the next generation of software. *Communications & Strategies*, *65*(1), 17–37.

O'Reilly, T., & Battelle, J. (2009). Web squared: Web 2.0 five years on (Whitepaper). Web 2.0 Summit , October 20–22, 2009, San Francisco, CA. Retrieved from: http://assets.en.oreilly.com/1/event/28/web2009_websquared-whitepaper.pdf.

Ortutay, B. (2009, September 21). Facebook to end Beacon tracking tool in settlement. *USA Today*. Retrieved from: http://www.usatoday.com/tech/hotsites/2009-09-21-facebook-beacon_N.htm.

Ovide, S. (2011, April 6). YouTube's history: Google's repeated revamps. *The Wall Street Journal*. Retrieved from: http://blogs.wsj.com/deals/2011/04/06/youtubes-history-googles-repeated-revamps/#.

The people formerly known as the audience [special report]. (2011). *The Economist*, July, *9400*(8741), 9–12.

Percival, S. (2009). *My Space marketing: Creating a social network to boom your business.* Indianapolis, IN: Que.

Picard, R. G. (2011). *Mapping digital media: Digitization and media business models.* London: Open Society Foundations.

Rivlin, G. (2006, October 15). Wallflower at the web party. *The New York Times*. Retrieved from: http://www.nytimes.com/2006/10/15/business/yourmoney/15friend.html?pagewanted=1.

Rosenbush, S. (2005, June 13). Hey, come to this site often? *Bloomberg Businessweek*, (3937), 66–67. Retrieved from: http://www.businessweek.com/magazine/content/05_24/b3937077_mz063.htm.

Rosenbush, S. (2006, March 28). Facebook's on the block. *Bloomberg Business Week*. Retrieved from: http://www.businessweek.com/technology/content/mar2006/tc2006 0327_21597_htm.

Seabrook, J. (2012, January 16). Streaming dreams. *The New Yorker*. Retrieved from: http://www.newyorker.com/reporting/2012/01/16/120116fa_fact_seabrook?currentPage=all.

Sellers, P. (2006, August 29). Myspace cowboys. *Fortune, 154*(5), 66–74. Retrieved from: http://money.cnn.com/magazines/fortune/fortune_archive/2006/09/04/8384727/index.htm.

Sengupta, S. (2012, February 26). Risk and riches in user data for Facebook. *The New York Times*. Retrieved from: http://www.nytimes.com/2012/02/27/technology/for-facebook-risk-and-riches-in-user-data.html?pagewanted=all.

Shedden, D. (2010). *New media timeline (1969–2010)*. Poynter Institute. Retrieved from: http://www.poynter.org/ latest-news/business-news/transformation-tracker/28803/new-media-timeline-1969-2010/.

Sifry, D. (2004, October 10). State of the blogosphere, October 2004. *Sifry's Alerts* [Web log post]. Retrieved from: http://www.sifry.com/alerts/archives/000245.html.

Smarty, A. (n.d.). The evolution of three home pages: Facebook, Twitter and LinkedIn. Retrieved from: http://www.seosmarty.com/the-evolution-of-three-home-pages-facebook-twitter-and-linkedin/.

Sorkin, A. R., & Peters, J. W. (2006, October 9). Google to acquire YouTube for $1.65 billion. *The New York Times*. Retrieved from: http://www.nytimes.com/2006/10/09/business/09cnd-deal.html.

Stone, B. (2008, November 30). Facebook aims to extend its reach across the web. *The New York Times*. Retrieved from: http://www.nytimes.com/2008/12/01/technology/internet/01facebook.html?_r=1&pagewanted=1&partner=rss&emc=rss.

Story, L., & Stone, B. (2007, November 30). Facebook retreats on online tracking. *The New York Times*. Retrieved from: http://www.nytimes.com/2007/11/30/technology/30face.html.

Swartz, J. (2011, April 12). Court sides with Facebook against Winklevoss twins. *USA Today*. Retrieved from: http://www.usatoday.com/tech/news/2011-04-1_facebook-winklevoss-settlement.htm.

Tartakoff, J. (2010, March 29). *The (short) history of Twitter's plans to make money*. PDA: The digital content blog. Guardian News and Media Ltd. Retrieved from: http://www.guardian.co.uk/media/pda/2010/mar/29/twitter-making-money.

Tebay, A. (2011, November 8). Korea's Cyworld takes second shot at going global, but service issues still linger. *The Next Web*. Retrieved from: http://thenextweb.com/asia/2011/11/08/koreas-cyworld-takes-second-shot-at-going-global-but-service-issues-still-linger/.

Technorati.com. (2011, November 4). State of the Blogosphere 2011: Introduction and methodology. Retrieved from: http://technorati.com/blogging/article/state-of-the-blogosphere-2011-introduction/page-2/ (p. 2).

The trouble with YouTube. (2006). *The Economist, 380*(8493), 57–58.

The value of friendship. (2012). *The Economist, 402*(8770), 23–26.

Thompson, C. (2008, September 5). Brave new world of digital intimacy. *The New York Times*. Retrieved from: http://www.nytimes.com/2008/09/07/magazine/07awareness-t.html?_r=1&oref=slogin.

Timeline. (n.d.). *Facebook Newsroom Timeline*. Retrieved February 25, 2012 from: http://newsroom.fb.com/content/default.aspx?NewsAreaId=20.

Trewe, M. (2011, December 7). Obtaining a Twitter follower through promoted tweets costs $2.50 to $4.00. *AdBeat*. Retrieved from: http://adbeat.com/real-estate-technology-new-media/obtaining-a-twitter-follower-through-promoted-tweets-costs-2-50-to-4-00/.

Tsukayama, H. (2012, January 12). YouTube: the future of entertainment is on the Web. *The Washington Post*. Retrieved from: http://www.washingtonpost.com/business/

technology/youtube-the-future-of-entertainment-is-on-the-web/2012/01/12/gIQAD pdBuP_story.html.

Twitter. (n.d.). CrunchBase. Retrieved February 24, 2012 from: http://www.crunchbase. com/company/twitter.

Twitter basics. (n.d.). Twitter help center. Retrieved February 24, 2012 from: https:// support.twitter.com/groups/31-twitter-basics.

W3Techs (Q-Success). (2011, November 1). *W3Techs – World Wide Web technology surveys.* Retrieved from: http://w3techs.com/.

Walsh, J. (2012, January 2). Wikimedia fundraiser concludes with record breaking donations [Web log post]. Retrieved from: http://blog.wikimedia.org/c/community/fundraising/ fundraiser-2011/.

Welcome to (the new) CitizenTube! (2008, April 23). *YouTube CitizenTube.* Retrieved from: http://www.citizentube.com/2008/04/welcome-to-new-citizentube.html.

What are political ads? (n.d.). Twitter help center. Retrieved February 24, 2012 from: https://support.twitter.com/articles/20169454.

What are promoted accounts? (n.d.). Twitter help center. Retrieved February 24, 2012 from: https://support.twitter.com/articles/282154-promoted-accounts.

What does LinkedIn do? (n.d.). Investor FAQs. LinkedIn investor relations. Retrieved February 19, 2012 from: http://investors.linkedin.com/faq.cfm.

Wikipedia. (n.d.). In Wikipedia. Retrieved February 8, 2012 from: http://en.wikipedia. org/wiki/Wikipedia.

Wikipedia: About. (n.d.). In Wikipedia. Retrieved February 8, 2012 from: http://en. wikipedia.org/wiki/Wikipedia:About.

Wikipedia Guidelines. (n.d.). Wikipedia.org. Retrieved February 8, 2012 from: http://en.wikipedia.org/wiki/Wikipedia:About.

Wood, D. B. (2006, December 18). The YouTube world opens an untamed frontier for copyright law. *The Christian Science Monitor.* Retrieved from: http://www.csmonitor. com/2006/1218/p01s03-usju.html.

YouTube model is compromise over copyrights. (2006, Sept. 19). *The Wall Street Journal.* Retrieved from: http://online.wsj.com/public/article/SB115862128600366836- pJip_ NHyQ7j0b44svDZ2kgHCYfs_20070918.html?mod=blogs.

Zakon, R. H. (2010). *Hobbes' Internet Timeline.* Retrieved from: http://www.zakon.org/ robert/internet/timeline/.

3

THE PARADOXES OF SOCIAL MEDIA

A Review of Theoretical Issues

Francisco J. Pérez-Latre

Introduction

The brave new world of social media has captured the attention of scholars and book authors around the world, which has led to the publication of a number of works on Twitter, Facebook, YouTube, LinkedIn and the like (Breitbarth, 2011; Comm, 2009; Holzner, 2008; Kirkpatrick, 2010; McFedries & Cashmore, 2009; Miller, 2008; O'Reilly & Milstein, 2009; Shih, 2009; Whitlock & Micek, 2008). Most of these books are practical and industry-based in nature and do not consider in depth the social media impact on audiences and communication strategies. Nevertheless, the vitality of book publishing in this subject illustrates the research relevance that social media and social networks are acquiring.

boyd and Ellison (2008) have summarized recent research and social network history. The authors, Berkeley and Michigan State professors, consider social media are fascinating topics for researchers because of their usefulness, audience size and market research potential. They define social networks as web-based services that allow users to build a public or semi-public profile within a system; articulate a user list with shared relationships; and observe the list of relationships of those persons with other people within the system (boyd and Ellison, 2008).

boyd and Ellison explain that SixDegrees (1997) was chronologically the first social network but it disappeared in 2000. The most important current social networks were established after 2002: Fotolog (2002), LinkedIn (2003), Myspace (2003), Last.FM (2003), Hi5 (2003), Orkut (2004), Flickr (2004), Facebook (2004), YouTube (2005), Bebo (2005), Ning (2005), and Twitter (2006). From 2003 on, social networks reached the mainstream, and started producing audience figures considered to be "massive." The audience growth of social networks has been explosive. In April 2009, Facebook had 200 million users worldwide: in March 2010, it had reached 400 million. By November 2011, Facebook's estimated audience is more than 775 million users.[1] Only 26% of the users are in the United States, indicating we are talking about a genuinely global phenomenon. Twitter shows more modest audience figures (19 million in March 2009;

75 million in March 2010). Nevertheless, the figures speak for themselves and will give Facebook, Twitter, YouTube and LinkedIn a place in the history of communications. Papacharissi (2009) has compared Facebook and LinkedIn as a means of communication, and also analyzed Twitter, and specifically its role in the Egyptian revolution of 2011 (Papacharissi & de Fatima Oliveira, 2011).

Books on Social Media

Arguably, four books have been especially influential and are often quoted in professional and academic circles in this context: (1) Tapscott and Williams' (2006) *Wikinomics*; (2) Jenkins's (2006) *Convergence Culture*; (3) Li and Bernoff's (2008) *Groundswell*; and (4) Qualman's (2011) *Socialnomics*.

Tapscott and Williams (2006) consider social networks as a part of a wider trend in communication landscapes. They characterize it as "mass collaboration." In their opinion, transparency, peer collaboration, audience participation and globalization are changing markets and companies. Social media like YouTube or Myspace are crucial. A new type of market is being shaped: copyright, communication strategy and message control by hierarchical management structures are increasingly under attack. Wikipedia is described as symbolic of this process that is influencing the communication of brands, fashion, markets, ideas and ideology.

Jenkins (2006) described three concepts that shape what he called "convergence culture": media convergence, participatory culture and collective intelligence. By media convergence, Jenkins means the content flow between multiple content platforms and the audience's migratory behavior in that people are fundamentally looking for brief entertainment experiences. By the term "participatory culture," the author underlined the contrast with the idea of a passive viewer in the days when producers and consumers had clearly different roles. Now the users interact with rules that we don't seem to understand fully yet. By collective intelligence, Jenkins elaborates on a trend to turn consumption into a collective process, sharing our knowledge to cope with the sheer volume of available information. Social media has developed in this unique convergence, participation and "crowd-sourcing" environment.

Li and Bernoff (2008), two Forrester Research[2] analysts, showed through 25 real-life case studies how companies increase their market knowledge, generate income, save money and mobilize their employees using "social technologies." Such firms followed the "groundswell" model, similar to a wave that sweeps markets. Li and Bernoff state that there is a definite social trend for people to use technologies to get what they need from other people, instead of relying on traditional institutions such as companies. The consequences are relevant: control by the company is weakened and reduced. Li and Bernoff stressed the need to understand how new relationships have been created in social media; the technologies have changed, but the impact on personal relationships has been even more profound.

Qualman (2011) also discusses the "social media revolution." The author describes an age of instant communication, transparency (we live according to what he terms the "glass–house effect"), narcissism and participation. It is a landscape where authenticity is a currency of exchange and mass communications do not work, as audiences go back to trust in people close to them, and the influence of traditional media declines. Qualman also explores Obama's rise to power and offers some future indications of what might happen in expressions such as "what happens in Vegas stays in YouTube" or "we will no longer look for the news, the news will find us."

Qualman looks at the social media phenomenon and assesses its impact on interpersonal relationships, showing how strategy, marketing and markets are influenced, and explores how some brands feel very comfortable in such a context. In his opinion, social media are more a revolution than an ephemeral fashion.

Discussion and Implications

Since 2006, researchers' attention has turned to social networks, especially in the United States, where they were established. Research has considered different aspects of social media.[3] Some papers have concentrated on the "management of impressions" by the audience, investigating how users introduce themselves and build "a profile," and the quality of relationships that are generated in this context (Back, Stopfer, Vazire, Gaddis, Schmukle, Egloff, & Gosling, 2010; Davis, 2010; Hargittai & Hsieh, 2010; Zywica & Danowski, 2008). Marwick (2005) analyzed the degree of authenticity of users' profiles. Looking into their different roles, Kumar, Novak, and Tomkins (2006) divided users into two different groups: passive users and "connectors," who participate fully in the networks' social evolution.

Most available research suggests that the majority of social networks serve a need to reinforce existing relationships. We could say that they cater to a need: building bridges between the online and offline worlds. Ellison, Steinfield and Lampe (2007) suggest that Facebook is used to strengthen "offline" friendships more than to meet new people (see also Back, et al., 2010). Such relationships could be thin, but often there are previous links, like attending the same college.

Another key research thread deals with issues of privacy and intimacy generated by social networks. Sometimes the need for a safe environment for children and adolescents was emphasized, as in works by George (2006) or Kornblum and Marklein (2006). It is especially worthwhile to study what Barnes (2006) defined as the "privacy paradox." Acquisti and Gross (2006) described the "disconnect" between the goal of protecting users' privacy and their social network behavior (increasingly narcissistic, to say the least), also described in Stutzman's research (2006). Dwyer, Hiltz, and Passerini (2007) explained that Facebook saw off Myspace precisely because of its better ability to deal with privacy. Researchers agree that the most serious crisis faced by social networks have been related to privacy and personal data protection. Myspace's audience decrease and Friendster's decline have been related to this (boyd, 2006).

Social networks might also be a tool for audience and market segmentation and the analysis of specific or "niche" audiences. Different authors have studied their use by audiences defined by gender (Van Doorn, 2010), ethnicity (Gajjala, 2007), language (Honeycutt & Cunliffe, 2010) or religion (Nyland & Near, 2007). Specifically, ethnicity has often been researched in the U.S., as some of the better-established social networks are used to connect ethnic minorities. Such is the case of AsianAvenue, AsianAve today (established in 1999), BlackPlanet (1999), and MiGente, launched in 2000. Along the same lines, Fragoso (2006) studied the role of national identity to explain Orkut's[4] spectacular success in Brazil. Some other authors have studied the role of social networks in different cultures, which opens up a very interesting field for research (Herring, Paolillo, Ramos Vielba, Kouper, Wright, Stoerger, Scheidt, & Clark, 2007). It is in fact worthwhile to find out whether social networks are more successful in some cultures or countries, or the rationale for local versus global social networks.

There are also a number of issues related to education. Some authors have researched students' reaction to educators' presence in Facebook (Hewitt & Forte, 2006) and how student–faculty relationships are influenced (Mazer, Murphy, & Simonds, 2007). Students are typically ahead of faculty in social media terms, as Kalamas, Mitchell and Lester (2009) have shown. This new landscape is a source of relevant educational challenges, such as those explored by Caravella, Ekachai, Jaeger and Zahay (2009) in their research on education in advertising. The impact of social media in learning is also discussed by other authors (Greenhow, 2011; Junco, 2012).

Researchers have also been looking to the future, trying to find out what the social networks' life cycle will be. Along these lines, boyd (2006) studied the rise and decline of Friendster, a social network established to compete with match.com in 2002. As its market share in the U.S. fell, Friendster was winning popularity in Asia (especially in the Philippines, Singapore, Malaysia and Indonesia), where it still was a relevant social network as recently as 2007 (Goldberg, 2007). Friendster's case is interesting to see what the future of social networks might be, and what kind of mistakes might be fatal to their future. In the past few years several authors have analyzed Myspace's audience decline (Davis, 2010; Wilkinson & Thelwall, 2010).

In hindsight, the 2008 U.S. election might well be considered a turning point in social media research. Social networks were showcased, and their use is almost universally recognized as being critical in the campaign's outcome. Books by Harfoush (2009), Libert and Faulk (2009) and Plouffe[5] (2009) have studied the campaign's communication strategy principles. Chris Hughes, one of Facebook's co-founders, had a critical role in designing the website mybarackobama.com that used social media to connect. According to McGirt (2009), the results were impressive: two million personal profiles were created on the website; 200,000 events were planned and 35,000 groups were established, and the campaign raised $30 million online. The campaign has often been considered a paradigm in strategic campaigns based on social media. Political strategies are increasingly based on two social media principles: dialogue and participation. A Harvard Business School case examines this subject (Piskorski & Winig, 2009). The influence of social media in politics is a frequent research topic (Baumgartner & Morris, 2010; Fuchs, 2011a, 2011b; Vitak, Zube, Smock, Carr, Ellison, & Lampe, 2011).

Researchers have looked at a variety of other public health, social, cultural, business or commercial issues, such as social networking sites and the marketing of alcohol (Griffiths & Casswell, 2010); the role of youth in cultural production (Greenhow, 2011); play and gaming in social media (Hjorth, 2010); social media's role in what some authors call the "surveillance society" (Fuchs, 2011b); and their implications for enterprises (Richter, Riemer, & Vom Brocke, 2011).

Media management scholars are also looking at the field. Picard (2009) discusses the role of social media technology in the news business. The author suggests that if the technology does not generate money, the reasoning needs to be clear as to why technology has been used, and strategies must be developed for each platform that links users to news organizations to measure performance and maximize the return on investment. In Picard's opinion, the enthusiasm of media companies for social media and the web 2.0 is not fully justified.

Some Preliminary Conclusions and Future Research

After Wikileaks, the widespread BlackBerry use in the London riots, the "occupy Wall Street campaign," or the "wired" Arab Spring (with its dangers and risks but also its great changes and hopes), it is hard to argue against the value of social media and the new communities it tends to create, often bypassing traditional media and institutions, and causing speedily profound effects. Facebook, with more than 800 million users worldwide, has already established a place in the history of communication (and a 2010 *Time* magazine Man of the Year for Zuckerberg). Twitter is already the leading place for breaking news.

In the media we have always faced lights and shadows, problems and opportunities. Somehow the world is in our hands; we are only one click away from updated and interesting content. Anyone can have a global audience. At the same time, being so close to news, entertainment and games is a source of distractions and is pushing the audience in the direction of instant gratification, close to addiction, and other social and psychological problems.

In this social media landscape, limiting Internet and mobile access is not the best educational option. However, at this point and after all the things we have learned, it would not be reasonable to ignore the dangers of digital media. Most of the issues already existed in analog media: excessive consumption, proliferation of content against human dignity, lack of editing and the exploitation of sensationalism. Let's consider four areas.

Online life cannot replace offline life. In other words, technology is at the service of humans and should make us more sociable. Technologies could potentially foster anonymity. In digital communication we often lack the visual and verbal clues we have in face-to-face encounters. But it is also true that now we have the ability to reach more people and be somewhat closer to them. The proliferation of "friends," a positive and interesting development in itself, also provokes the potential growth of encounters with strangers and other issues. The risk of stalking and "cyberbullying" increases.

Some audiences show a disturbing lack of empathy that could be facilitated by the "automatism" and distance of online communications. Part of the audience, more than talking, prefers to send messages. Texting is replacing talking. Total connectivity is already leading to symptoms of addiction and lack of memory.

One of the paradoxes of digital communication is the tension between isolation and thirst for contact with friends and colleagues. On one hand, some seem to take refuge in virtual relations replacing direct conversations, because they lack empathy and "social competence." On the other, the number of "friends" increases and the relationship to persons closer to us intensifies. Isolation would be an indicator that communication is not properly working. If we make adequate use of digital communications, then we will get closer to the people that matter to us. Getting closer to people is a constant of human communication that always finds new ways to reassert itself.

Sometimes the distinction between online life and offline life can be confusing. Online or virtual life is real (although it is not "physical"). In other words, online life is as real as life itself, an opportunity for us to display personalities and exercise virtue (or show our defects). Those who show respect in real life, also do it online. The web is a public square where we are always portrayed. That is why there is a need for etiquette in this age of "trolls" and angry mobs. If you look at comments on blogs, Twitter, Facebook, YouTube or online newspapers you will find users who, hiding in anonymity, insult, sow the seeds of hatred and are generally hostile and angry. The net is an extension of personal relationships. There is a need to promote honest and open communication, optimism, respect and good manners. There is a pending revolution: the revolution of kindness.

The "narcissism epidemics" (Twenge & Campbell, 2009) is another fascinating issue. People become narcissistic on the web to an extent that probably was unknown in human history. But, somewhat paradoxically, they make that compatible with an extraordinary zeal to protect their privacy. Some have talked about a "me generation" that is actively seeking "visibility." They seem to be tireless self-promoters in the search of an ever increasing popularity. In social media we "create profiles" (a significant expression) that are improved versions of ourselves. This is an often ambiguous process that is part of the same process that allows us to have a global network of "friends" and followers. In fact, entire social networks like Friendster failed because of the lack of privacy protection, and arguably some of the worst Facebook crises are related to this.

The "cloud" stores significant amounts of information on citizens: pictures, words, videos. We often have lost track of the content and forgotten its existence but it is still there and could surface at any time, causing possible havoc. We do not keep our "box of letters." Are we losing our memory and even our capacity to archive? That is one of the reasons behind some movements to demand the power to "erase" our online history. There is an open conversation about a "right to be forgotten," selecting contents with respect to consumer image and dignity. In general, the audience needs more knowledge to understand the risks behind the age of "total transparency." Sharing absolutely everything is probably not a good idea. The "self-promoter" can find himself in very dangerous territory.

The extraordinary abundance of information is another fascinating topic that affects media and other content consumption, but also media quality (Kovach & Rosenstiel, 2010). We have access to a previously unthinkable amount of data but we often lack the context for it and even the possibility of interpreting it. The increase in the quantity of information is not going to make us necessarily wiser.

We have built amazing information highways, but have forgotten to teach how to drive. With more news and data, we will need more filtering and better selection. There is a stronger need to establish a hierarchy of information, gatekeeping, and search for solid evidence. The best information sources have an added value. Audiences will need additional ability to assess and select the best menu and make the best use of their time. At the same time, the abundance of information is more a blessing than a problem. The public has access to more content (often for free), and has the potential to expand their information, research and knowledge access.

Digital communication and mobile tools have enormously increased the speed of breaking news, the global diffusion of trends and ideas and real-time participation in events. The speed of information is provoking outstanding effects on reputation, natural catastrophes and humanitarian crises, political campaigns, grassroots movements and economic crises. At the same time, speed is a source of multiple errors, helps to spread toxic rumors that can be lethal, and generally makes fact-checking and quality more difficult. Now everybody is a journalist, but nobody is an editor. Speed is already crucial. But we need to underline the need for reflection and pause to avoid costly mistakes. We need to emphasize quality and accuracy.

There needs to be attention not only to the ability to communicate but also the content of the communication. The leaders of the riots in Britain were sophisticated BlackBerry users, but the content of their messages speaks of broken personalities that go viral, spreading damage. At the same time, the Arab Spring would probably not have been possible without significant communication technologies in place in Tunisia or Egypt.

We are "always on," connected to the world, using computers or mobile phones, Twitter, Facebook, LinkedIn, or email. We need to be online to be close to friends, family and colleagues, or keep in touch with professional networks.

There is no easy way out: if you are not part of the networks, you can really fall behind professionally. But permanent connection is also a source of new anxieties, and the traditional borders between professional and personal life are increasingly blurred. At the same time there are interesting movements that promote "slower" forms of communication, calling openly for an ability to disconnect (Carr, 2011). Some people are looking to open "offline" spaces and expanded times for friendship and relaxation. They try to "disconnect to connect."

To some extent, researchers are finding a very real "nostalgia of disconnection" that becomes all the more valuable because too many people are unable to achieve it. Again, paradoxically, those who are always connected will not be able to start and pursue valuable long-term projects. They will become enslaved to the continuous flux of news, gaming and entertainment and thus will see their efficiency and productivity reduced.

Research suggests some differences between social media and the rest of "online media." Social media calls for a new audience relationship framework. Some rules seemed to be emerging for environments shaped by such audiences: authenticity, participation, transparency, and relevance. There seems to be a premium in avoiding commercial interruptions. Communications between individuals that are potentially always connected to the Internet, and often on the move, will be an area of growing interest for researchers.

Consumers are driving markets, and the Internet changes the way consumers learn, gather information and relate to each other. Advertising tries to arouse consumer participation in all the brands' contact points. Social networks have become a significant research tool and a way to communicate directly with consumers. Strategic planners in advertising use social networks for consumer intelligence, trying to deepen users' knowledge. This represents another area for further research.

In social networks, although their audience growth has been spectacular, there are still significant doubts regarding business models. Their early life has been funded by large bets by investors based on non-proven expectations about their potential. But this market situation will not last forever. Therefore, research on advertising effectiveness will be crucial. What are going to be the most interesting advertising messages in a social media environment? What is going to be effective? Advertising is a key source of income for social media survival but interruption-based models are unlikely to work.

Nevertheless, researchers will still be looking to understand not only the ever-changing technology, but also audience relationships. Markets have become conversations and the consequences are far-reaching. It is interesting to see to what extent we go back to the beginning. From mass communication media the flow of messages goes back to person-to-person communication, as Lazarsfeld explained in his classic work, *Personal Influence* (1955). When Lasswell defined mass media rules, he was indicating that a radio station or a newspaper could be compared with a person communicating messages. But now the emphasis is again on person-to-person communication and it is increasingly clear that an individual who reads something and discusses it with others cannot be considered only as a social entity, analogous to a newspaper or magazine: the individual needs to be studied in the double capacity as both communicator and contact point in a mass communication network (Lazarsfeld, 1955).

The need for human contact and interaction is a constant that always finds new ways to express itself. Some could argue that the present passion for social media will give way to some skepticism. But we seem to be witnessing more than an ephemeral passion. Qualman (2011) describes a "social media revolution." In any case, and paraphrasing Lazarsfeld, we have person-to-person communication once more at the very core of media, communications strategies and academic conversations.

A review of theoretical issues raises key questions that will need to be explored by researchers more thoroughly in the future. Some are related to advertising effectiveness and the place for advertising messages in social media platforms that are deemed personal territory; some are related to the way online and offline media connect and interact; some are on communication effects, the way information is learned in social media environments and the impact of speed in communication; some are on the increasing need to foster a dialogue with audiences that are used to participate and interact. As "localization apps" go mainstream, there will be more interest in social media and "geolocalization." There will also be increasing research on how mobile platforms relate to social media use and with "social TV," where users participate in actual TV programs through Facebook and Twitter, apparently using several "media" platforms simultaneously.

Some other "paradoxes" also require further research: the tension between privacy and increased transparency; the relationship between "online" and "offline," virtual and real lives in a "blurred context"; the ability of audiences to organize information in an age of increasing overload; the "downsides" of being always connected in this economy of attention and how the value of information has always been related to scarcity.

Notes

1   See http://www.checkfacebook.com/ for updated Facebook use figures.
2   Forrester is a company specializing in digital audiences research.
3   danah boyd, one of the key researchers in the field, keeps an updated bibliographical list of social networks at http://www.danah.org/researchBibs/sns.php. She also keeps an updated list on Twitter and microblogging at: http://www.danah.org/research Bibs/twitter.php.
4   Orkut is a social network established by Google.
5   David Plouffe was Obama's campaign manager.

References

Acquisti, A., & Gross, R. (2006). Imagined communities: Awareness, information sharing, and privacy on the Facebook. In P. Golle, & G. Danezis (Eds.), *Proceedings of 6th workshop on privacy enhancing technologies* (pp. 36–58). Cambridge: Robinson College.

Back, M. D., Stopfer, J. M., Vazire, S., Gaddis, S., Schmukle, S. C., Egloff, B., & Gosling, S. D. (2010). Facebook profiles reflect actual personality, not self-idealization. *Psychological Science, 21*(3), 372–374.

Bae Brandtzæg, P., & Lüders, M. (2010). Too many Facebook "friends"? Content sharing and sociability versus the need for privacy in social network sites. *International Journal of Human–Computer Interaction, 26*(11), 1006–1030.

Baker, S. (2009, June 1). What's a friend worth? *BusinessWeek*, pp. 32–36.

Barnes, S. (2006). A privacy paradox: Social networking in the United States. *First Monday, 11*(9). Retrieved from: http://www.firstmonday.org/issues/issue11_9/barnes/index.html.

Baumgartner, J. C., & Morris, J. S. (2010). MyFaceTube politics: Social networking websites and political engagement of young adults. *Social Science Computer Review, 28*(1), 24–44.

Bohnert, D., & Ross, W. (2010). The influence of social networking websites on the evaluation of job candidates, *Cyberpsychology, Behavior, & Social Networking, 13*(3), 341–347.

boyd, d. (2006). Friendster lost steam. Is MySpace just a fad? *Apophenia Blog*. Retrieved from: http://www.danah.org/papers/FriendsterMySpaceEssay.html.

boyd, d.m., & Ellison, N. (2008). Social network sites: Definition, history and scholarship. *Journal of Computer-Mediated Communication, 13*(1), 210–230.

Breitbarth, W. (2011). *The power formula for LinkedIn success: Kick-start your business, brand, and job search*. Austin, TX: Greenleaf.

Bringué, X., & Sádaba, C. (2011). *Menores y redes sociales*. Madrid: Fundación Telefónica.

Caravella, M., Ekachai, D. G., Jaeger, C., & Zahay, D. (2009). Web 2.0 Opportunities and challenges for advertising educators. *Journal of Advertising Education, 13*(1), 58–63.

Carr, N. (2011). *The shallows: What the Internet is doing to our brains*. New York: W.W. Norton & Company.

Collins, T. (2009). *The little book of Twitter: Get tweetwise*. London: Michael O'Mara Books Limited.

Comm, J. (2009). *Twitter power: How to dominate your market one tweet at a time*. Hoboken, NJ: Wiley.

Cooke, M., & Buckley, N. (2007). Web 2.0, social networks and the future of market research. *International Journal of Market Research, 50*(2), 267–291.

Coyle, C. L., & Vaughn, H. (2008). Social networking: Communication revolution or evolution? *Bell Labs Technical Journal, 13*(2), 13–17.

Davis, J. (2010). Architecture of the personal interactive homepage: Constructing the self through MySpace. *New Media and Society, 12*(7), 1103–1119.

Dwyer, C., Hiltz, S.R., & Passerini, K. (2007). Trust and privacy concern within social networking sites: A comparison of Facebook and MySpace. In *Proceedings of AMCIS 2007*, Keystone, CO. Retrieved from: http://csis.pace.edu/~dwyer/research/Dwyer AMCIS2007.pdf.

Ellison, N. B., Steinfield, C., & Lampe, C. (2007). The benefits of Facebook "friends:" Social capital and college students' use of online social network sites. *Journal of Computer-Mediated Communication, 12*(4), 1143–1168.

Fragoso, S. (2006). WTF a crazy Brazilian invasion. In F. Sudweeks, & H. Hrachovec (Eds.), *Proceedings of CATac 2006*, Murdoch University, Murdoch, Australia.

Fuchs, C. (2011a). Social networking sites and complex technology assessment. *International Journal of E-Politics, 1*(3), 19–38.

Fuchs, C. (2011b). studiVZ: Social networking sites in the surveillance society. *Ethics and Information Technology, 12*(2), 171–185.

Gajjala, R. (2007). Shifting frame: Race, ethnicity, and intercultural communications in online social networking and virtual work. In M. B. Hinner (Ed.), *The role of communication in business transactions and relationships* (pp. 257–276). New York: Peter Lang.

George, A. (2006, September 18). Living online: The end of privacy? *New Scientist, 2569*. Retrieved from: http://www.newscientist.com/channel/tech/mg19125691.700-living-online-the-end-of-privacy.html.

Goldberg, S. (2007). Analysis: Friendster is doing just fine. Digital Media Wire, May 13. Retrieved June 2010 from: http://www.dmwmedia.com/news/2007/05/14/analysis-friendster-is-doing-just-fine.

Greenhow, C. (2011). Learning and social media: What are the interesting questions for research? *International Journal of Cyber Behavior, Psychology and Learning, 1*(1), 36–50.

Griffiths, R., & Casswell, S. (2010). Intoxigenic digital spaces? Youth, social networking sites and alcohol marketing. *Drug and Alcohol Review, 29*(5), 525–530.

Harfoush, R. (2009). *Yes we did: An inside look at how social media built the Obama brand.* Berkeley, CA: New Riders.

Hargittai, E. (2007). Whose space? Differences among users and non-users of social network sites. *Journal of Computer-Mediated Communication, 13*(1), 276–297.

Hargittai, E., & Hsieh, Y. P. (2010). Predictors and consequences of differentiated practices on social network sites. *Information, Communication & Society, 13*(4), 515–536.

Herring, S.C., Paolillo, J.C., Ramos Vielba, I., Kouper, I., Wright, E., Stoerger, S., Scheidt, L. A., & Clark. B. (2007). Language networks on LiveJournal. In *Proceedings of Fortieth Hawai'i International Conference on System Science*. Los Alamitos, CA: IEEE Press.

Hewitt, A., & Forte, A. (2006). Crossing boundaries: Identity management and student/faculty relationships on the Facebook. Poster presented at CSCW, Banff, Alberta, November.

Hjorth, L. (2010). The game of being social: Web 2.0, social media, and online games. *Iowa Journal of Communication, 42*(1), 73–92.

Hjorth, L., & Arnold, M. (2011). The personal and the political: Social networking in Manila. *International Journal for Learning and Media, 3*(1), 29–39.

Holzner, S. (2008). *Facebook marketing: Leverage social media to grow your business.* London: Que Publishing.

Honeycutt, C., & Cunliffe, D. (2010). The use of the Welsh language on Facebook: An initial investigation. *Information, Communication and Society, 13*(2), 226–248.

Jenkins, H. (2006). *Convergence culture: Where old and new media collide.* New York: New York University Press.

Junco, R. (2012). Too much face and not enough books: The relationship between multiple indices of Facebook use and academic performance. *Computers in Human Behavior, 28*(1): 187–198.

Kalamas, M., Mitchell, T., & Lester, D. (2009). Modeling social media use: Bridging the gap in higher education. *Journal of Advertising Education, 13*(1), 44–57.

Kirkpatrick, D. (2010). *The Facebook effect: The inside story of the company that is connecting the world.* New York: Simon & Schuster.

Kornblum, J., & Marklein, M.B. (2006, March 8). What you say online could haunt you. *USA Today*. Retrieved from: http://www.usatoday.com/tech/news/internetprivacy/2006-03-08-facebook-myspace_x.htm.

Kovach, B., & Rosenstiel T. (2010). *Blur: How to know what's true in the age of information overload*. New York: Bloomsbury.

Kozinets, R.V. (2002). The field behind the screen: Using netnography for marketing research in online communities. *Journal of Marketing Research*, *39*(1), 61–72.

Kozinets, R.V. (2006). Click to connect: Netnography and tribal advertising. *Journal of Advertising Research*, *46*(3), 279–288.

Kumar R., Novak, J., & Tomkins, A. (2006). Structure and evolution of online social networks. In *Proceedings of 12th International Conference of Knowledge Discovery in Data Mining* (pp. 611–617). New York: ACM Press.

Kushner, S. (2011). Virtually dead: Blogospheric absence and the ethics of networked reading. *The Communication Review*, *14*(1), 24–45.

Lampe, C., Ellison, N. B., & Steinfield, C. (2006). A Face(book) in the crowd: Social searching vs. social browsing. In *Proceedings of the 2006 20th Anniversary Conference on Computer Supported Cooperative Work* (pp. 167–170). New York: ACM Press.

La Rocca, G. (2010). Follow me on academia.edu: Analysis of a distraction online and of its consequences on daily life. *Journal of Comparative Research in Anthropology and Sociology*, *1*(2), 89–104.

Lazarsfeld, P. (1955). *Personal influence: The part played by people in the flow of mass communications*. New York: Free Press.

Li, C., & Bernoff, J. (2008). *Groundswell: Winning in a world transformed by social technologies*. Boston: Harvard Business Press.

Libert, B., & Faulk, R. (2009). *Obama Inc.: El éxito de una campaña de marketing*. Madrid: Prentice Hall/Financial Times.

Marwick, A. (2005). "I'm a lot more interesting than a Friendster profile." Identity presentation, authenticity and power in social networking services. Paper presented at Internet Research 6.0, Chicago, October.

Mazer, J. P., Murphy, R. E., & Simonds, C. J. (2007). I'll see you on Facebook: The effects of computer-mediated teacher self-disclosure on student motivation, affective learning, and classroom climate. *Communication Education*, *56*(1), 1–17.

McFedries, P., & Cashmore, P. (2009). *Twitter tips, tricks, and tweets*. Indianapolis: Wiley Publishing.

McGirt, E. (2009, March 17). How Chris Hughes helped launch Facebook and the Barack Obama campaign. *Fast Company*, *134*. Retrieved from: http://www.fastcompany.com/magazine/134/boy-wonder.html

Miller, M. (2008). *YouTube for business: Online video marketing for any business*. London: Que Publishing.

Morris, T. (2009). *All a Twitter: A personal and professional guide to social networking with Twitter*. London: Que Publishing.

Nyland, R., & Near, C. (2007). Jesus is my friend: Religiosity as a mediating factor in Internet social networking use. Paper presented at the AEJMC Midwinter Conference, Reno, NV, February 23–24.

O'Leary, N. (2009, November 2). The Hispanic market is set to soar. *Adweek.com*. Retrieved from: http://www.adweek.com/aw/content_display/news/agency/e3i26911e62ce1ee0f7f41748d31d4e42a0?pn=1.

O'Reilly, T., & Milstein, S. (2009). *The Twitter book*. Sebastopol, CA: O'Reilly Media.

Papacharissi, Z. (2009). The virtual geographies of social networks: A comparative analysis of Facebook, LinkedIn and ASmallWorld. *New Media & Society*, 11(1 & 2), 199–220.

Papacharissi, Z., & de Fatima Oliveira, M. (2011). The rhythms of news storytelling on Twitter: Coverage of the January 25th Egyptian uprising on Twitter. Paper presented at the World Association for Public Opinion Research Conference, Amsterdam, September 2011.

Pempek, T. A., Yermolayeva, Y. A., & Calvert, S. L. (2009). College students' social networking experiences on Facebook. *Journal of Applied Developmental Psychology*, *30*(3), 227–238.

Pérez-Latre, F. J., Portilla, I., & Sánchez-Blanco, C. (2011). Social media, audiences and advertising: A literature review. *Comunicación y Sociedad*, *24*(1), 65–74.

Picard, R. (2009). Blogs, tweets, social media, and the news business. *Nieman Reports*, *63*(3), 10–12.

Piskorski, M.J., & Winig, L. (2009). *Barack Obama. Organizing for America 2.0, case number N9-709-493*. Boston: Harvard Business School Publishing.

Plouffe, D. (2009). *The audacity to win: The inside story and lessons of Barack Obama's historic victory*. New York: Viking.

Pollet, T. V., Roberts, S.G.B, and Dunbar R. (2011). Use of social network sites and instant messaging does not lead to increased offline social network size, or to emotionally closer relationships with offline network members. *Cyberpsychology, Behavior, and Social Networking*, *14*(4), 253–258.

Qualman, E. (2011) *Socialnomics: How social media transforms the way we live and we do business*. Hoboken, NJ: John Wiley & Sons, Inc.

Raacke, J., & Bonds-Raacke, J. (2008). MySpace and Facebook: Applying the uses and gratifications theory to exploring friend-networking sites. *CyberPsychology & Behavior*, *11*(2), 169–174.

Richter, D., Riemer, K., & Vom Brocke, J. (2011). Internet social networking: Research state of the art and implications for enterprise 2.0. *Business and Information Systems Engineering*, *3*(2), 89–101.

Robards, B., & Bennett, A. (2011). MyTribe: Manifestations of belonging on social network sites. *Sociology*, *45*(2), 303–317.

Rosengren, K. E. (1974). Uses and gratifications: A paradigm outlined. In J. G. Blumler, & E. Katz (Eds.), *The uses of mass communications: Current perspectives on gratifications research* (pp. 269–286). Beverly Hills, CA: Sage.

Sheldon, P. (2008). Student favorite: Facebook and motives for its use. *Southwestern Mass Communication Journal*, *23*(2), 39–53.

Shih, C. (2009). *The Facebook era: Tapping online social networks to build better products, reach new audiences, and sell more*. Boston: Prentice Hall PTR.

Siibak, A. (2010). Performing the norm: Estonian pre-teens' perceptions about visual self-presentation strategies on social networking website rate. *Medien Journal: Zeitschrift für Kommunikationskultur*, *4*, 35–47.

Steinfield, C., Ellison, N. B., & Lampe, C. (2008). Social capital, self-esteem, and use of online social network sites: A longitudinal analysis. *Journal of Applied Developmental Psychology*, *29*(6), 434–445.

Stutzman, F. (2006). An evaluation of identity-sharing behavior in social network communities. *Journal of the International Digital Media and Arts Association*, *3*(1), 10–18.

Subrahmanyam, K., Reich, S. M., Waechter, N., & Espinoza, G. (2008). Online and offline social networks: Use of social networking sites by emerging adults. *Journal of Applied Developmental Psychology*, *29*(6), 420–433.

Swartz, J. (2009, September 22). Real-time web keeps social networkers connected. *USA Today*. Retrieved from: http://www.usatoday.com/tech/news/2009-09-22-social-networking-real-time-web_N.htm.

Tapscott, D., & Williams, A. D. (2006). *Wikinomics: How mass collaboration changes everything*. New York: Portfolio.

Thelwall, M., & Wilkinson, D. (2010). Public dialogs in social network sites: What is their purpose? *Journal of the American Society for Information Science and Technology, 61*(2), 392–404.

Thelwall, M., Wilkinson, D., & Uppal, S. (2010). Data mining emotion in social network communication: Gender differences in MySpace. *Journal of the American Society for Information Science and Technology, 61*(1), 190–199.

Twenge, J.M., & Campbell, W. K. (2009). *The narcissism epidemic: Living in the age of entitlement*. New York: Free Press.

Utz, S. (2010). Show me your friends and I will tell you what type of person you are: How one's profile, number of friends, and type of friends influence impression formation on social network sites. *Journal of Computer-Mediated Communication, 15*(2), 314–335.

Valenzuela, S., Park, N., & Kee, K. F. (2009). Is there social capital in a social network? Facebook use and college students' life satisfaction, trust, and participation. *Journal of Computer-Mediated Communication, 14*(4), 875–901.

Vander Veer, E. (2008). *Facebook: The missing manual*. Sebastopol, CA: Pogue Press, O'Reilly Media.

Van Doorn, N. (2010). The ties that bind: The networked performance of gender, sexuality and friendship on MySpace. *New Media & Society, 12*(4), 583–602.

Vitak, J., Zube, P., Smock, A., Carr, C. T., Ellison, N., & Lampe, C. (2011). It's complicated: Facebook users' political participation in the 2008 election. *Cyberpsychology, Behavior, & Social Networking, 14*(3), 107–114.

Weare, C., & Lin, W-Y. (2000). Content analysis of the World Wide Web: Opportunities and challenges. *Social Science Computer Review, 18*(3), 272–292.

Whitlock, W., & Micek, D. (2008). *Twitter revolution: How social media and mobile marketing is changing the way we do business & market online*. Las Vegas: Xeno Press.

Wilkinson, D., & Thelwall, M. (2010). Social network site changes over time: The case of MySpace. *Journal of the American Society for Information Science and Technology, 61*(11), 2311–2323.

Zywica, J., & Danowski, J. (2008). The faces of "Facebookers": Investigating social enhancement and social compensation hypotheses: Predicting Facebook and offline popularity from sociability and self-esteem, and mapping the meanings of popularity with semantic networks. *Journal of Computer-Mediated Communication, 14*(1), 1–34.

4

BUSINESS MODELS OF MOST-VISITED U.S. SOCIAL NETWORKING SITES

Jiyoung Cha

Introduction

Social networking sites have relatively short histories in the United States, but the growth of U.S. social networking sites has accelerated. It is becoming prevalent for offline businesses to use social networks to market their goods and services, and for media firms to present and publicize at least some of their content on popular social networking sites along with their own traditional distribution platforms and websites. Although social networking sites now receive acute attention from consumers, media, businesses, advertisers, and investors, lingering questions still remain. Such questions include whether social networking sites actually generate profit and whether they have stable business models. These doubts parallel the questions that scholars had about popular websites during the Internet bubble.

As witnessed during the Internet bubble, the number of users of a website does not directly translate to the amount of revenue that the website draws. The question about business models of online businesses includes one hotly debated factor—whether consumers will pay for online content (Ha & Ganahl, 2009). Moreover, consumer reluctance to pay online may not be limited to content. Consumers are accustomed to free *services* available online. As a result, the challenges that social networks encounter include how to create unique values and services that consumers will pay for, whether social networks have revenue sources other than advertising, how they can monetize consumers who are reluctant to pay for online services, and whether a social networking site can survive in the long term.

As social networking sites become an ever-increasingly essential medium for society and culture, academic research examining the use of social networking sites has grown markedly (e.g., Liu, 2008; Quan-Haase & Young, 2010). Nevertheless, there exists scant scholarly research regarding the business aspect of social networking sites. Given that fact, as well as general skepticism regarding business models of social networks, this chapter aims to examine the business models of specific major U.S. social networking sites, and identify their key differences.

Literature Review

Business Models

Information/Internet industries have encountered major challenges because it is difficult to transform online information into a commodity. The majority of consumers consider online services to be complementary. With the rise of online businesses, a business model concept has received substantial attention. Nevertheless, studies have pointed out that there is no universally established definition of a business model (e.g., Ho, Fang, & Lin, 2010; Morris, Schindehutte, & Allen, 2005). Some studies focused only on the financial aspect of a business, defining a business model as a statement of how a firm makes money and generates profit in the long term (e.g., Stewart & Zhao, 2000; Zhang, 2010). In these studies, the term "business model" was used interchangeably with "revenue" models or "economic" models.

This chapter suggests that a business model is not the same as a revenue model or economic model. Business models should not be concerned merely with the financial aspect of a business; they should deal with other aspects such as value creation, defining customers, and identifying competencies needed to stay in business. Indeed, numerous studies have approached the business model from a more holistic view, distinguishing it from a revenue model or strategy (e.g., Amit & Zott, 2001; Morris, et al., 2005). Many researchers view revenue streams as a component of a business model (e.g., Amit & Zott, 2001; Dubosson-Torbay, Osterwalder, & Pigneur, 2002; Morris, et al., 2005). From the holistic view of a firm, Amit and Zott (2001, p. 511) refer to a business model as "the content, structure, and governance of transactions designed so as to create value through the exploitation of business opportunities." Morris, Schindehutte, and Allen suggest that a business model "describes a company's unique value proposition, how the firm uses its sustainable competitive advantage to perform better than its rivals over time, whether, as well as how the firm makes money now and in the future" (2005, p. 28).

Furthermore, an array of research has identified the key components of a business model, especially in the context of e-business (e.g., Afuah & Tucci, 2001; Donath, 1999; Dubosson-Torbay, et al., 2002; Eisenmann, 2002; Petrovic, Kittl, & Teksen, 2001; Timmers, 1998). Dubsson-Torbay, Osterwalder, and Pigneur (2002) included product innovation, customer relationships, infrastructure management, and financial aspect as components of an e-business model. The business model suggested by Afuah and Tucci (2001) encompasses customer values, scope, price, revenue, connected activities, implantation, capabilities, and sustainability. Petrovic, Kittl, and Teksen (2001) included value model, resource model, production model, customer relations model, revenue model, capital model, and market model. The business model suggested by Eisenmann (2002) is composed of products/services provided by the company, customers, revenue sources, technologies utilized, partnerships, and cost changes along with growth.

Although the aforementioned studies use different terms to identify components of a business model, Morris, Schindehutte, and Allen (2005) suggest that the basis of a business model consists of the value chain concept (Porter, 1985) and strategic positioning (Porter, 1996). Similarly, Amit and Zott (2001) assert that a business model is built upon the value chain concept (Porter, 1985) and strategic network theory (Dyer & Singh, 1998). Despite the slight differences among the studies that identified the components of a business model, their commonalities can be summarized as value creation, target market, sources of competence, and revenue sources.

Theoretical Framework

This chapter establishes a framework to analyze business models of social networking sites. The framework is built upon several criteria: reasonably simple, logical, measurable, comprehensive, and operationally meaningful (Morris, et al., 2005). The characteristics allow the framework to be applied to various social networking sites as well as general e-business contexts. The integration of previous studies has resulted in a business model framework composed of four components. The four components are: (1) value creation; (2) target market; (3) sources of competencies; and (4) revenue. Figure 4.1 presents the theoretical framework to analyze a business model.

The first component of a business model is value creation. It addresses the value that the firm provides to customers and how the firm creates value. This component focuses on the nature of the product/service, the scope of the product/service, the way that the product/service is created, the firm's role in production or service delivery, and how the offering is made available to customers (Afuah & Tucci, 2001; Dubosson-Torbay, et al., 2002; Morris, et al., 2005). The value creation is also directly related to how the firm positions itself in the market. Although Morris, Schindehutte, and Allen viewed positioning as a separate component from value creation, the current study considers positioning as an element of the value creation process. The value that a firm creates, and how the firm creates value, cannot be separated from how the firm positions itself in the marketplace. The value creation component is commonly found in prior studies that identified the components of a business model (e.g., Afuah & Tucci, 2001; Chesbrough & Rosenbloom, 2002; Dubosson-Torbay, Osterwalder, & Pigneur, 2002; Magretta, 2002; Morris, et al., 2005).

The second component of a business model concerns the target market (Chesbrough & Rosenbloom, 2002; Dubosson-Torbay, et al., 2002; Hoque, 2002; Kim & Mauborgne, 2000; Magretta, 2002; Morris, et al., 2005). The target market component addresses the question for whom the firm creates and delivers the value. Specifics of the component include identification of customer types, their geographic areas, geographic dispersion, and interaction requirements with customers. Customer types can be divided into business-to-consumer (B2C),

Value creation

How the firm creates value

- Nature of product/service
- Scope of products/services offering (single or multiple products)
- Distribution of product/service
- Positioning of the firm

Target market

For whom the firm creates value

- Customer types
- Geographic areas
- Geographic dispersion
- Interaction requirements with customers

Business model of social networking sites

Sources of Competencies

What the sources of core competencies are

- Technology
- Marketing
- Supply chain management
- Networking
- Resource leveraging
- Branding

Revenue

How the firm makes money

- Revenue sources
- Prices

FIGURE 4.1 Framework for a business model

business-to-business (B2B), the combination of both, and consumer-to-consumer (C2C). With respect to B2C, the target market can be divided further into subgroups in terms of demographics or other characteristics of customers. Therefore, whether the firm chooses a broad or niche market is a focus of discussion as well. Geographic areas indicate where the product/service is available. Geographic dispersion refers to whether the business takes place at the local, regional, national, or international levels (Morris, et al., 2005).

The third component consists of capabilities and resources for the firm's competencies (Amit & Zott, 2001; Dubosson-Torbay, et al., 2002; Hedman & Kalling, 2003; Kim & Mauborgne, 2000; Morris, et al., 2005). To sustain competitive position in a market for the long term, firms must have unique resources and capabilities in terms of technology, marketing, brands, supply chain management, image of operational excellence, availability, consistency, patents, culture, speed, and resource leveraging (Morris, et al., 2005; West, 2007). Partner networking is also a source of a firm's competencies. Strategic networks are "stable interorganizational ties which are strategically important to participating firms" (Gulati, Nohria, & Zaheer, 2000, p. 203). Through strategic networks, firms can have greater access to markets, information, and technologies (Amit & Zott, 2001). Forms of partner networking include strategic alliances, joint ventures, and long-term buyer–supplier partnerships (Gulati, et al., 2000).

The fourth component is revenue. This component involves how a firm monetizes the value that it creates and how the firm sustains its revenue (Dubosson-Torbay, et al., 2002). The firm's revenue model encompasses the revenue sources and the prices of the products/services (Amit & Zott, 2001; Chesbrough & Rosenbloom, 2002). The existing literature provides various classifications for Internet-based revenue models (e.g. Jelassi & Enders, 2005; Dubosson-Torbay, et al., 2002). Dubosson-Torbay, Osterwalder, and Pigneur (2002) suggest that the revenues of a firm can come from customer subscriptions, advertising and sponsoring, commissions and transaction cuts from provided services, revenue-sharing with other firms, and selling products. Enders, Hungenberg, Denker, and Mauch (2008) classified revenue models for social networking sites into three categories: (1) advertising models; (2) subscription models; and (3) transaction models.

To become a stable social networking site that attracts frequent and regular visitors, it is essential that the website attracts a critical mass (Zeng & Reinartz, 2003). Critical mass refers to a certain minimum number of users that substantially contributes to the takeoff of the social networking site. To make money, a site might develop an advertising model, in which advertisements are solicited and placed on the site. In this case, attracting large and/or highly differentiated users is key to successfully maximizing revenues (Laudon & Traver, 2007). Multi-segmentation or mass customization, which offers customized services tailored to multiple niche markets, are examples of ways to attract highly differentiated users. In another bid to make money, a site might adopt a subscription model, in which it charges its users for access to some or all of its content or services (Laudon & Traver, 2007). An important success element for subscription-based models is the creation of high levels of unique customer value, which will increase customer willingness to pay for a service (Enders, et al., 2008). The transaction model consists of charging a fee for enabling or executing a transaction (Laudon & Traver, 2007).

Method

Data Collection

This study used case studies to examine the business models of major U.S. social networking sites. Existing scholarly research has scarcely touched upon business models in the context of social networking sites, and this study aims to fill that gap. Researchers employ a qualitative study approach to examine complex situations and problems (Hoepfl, 1997). Specifically, a case study is appropriate when a holistic, in-depth investigation is needed (Feagin, Orum, & Sjoberg, 1991). Case studies are justifiable from the perspective of epistemology when behavioral events cannot be controlled, and when the research focuses on contemporary events (Yin, 2003). A case study approach is also widely used in the field of media management (Hollifield, 2001). For the aforementioned reasons, a case study approach was chosen to examine contemporary business models of leading social networking sites within their real-time context.

Specifically, this study is a comparative case study of four leading U.S. social networking sites as units of analysis. In conducting case studies, it is important to sample theoretically useful cases. In particular, best practice models serve as good candidates for a case research methodology (Eisenhardt, 1989; Teagarden, et al., 1995). Given the concern about the presence and stability of business models on the Web in general, as well as in the context of social networking sites, the leading U.S. social networking sites can serve as best practice models for social networking sites. According to Quantcast (2011), the top four social networking sites are Facebook, Myspace, Twitter, and LinkedIn, according to the estimated unique monthly visitors. Table 4.1 presents the profiles of the social networks. By using the comparative case design approach instead of a single case analysis, not only does this study identify business models of major U.S. social networking sites, it also examines whether there are differences among those sites in terms of business models. To ensure the validity of research design, the data for this study were obtained from various sources as suggested by Yin (2003). The sources came from company websites, annual reports of companies, newspapers articles, trade journals, and published interviews with CEOs, executives, and managers of each company.

Results

What Value the Firm Offers and How the Firm Creates Value

The nature of the service that Facebook sells to customers is that of staying connected with the people they already know. In this way, Facebook differentiated itself from existing social networking sites that place more emphasis on networking with strangers (Gustafson, 2011). To fulfill its core value, Facebook developed an easy-to-use interface and constantly adds more communication features to help customers connect with each other. Facebook uses a simple template that allows anybody to set up a profile easily without fundamental web design knowledge. Facebook required customers to use their real names and encouraged them to enter basic personal information. Such Facebook policies have fueled privacy concerns, but the systems also helped users to easily find friends and colleagues. In addition, Facebook offers instant messaging, email, a notice feature to announce events, and a feature called "people you already know," which suggest people the user may know based on his/her existing networks. As the site continues its rapid growth, Facebook's core value is evolving into becoming a one-stop communication and

TABLE 4.1 Profile of most-visited U.S. social networking sites, 2011

Basic Profile	Facebook	Myspace	Twitter	LinkedIn
Year of launch	2004	2003	2006	2002
No. of users	800 million	125 million	200 million	135 million
Users inside the U.S.	25%	61%	40%	44%
Users outside the U.S.	75%	39%	60%	56%
Revenue (2010)	$2 billion	$347 million	$45 million	$161 million
Revenue (2011)	$4.27 billion	n/a	$140 million	n/a
Headquarter	Menlo Park, CA	Beverly Hills, CA	San Francisco, CA	Mountain View, CA
International offices	Dublin, Ireland	London, UK	Dublin, Ireland	Dublin, Ireland
	London, UK	Berlin, Germany	London, UK	London, UK
	Hamburg, Germany	Sydney, Australia	Tokyo, Japan	Mumbai, India
	Hong Kong, China			Amsterdam, The Netherlands
	Hyderabad, India			Toronto, Canada
	Madrid, Spain			Bangalore, India
	Milan, Italy			Delhi, India
	Paris, France			Melbourne, Australia
	Selangor, Malaysia			Paris, France
	Singapore			São Paulo, Brazil
	Stockholm, Sweden			Singapore
	Sydney, Australia			Stockholm, Sweden
	Tokyo, Japan			Sydney, Australia
				Tokyo, Japan
Languages	70 languages	15 languages	17 languages	11 languages

Sources: CrunchBase (2011); Facebook (2011); Hernandez (2011); Jeffbullas.com (2011); E. Lee (2011); LinkedIn (2011); Myspace (2011); O'Dell (2011); Sec.gov (2011); Twitter Blog (2011); Womack (2011)

entertainment center that users can share with people they already know in everyday life.

Myspace once had a value similar to that of Facebook—helping customers to network. Networking is still part of the equation, but Myspace has changed its core value from social networking to social entertainment in the wake of Facebook's dominance in the former category. Myspace launched its new design emphasizing social entertainment in October 2010. Myspace positions itself as an online playground where people can share their favorite entertainment with others. On the site, entertainment fans connect with independent artists, such as comedians, musicians, and authors. The content types of Myspace include music, video, games, TV, and movies. In particular, Myspace specializes in music content. Songs, music videos, charts, new releases, music news, and so on are provided on the venue.

LinkedIn has a different value proposition than either Facebook or Myspace— namely, professional networking. The mission of LinkedIn is to help users to stay informed about their contacts and industry, to find the people and knowledge they need to achieve their goals, and to control their professional identities online. Professionals at LinkedIn can easily connect to co-workers, clients, recruiters, and people with similar professional interests. Companies can post job openings and necessary qualifications on LinkedIn. Job seekers can visit company profiles and find information about job openings.

The value that Twitter creates is real-time information networking. While there exist numerous websites that produce and deliver information or content, the core value of Twitter is to enable individual consumers and businesses to share interesting information in a succinct and timely manner with others. Twitter per se does not generate any of the content, albeit information-sharing is its core value. Individual users and businesses create information themselves, or simply link the information produced by somebody else. The tagline of Twitter, "the best way to discover what's new in your world," reflects the value that Twitter offers—to enable people to share information and be informed up to the second.

For Whom the Firm Creates Value

Value proposition is directly related to the types of consumers targeted by a social networking site. Facebook, Myspace, and Twitter all target the general population. On the other hand, the targeted consumers of LinkedIn are professionals, job-seekers, and businesses. Although Facebook, Myspace, and Twitter target a general population, Myspace specifically targets a younger generation than do Facebook and Twitter. Considering its new aim to position itself as a social entertainment destination, Myspace primarily targets young people under 35 years old who enjoy music, movies, and games—a demographic known as Generation Y (Myspace, 2011).

The actual user data also indicates that the leading social networks do attract different demographic groups. Facebook and Twitter users more closely reflect the general U.S. Internet population than those of Myspace and LinkedIn with respect to gender, age, ethnicity, income level, and education level (Quantcast, 2011). Myspace users in the U.S. are younger, less educated, and more ethnically diverse than general U.S. Internet users. Americans under the age of 18 are 195% more likely to use Myspace than are general U.S. Internet users. Hispanic Americans and African Americans are 100% and 51% more likely than general U.S. Internet users to use Myspace, respectively (Quantcast, 2011). LinkedIn users in the U.S. are more educated, wealthier, and older than general U.S. Internet users. Americans who completed graduate schools are 61% more likely than general U.S. Internet users to use LinkedIn. Americans who earn annual incomes of $100,000 or more are 28% more likely than general U.S. Internet users to use LinkedIn. Americans between the ages of 35 and 49 are 19% more likely to use LinkedIn than general U.S. Internet users (Quantcast, 2011).

Given the value proposition of LinkedIn as a professional networking site, LinkedIn also explicitly targets businesses as well as individuals. For example, it has a page template designed for companies. Companies can present their basic information and update users about new developments. As of 2011, more than 2 million companies had LinkedIn Company Pages (Vivekavonrosen, 2011). To attract companies, LinkedIn also offers hiring solutions that integrate sourcing of candidates, distribution of jobs, and promoting of brands. Seventy-five of the Fortune 100 companies have used LinkedIn hiring solutions (Vivekavonrosen, 2011).

All of the four social networking sites were launched in the U.S., but their target consumers are not limited to people in the U.S. market. Facebook has been aggressive in expanding its footprint into other countries in response to its high penetration in the U.S. and the decelerating growth of the North American market. Facebook has huge numbers of users in Australia, Canada, India, France, Germany, Italy, Spain, and the United Kingdom. More recent growth sources of Facebook consist of users in developing countries, including Mexico, Brazil, and India (A. Lee, 2011). More than 75% of Facebook users are now outside the U.S. (Facebook, 2011).

LinkedIn is also aggressive in targeting foreign markets, because professionals increasingly have international business relationships. It tends to develop localized services, although technological development is still centralized in the U.S. (Kiss, 2008). Of the 135 million LinkedIn registered users in 2011, more live outside the U.S. (59%) than inside the U.S. (41%) (LinkedIn, 2011). In particular, LinkedIn has many users in European countries, including the United Kingdom, the Netherlands, France, Italy, Spain, and Germany (Quantcast, 2011). The growth of LinkedIn users in Brazil, Mexico, India, and France is exponential (Birch, 2011).

Similar to LinkedIn and Facebook, Twitter has been targeting foreign markets. In 2010, Twitter offered its service in eight different languages (English, French, Korean, Japanese, Italian, Spanish, German, and Portuguese). Currently, the primary target consumers of Twitter are the people who can speak those languages.

Twitter also plans to add Indonesian, Russian, and Turkish. It is also testing a service that enables translation of tweets to nine other foreign languages. Twitter announced that 60% of its registered users reside outside the U.S., whereas 40% are inside the U.S. (Twitter Blog, 2010).

Myspace used to aggressively target foreign markets, but it is currently downsizing international expansion. Myspace still retains its offices in London, Sydney, and Berlin, but it has downsized or restructured its offices in Argentina, Brazil, Mexico, France, Russia, Sweden, Spain, and India (Rao, 2009).

What the Sources of Competencies Are

The core competency of Facebook comes from its network size. Facebook is one of the most popular social networking sites in Canada, France, Australia, Germany, Italy, Spain, the United Kingdom, and of course the United States. For community-oriented Web proprietors, network externalities are a critical factor for success. Researchers suggest that companies with the greatest installation of network bases will dominate the market (Arthur, 1996; Brynjolfsson & Kemerer, 1996; Katz & Shapiro, 1985; Lee & O'Connor, 2003). In the aforementioned countries where Facebook took the top spot in the online social network market, many people will join Facebook because it has the largest existing user base.

Facebook also uses strategic alliances very effectively for its branding. The partnership with Microsoft is one of the reasons why Facebook became a profitable company and grew as a strong brand. The two companies have had an exclusive advertising deal since August 22, 2006. Under the terms, Microsoft exclusively sells standard banner advertising on Facebook, both in the U.S. and internationally; (Microsoft News Center, 2007; Tartakoff, 2010). Facebook also has had a partnership with Microsoft for social searching since October 2010 (Krazit, 2010). If somebody searches for something on Microsoft's Bing, the user can designate whether they like the goods or the service. This is a "Like" feature that is used on Facebook. What the user likes is also shared with their Facebook friends. In addition, Facebook has established partnerships with many established media firms. It partnered with CNN to report the inauguration of President Barack Obama in 2009. Its partnership with Yahoo! allows users of both sites to share activity updates and content. Facebook also rolled out a video-renting service in partnership with Warner Brothers in 2011. Through this array of strategic partnerships and alliances with well-established media firms, Facebook is able to present anywhere and anytime, which fuels its growth as a dominant and omnipresent brand.

Facebook is also reinforcing its presence on mobile platforms. It acquired Beluga, a group mobile messaging service company, which enables Facebook users to send text messages using their mobile phones to their Facebook friends individually or as a group (Albanesius, 2011; Debrais, 2011). In early 2011, Facebook acquired mobile ad start-up Rel8tion to improve hyper-local ad targeting to its 200 million-plus mobile subscribers (Albanesius, 2011). In 2011,

Strobe Corp., a HTML5-based mobile app development startup, was acquired by Facebook (Taylor, 2011a). Facebook also added a new acquisition, Snaptu, to optimize apps for feature phones—that is, mobile phones with limited value-added features—realizing that 80% of U.S. mobile phone users are still using feature phones (Gahran, 2011). Expanding its footprint, Facebook has forged partnerships with 474 mobile operators around the globe to promote its mobile products (Facebook, 2011). Facebook is also working with HTC, a Taiwan-based mobile phone manufacturer, to build the first official Facebook phone. This phone's core functions will be built upon social networking (Warman, 2011). These aggressive actions regarding mobile platforms are, again, in line with Facebook's desire for ubiquity—accessible anywhere and anytime.

The core competency of Myspace consists of its resources for music content and services. Myspace originated as a website where independent musicians could promote songs to the public. Thus, Myspace offers more music content and relevant information than any other social network (Arrington, 2009). Myspace users can add a maximum of 100 songs to their playlists for free. In contrast, playing songs is not as feasible on Facebook, Twitter, and LinkedIn, unless users link online videos or songs from other music sites. To provide free streaming music, mp3 downloads, ringtones, merchandise, and ticket sales, Myspace created a joint venture, Myspace Music, with major music labels Sony BMG, Universal Music Group, EMI Music, Sony ATV/Music Publishing, and Warner Music Group in 2008 (Arrington, 2008; Business Wire, 2008). To further expand its music catalog, Myspace Music has inked deals with Nettwerk Music Group, INgrooves, IRIS Distribution, and RoyaltyShare (Crum, 2009). Myspace has 5 million bands on its Web-based catalog (Associated Press, 2009; Locke, 2008). To reinforce its other entertainment content, Myspace has formed partnerships with U.S. major content creators, such as MTV, the *Los Angeles Times*, Access Hollywood, *The New York Times*, the *Village Voice*, and Just Jared (Jennings, 2010).

With respect to Twitter, a core competency comes from timeliness. Twitter enables users to share interesting information almost instantly. A plane landing in the Hudson River in New York in 2009 garnered Twitter huge attention from media and the public. There exist similar anecdotes that show the timeliness of Twitter in delivering breaking news. It has become common practice for television news programs to have Twitter accounts so that other Twitter users can share interesting news. Twitter also has forged deals with major U.S. search engines, such as Bing and Yahoo, to turn tweets into real-time searches and to introduce Twitter to non-users. To boost its timeliness and accessibility, Twitter integrates different types of platforms. Twitter users can utilize mobile devices, instant messaging, and the Web. Like Facebook, Twitter aggressively utilizes mobile platforms. Although more Facebook users accessed Facebook through mobile browsers than did Twitter users in 2011, Twitter use on mobile devices is growing more rapidly than Facebook mobile use. From January 2009 to January 2010, access to Twitter via mobile browsers increased 347%, whereas Facebook experienced a 112% growth (Comscore, 2010). People might read longer news articles on mobile devices, but they are more likely to check out the short messages on portable devices, especially with breaking news (Hachman, 2011a).

Another competency of Twitter is rooted in its popularity with public figures and celebrities. Public figures and celebrities who tweet range from politicians to pop singers, including President Barack Obama, Al Gore, Lady Gaga, Justin Bieber, Britney Spears, Jack Welch, etc. The use of Twitter by celebrities and public figures is prevalent. Twitter users include 75% of the NBA's players, 82% of the U.S. House, 85% of Billboard's top 100 musicians, and 93% of the top Food Network chefs (Hachman, 2011b). The fact that many famous people use Twitter is an inherently seamless and powerful marketing strategy.

When LinkedIn was introduced, some industry experts predicted that it would not succeed because social networking does not work in a business context. Media experts, such as Jyri Engestrom, predicted that choosing non-social objects as the social network's target would be problematic (Howell, 2007). Despite the negative projections, the social network succeeded in attracting users and finally generated a profit in 2010. Contrary to Engestrom's assertion, a competence of Linkedin is that the site indeed focuses on a narrower niche market—professionals and job-seekers—compared to other social networks. Although Facebook and Myspace have attracted numerous users, people are less likely to post their résumés and professional achievements along with their photos and mundane conversations about everyday life. Fulfilling the needs of consumers that differ from the needs fulfilled by Facebook and Myspace is one of the reasons why LinkedIn has grown.

Another core competency of LinkedIn is its network size of recruiters. In 2010, approximately 3,900 companies—including 69 of the Fortune 100 companies—used LinkedIn's hiring solutions to find candidates for positions (Sec.gov., 2011). Microsoft, Ebay, Target, Accenture, Nokia, Oracle, and IBM are some of the companies that have recruited employees through LinkedIn (Hempel, 2010). One reason why more and more recruiters use LinkedIn is that the site enables companies to locate highly qualified candidates who may be passive job-seekers, whereas existing recruiting sites focus on active job-seekers. To draw more recruiters, LinkedIn has entered into partnerships with various businesses. In 2004, it formed a partnership with the DirectEmployers Association, a group that Fortune 500 companies founded to deal with online recruiting issues. It allows higher-level managers to search for candidates recommended by their colleagues for available positions (DirectEmployers, 2004). LinkedIn has also formed partnerships with big recruiters like PricewaterhouseCoopers, Dematteo Monness, SAP, and CIO to attract job-seekers, such as college students and senior IT executives.

How the Firms Make Money

Facebook generates revenues from three sources: advertising, commerce, and syndication with advertising, which is the primary revenue source. Advertisements on Facebook appear in the right-hand column of many types of Facebook pages, such as Apps, Photos, Groups, Profiles, and the Home page. Advertisers can choose a maximum bid to place the advertisement. According to e-Marketer, Facebook generated an estimated $1.86 billion from worldwide advertising in 2010. The same report revealed that $1.21 billion of this income came from the U.S., whereas $740 million came from outside the U.S. (E. Lee, 2011). Although Facebook currently generates more advertising revenue in the United States, the ad revenue from other countries is projected to grow rapidly, as its market outside the U.S. continues to grow. Facebook succeeded in attracting large advertisers, such as AT&T, Ford Motor Co., and Research in Motion, in 2010 (Oreskovic, 2010). However, more advertising revenue actually came from smaller companies. Approximately 60% of Facebook's U.S. advertising revenue was generated by smaller companies, while big corporations generated 40% (Horn, 2011a; E. Lee, 2011).

Another revenue source of Facebook is commerce. Users purchase Facebook Credits, virtual currency that is used to buy games, applications, and other virtual items available only on Facebook. The commerce on Facebook is limited to virtual items. Virtual items refer to goods and services whose purchase and use are restricted to a particular online space. On the other hand, real items are defined as goods or services that can be used offline—regardless of whether these goods or services are bought online or offline (Cha, 2011). Similar to Apple and its iPhone and iPod Touch application store sales, Facebook takes 30% of total Facebook Credit revenue, while the game or application developers take 70% of the Credit revenue (Axon, 2010).

One Facebook Credit costs 10 cents. Users have three options in purchasing Facebook Credits: (1) 15 Credits for $1.5; (2) 50 Credits for $5; and (3) 100 Credits plus free 10 Credits for $10. Users can buy Credits in the currency of U.S. dollars, the Euro, the British pound, the Venezuelan Bolivar, and the Danish Krone (Helft, 2010). Facebook Credits are available in the form of gift cards in offline retail stores in the U.S. The gift cards, worth $15, $25, or $50, are sold in store branches and on the websites of Target, Walmart, and Best Buy. The Facebook revenue from commerce through Facebook Credits has been growing. In 2009, the revenue from Facebook commerce accounted for only approximately 5% of the total revenue. In 2011, Facebook commerce revenue is expected to account for 11% of total revenue (Learmonth, 2011).

Syndication is another source of Facebook revenue. Facebook users' publicly available status updates are linked with their other search results. Thus, search engines can provide Internet users with "real-time" search results (Miller, 2010). Facebook has licensed its users' publicly available status updates to search engine companies such as Microsoft (Bing) and Google. Google, which had inked deals with Facebook, Myspace, and Twitter for real-time searches, removed real-time social searches from its search engine result pages in early 2011—perhaps because it can now implement real-time searches with its own social networking site, Google+.

Myspace revenue comes from advertising and commerce. The advertising models of Myspace have four streams: (1) branded sponsorship; (2) display ads; (3) search ads; and (4) in-stream audio ads. Google has been a long-term partner for search and display advertising on Myspace (Boulton, 2010). Myspace sells display ads through Google's DoubleClick Ad Exchange and its display advertising network (Diana, 2010). On Myspace Music, users can stream music on demand, create playlists, and add widget music players to their profiles for free. The music streaming is advertising-supported. When Myspace Music users listen to a song initially and to another 100 streams, they see display ads. After 100 streams, the listeners will hear 30-second in-stream audio ads (Maloney, 2011). Advertising revenue on Myspace Music is split between the joint venture partners, regardless of play counts (Arrington, 2008). The commerce revenue model comes into play when users want to download music. Users can download songs at iTunes or Amazon via Myspace Music. Myspace shares the sales of song downloads with iTunes and Amazon.

The revenue sources of Twitter are advertising and syndication. Twitter generated $45 million in 2010, and is estimated to generate nearly $140 million in 2011 (O'Dell, 2011). The advertising revenue is based on three forms of advertising: (1) Promoted Tweet; (2) Promoted Trend; and (3) Promoted Account (McHugh, 2011). Relevant Promoted Tweets appear if a user searches for something. Twitter charges for Promoted Tweets on a cost per engagement (CPE) basis. That is, the number of people who follow the Promoted Tweet determines the cost of a Promoted Tweet. Twitter generated the Promoted Tweet revenues from approximately 30 large companies, including PepsiCo and Virgin America. Promoted Tweets were not available to small and mid-sized advertisers until very recently (Khalil, 2010).

Promoted Trends have emerged as a major source of revenue. Promoted Trends enable users to see time-, context-, and event-sensitive trends promoted by advertisers. These paid Promoted Trends appear at the top of the Trending Topics list on Twitter and are clearly marked as "Promoted." Advertisers who purchase Promoted Trending can display their messages at the top of the "trend" section of users' pages. Advertisers can also customize their trends based on geographic locations. Twitter charges a flat daily fee for a Promoted Trend, between $70,000 and $80,000. Twitter Trend has been very successful as it sells out almost every day. As a result, Twitter is planning to increase the average price from $100,000 to $120,000 (Taylor, 2011b).

Promoted Accounts recommend accounts that people do not currently follow but may find interesting. Like Promoted Tweets, Promoted Accounts are charged on a cost per engagement (CPE) basis. Twitter charges an advertiser from $1 to $3 for every new user that follows the advertiser's Promoted Account (Anmenion. com, 2011). Accounts can be targeted based on interest, keywords, current followers, and can be geo-targeted at the country level (Dugan, 2011). The revenue from the three forms of advertising was $45 million in 2010. All of the revenue came from the U.S. market—but the advertising revenue from other countries is expected to grow slowly beginning in 2011 (Schroeder, 2011).

Another revenue source of Twitter is syndication. Twitter syndicates tweets generated by its users, and this syndication allows search engines to integrate these tweets with their other search results. By doing so, search engines can provide "real-time" search results, which include tweets of the latest current events (Miller, 2010). Twitter licensed its tweet-streams to Microsoft (Bing), Google, and Yahoo in the U.S. For instance, Internet users can search real-time tweets regarding a certain subject on Bing Social. The licensing of its tweets earned Twitter $25 million per year from Google and Microsoft; it also shares the advertising revenue that results from real searches using search engines (Buskirk, 2009; Reuters, 2009). Twitter continues to provide its public tweets to Bing and Yahoo, but the partnership between Twitter and Google dissolved in early 2011. Twitter has also been expanding its licensing revenue stream to major search engines in other countries, such as Daum—one of the most visited Internet portals in South Korea—and Yahoo Japan. Twitter's syndication has also expanded to traditional media companies. In 2011, Twitter inked a deal with Mass Relevance, which allows the latter to aggregate publicly available tweets and re-syndicate them to traditional media firms such as MTV Networks and CNN (Hawkins, 2011).

LinkedIn has three revenue sources: (1) paid subscriptions; (2) advertising; and (3) hiring solutions. It generated net revenue of $161 million through these streams in 2010 (Sec.gov, 2011). Paid subscriptions to a premium service on LinkedIn enable the users to be listed at the top of the hiring manager application, to directly contact other users outside their networks, to see who has looked at their profile without limits, to get more powerful search tools to deliver desired results, and to send more simultaneous requests for introductions. For individual consumers, the company offers three tiers of premium subscription services: (1) basic; (2) job seeker; and (3) job seeker plus. Individual paid subscriptions range from $15.95 to $49.95 per month. For businesses, LinkedIn also provides three tiers (business, business plus, and executive) with two price options for each tier. The paid subscription for businesses ranges from $19.95 to $99.95. In 2010, LinkedIn generated 27% of its revenue from paid subscriptions (Sec.gov, 2011).

Another revenue stream is advertising. In 2010, LinkedIn generated 32% of its revenue from advertising, which is slightly more than what it generated from paid subscriptions (Sec.gov, 2011). It charges per click (CPC) or per thousand impressions (CPM). LinkedIn allows advertisers to bid for the type of advertisement they want. The bid starts from $2.00 if advertisers opt for the CPC option. Because LinkedIn targets professionals, its customers tend to be more educated, high-earning, and influential in business than general Internet users (Quantcast, 2011; Sec.gov., 2011). With respect to advertising, LinkedIn does not compete with other social networking sites targeting the general public. Rather, it competes with professional publications like the *Wall Street Journal*, *Bloomberg*, and *Washington Post* for advertising (Thomases, 2010).

Hiring solutions account for the third and largest revenue stream of LinkedIn. This is a paid recruiting service that LinkedIn provides for businesses. The price of a hiring solution ranges from $49.95 to $499.95/month or higher. These hiring solutions serve both active job-seekers and passive candidates who are not actively looking to change jobs (Noyes, 2011). Hiring solutions generated $66 million, or 41%, of LinkedIn's total revenue in 2010. The hiring solution revenue stream has been also growing at a much faster pace than the other two revenue streams (Schrum, 2010). LinkedIn's revenue from hiring solutions grew to 41% of revenue in 2010 from 23% in 2007, whereas paid subscriptions decreased to 27% in 2010 from 53% in 2007. Revenue from advertising increased from 24% in 2007 to 33% in 2008 and then remained at about 32% until 2010 (sec.gov, 2011). Table 4.2 summarizes the business models of the four social networks.

Discussion

This chapter has explored business models of four leading U.S. social networking sites. The findings revealed that these most-visited social networks have different values, target consumers, sources of competencies, and revenue models. First, the values and positioning that Facebook, Myspace, Twitter, and LinkedIn create are different. The differentiated values and target consumers explain why Twitter and LinkedIn have rapidly grown along with Facebook. On the other hand, the extensive original overlap between Facebook and Myspace in terms of value propositions and target audiences significantly transformed Myspace's value proposition and target audience.

Firms wanting to enter the social networking market should differentiate their value, positioning, and target consumer base from existing major social networks. For community-oriented Web proprietors, researchers suggest that companies with the largest number of installed network bases will dominate the market (Arthur, 1996; Brynjolfsson & Kemerer, 1996; Katz & Shapiro, 1985; Lee & O'Connor, 2003). Network externalities are not sufficient alone to explain why people use a certain social networking site. When network externalities are compared with intrinsic motives for using a site, the motives for using a site are found to be more critical in influencing how often people use the social network (Kim & Cha, 2011). It is probable that consumers will use more than one SNS concurrently if the sites fulfill different consumer needs. However, if a substantial overlap exists between the two SNSs with respect to which needs fulfillment consumers seek from the SNSs—and the two sites reach a certain level of user base—then one of the SNSs that best fulfills those specific needs of consumers can lure users away from the other, and ultimately dominate the market (Kim & Cha, 2011).

As society becomes increasingly globalized, it is worth noting the aggressive international expansion of U.S. social networking sites. The major U.S. social networks, except for Myspace, are expanding their reach to international markets,

TABLE 4.2 Summary of business models

Business model	Facebook	Myspace	Twitter	LinkedIn
Value creation (initial)	Social networking	Social networking	Real-time information sharing	Professional networking
Value creation (current)	One-stop global communication center	Social entertainment	Real-time information sharing	Professional networking
Target markets	General public Expanding international markets	Generation Y Downsizing international markets	General public Expanding international markets	Professionals Job seekers Businesses Expanding international markets
Sources of competency	1. Network size 2. Branding through strategic alliances 3. Mobile platforms	1. Music content and services	1. Timeliness 2. Celebrity marketing 3. Mobile platforms	1. Niche target 2. Presence of various recruiting firms
Revenue sources	1. Advertising 2. Commerce 3. Syndication	1. Advertising 2. Commerce	1. Advertising 2. Syndication	1. Advertising 2. Paid subscriptions 3. Hiring solutions

often with visible success. Considering that this international expansion may accelerate, and that some U.S. social networking sites are rapidly gaining popularity in some countries, these U.S. sites may pose a formidable threat to countries' local social networks. Those local social networking sites will have to fulfill different needs of their users, and do so more satisfactorily than the leading U.S. social networking sites, in order to survive the threat.

The four social networks generate revenues from advertising, commerce, paid subscriptions, syndication, and other specialized services. The major social networks all employ multiple revenue streams rather than a single revenue stream. However, they still overwhelmingly rely on advertising to earn revenue. LinkedIn is the exception; its revenue is spread relatively evenly among paid subscriptions, advertising, and hiring solutions. Advertisers and investors remain in flux as interesting new technologies and websites emerge (Cha, 2009). A heavy reliance on any one revenue stream poses a risk. It is imperative for social networks to spread revenue over diverse sources or develop other revenue streams. Building various and reliable revenue streams also allows social networks to be flexible in investing in new or existing services, especially in turbulent economic conditions.

Recall that the advertising models of Twitter are different from typical online advertising. Twitter's advertising model consists of *indirect* promotion of products/services through *publicity*, whereas typical online advertising directly promotes products/services. It may be observed that Twitter's advertising model is based on public relations and customer relationship management, rather than traditional advertising. When Twitter users voluntarily follow a company or product/service, they are displaying more active engagement with the company or product/service. Thus, consumers who follow a company on Twitter are more likely to bond with the brand. Indeed, a recent study found that people are more likely to buy or recommend a brand if they follow it on Twitter (CMB, 2010).

Despite heavy reliance on advertising for revenue, the major social networking sites also monetize their huge user bases to some degree, using direct user monetization and indirect user monetization. Direct user monetization refers to generating revenue directly from the social networking site's users through commerce and paid subscriptions, such as Facebook Credits or LinkedIn premium subscriptions. Indirect user monetization refers to generating revenue indirectly from users through byproducts created by the social networking site's users. Indirect user monetization allows users to use the social networking platform free of charge. In return, the social networking site generates revenue by syndicating the aggregated content generated by the users. Twitter syndicates tweets generated by its users and offers them to search engines and traditional media firms. Facebook also generates revenue by licensing the users' publicly available status updates to search engines. Syndication, an indirect user monetization model, has a huge potential to grow for three reasons. First, consumers are accustomed to complementary product/services online. Second, consumers tend to eschew being directly targeted as sources of monetization. Third, the timeliness and richness of information generated during social networking and interacting are unique—differentiated from the nature of information generated by traditional media. Figure 4.2 presents a classification of the revenue models of the most-visited U.S. social networking sites, according to direct monetization of users and outsiders.

The monetization of users among the leading social networks indicates that they are striving to differentiate their revenue models from previous online giants who disappeared after the Internet bubble burst in 2000, and to reduce financial risk by diversifying revenue streams. Nevertheless, the monetization of users is still in its infancy among the social networks. Commerce, in the context of social networking sites, has great potential to grow as a revenue stream because the commerce revenue model takes full advantage of the inherent nature of social networking sites. While online businesses that sell goods and services spend money and time to attract users and promote their services, leading social networks already have well-established, robust user bases. The inherent nature of social networking sites keeps users coming back on a regular basis, which also likely increases the exposure of these returnees to the goods and services marketed on the sites. Social networking sites can also carry virtual items since they are Internet-based systems.

Facebook is the only social networking site that aggressively utilizes commerce of virtual items. Facebook has increased its variety of virtual items and sells them through a variety of applications. Facebook users seamlessly buy virtual items that facilitate their use of the applications. Users can also purchase Facebook Credits in the form of gift cards in major brick-and-mortar retail stores. This adds a tangible value and visibility to virtual items, and also lessens consumers' privacy and security concerns—concerns that hinder e-commerce. Considering the growth of online games, mobile Facebook use, and global virtual item sales, the revenue from commerce should become a bigger slice of Facebook's total revenue pie.

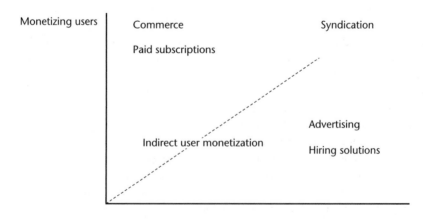

FIGURE 4.2 Revenue models of social networking sites

The data collected about Facebook shows that its advertising revenue from smaller advertisers is greater than that from large advertisers, similar to Google. The phenomenon can be explained from the theory of the long tail, which posits that revenues from niche markets in the long tail of the demand curve can be greater than the revenue that comes from hit markets in the short head of the demand curve in the context of an online business (Anderson, 2006). Advertising on Twitter was limited to big advertisers until 2010, but Twitter is now attracting smaller advertisers. Large advertisers can provide a big boost to social networking sites by attracting more advertisers, helping publicize a site, and providing cash flow in the introduction stage of its product lifecycle. On the other hand, monetizing via small advertisers is very critical in order for social networks to grow and stay stable in business at later stages of their product lifecycle. The nature of social networking sites, which enables advertisers to single out specific or niche target consumers, is appealing to small advertisers. To attract these small advertisers, social networking sites should diversify price tiers, offer initial low advertising prices, and offer more product choices.

This chapter has offered a theoretical foundation to analyze the business aspect of community-based businesses, and elucidated the business models of the four leading U.S. social networks. Although the data was based on multiple sources to ensure reliability and validity, the results need to be interpreted with caution, because they were based on publicly available information. Although some U.S. social networks are globally popular, other countries in the world also have popular local social networks, such as Cyworld in South Korea, Bebo in the UK, Tuenti in Spain, Skyrock in France, and Mixi in Japan. Culture presumably plays a role in building a business model for a firm. Therefore, future studies could examine whether there exists uniqueness in business models of social networks among different countries.

References

Afuah, A., & Tucci, C. (2001). *Internet business models and strategies.* New York: McGraw-Hill.

Albanesius, C. (2011). Facebook acquires group messaging service Beluga. *PC Magazine.* Retrieved March 5, 2011 from: http://www.pcmag.com/article2/0,2817,2381245,00.asp.

Amit, R., & Zott, C (2001) Value creation in e-business. *Strategic Management Journal, 22,* 493–520.

Anderson, C. (2006). *The long tail: Why the future of business is selling less of more.* New York: Hyperion.

Anmenion.com. (2011). Twitter tells advertisers to dig deeper: "Promoted Trends" gets a price hike. Retrieved February 13, 2011 from: http://armenion.com/?p=2232.

Arrington, M. (2008, April 2). Confirmed: MySpace to launch new music joint venture with big labels. Retrieved March 5, 2011 from: http://techcrunch.com/2008/04/02/myspace-to-launch-new-music-joint-venture-with-big-labels/.

Arrington, M. (2009, January 31). MySpace CEO talks MySpace revenue, music, mobile and his Murphy bed. *TechCrunch*. Retrieved from: http://techcrunch.com/2009/01/31/myspace-ceo-talks-myspace-revenue-music-mobile-and-his-murphy-bed/.

Arthur, B. (1996). Increasing returns and the new world of business. *Harvard Business Review*, (July–Aug.), 100–109.

Associated Press. (2009, April 19). MySpace Music hopes to profit from free songs. *MSNBC*. Retrieved February 13, 2011 from: http://www.msnbc.msn.com/id/30295071/ns/business-us_business/.

Axon, S. (2010, March 10). Farmville adds Facebook credits payment option. *Mashable*. Retrieved February 13, 2011 from: http://mashable.com/2010/03/10/farmville-facebook-credits/.

Birch, G. (2011, March 22). 100 Million users: The international appeal of LinkedIn. *Multilingual Search*. Retrieved March 24, 2011 from: http://www.multilingual-search.com/100-million-users-the-international-appeal-of-linkedin/22/03/2011/.

Boulton, C. (2010, December 17). Google, MySpace add display ads to search, ad tie. *Search Engine News*. Retrieved February 11, 2011 from: http://www.eweek.com/c/a/Search-Engines/Google-MySpace-Ad-Display-Ads-to-Search-Ad-Tie-864254/.

Brynjolfsson, E., & Kemerer, C. F. (1996). Network externalities in microcomputer software: An econometric analysis of the spreadsheet market. *Management Science*, *42*(12), 1627–1647.

Business Wire. (2008, September 25). EMI Music and Sony ATV sign on to groundbreaking "MySpace Music" joint venture alongside Sony BMG Music Entertainment, Universal Music Group, and Warner Music Group. Retrieved March 5, 2011 from: http://www.businesswire.com/news/home/20080924006367/en/EMI-Music-Sony-ATV-Sign-Groundbreaking-MySpace.

Buskirk, E. V. (2009, December 21). Twitter earns first profit selling search to Google, Microsoft. *Wired*. Retrieved March 13, 2011 from: http://www.wired.com/epicenter/2009/12/twitter-earns-first-profit-selling-search-to-google-microsoft/.

Cha, J. (2009). Shopping on social networking Web sites: Attitudes toward real versus virtual items. *Journal of Interactive Advertising*, *10*(1), 77–93.

Cha, J. (2010). Factors affecting the frequency and amount of social networking site use: Motivations, perceptions and privacy concerns. *First Monday*, *15*(12). Retrieved March 10, 2011 from: http://firstmonday.org/htbin/cgiwrap/bin/ojs/index.php/fm/article/view/2889/2685.

Cha, J. (2011). Exploring the Internet as a unique shopping chance to sell both real and virtual items: A comparison of factors affecting purchase intention and consumer characteristics. *Journal of Electronic Commerce Research*, *12*(2), 115–132.

Chesbrough, H., & Rosenbloom, R. S. (2002). The role of the business model in capturing value form innovation: Evidence from Xerox Corporation's technology spin-off companies. *Industrial and Corporate Change*, *11*(3), 529–555.

CMB. (2010, April 5). Consumers engaged via social media are more likely to buy, recommend. Retrieved March 26, 2011 from: http://blog.cmbinfo.com/press-center content/bid/46920/Consumers-Engaged-Via-Social-Media-Are-More-Likely-To-Buy-Recommend.

ComScore. (2010, March 3). Facebook and Twitter access via mobile browser grows by triple-digits in the past year. Retrieved March 10, 2011 from: http://www.comscore.com/Press_Events/Press_Releases/2010/3/Facebook_and_Twitter_Access_via_Mobile_Browser_Grows_by_Triple-Digits.

Crum, C. (2009, January 15). MySpace music makes some deals to bolster catalog. WebProNews. Retrieved March 10, 2011 from: http://www.webpronews.com/myspace-music-makes-some-deals-to-bolster-catalog-2009-01.

CrunchBase. (2011). Myspace. Retrieved October 10, 2011 from: http://www.crunch base.com/company/myspace.

Debrais, M. (2011, March 3). Social networking website Facebook focuses on mobile services and joins Beluga. Staho.com. Retrieved March 5, 2011 from: http://www.staho.com/social-networking-website-facebook-focuses-on-mobile-services-and-joins-beluga/2012199/.

Diana, A. (2010). Google, Myspace renew search deal. *InformationWeek*. Retrieved November 1, 2011 from: http://www.informationweek.com/news/global-cio/roi/228800816.

DirectEmployers. (2004). Linkedin "links up" with direct employers to transform online recruiting for Fortune 500 employers. Retrieved from: http://www.directemployers.org/2004/03/17/linkedin-links-up-with-directemployers-to-transform-online-recruiting-for-fortune-500-employers/.

Donath, P. (1999). Taming e-business models. *ISBM Business Marketing Web Consortium*, *3*(1), 1–24.

Dubosson-Torbay, M., Osterwalder, A., & Pigneur, Y. (2002). E-business model design, classification, and measurement. *Thunderbird International Business Review*, *44*(1), 5–23.

Dugan, L. (2011, April 28). Want to purchase a promoted Tweet? Be prepared for 3 month commitment, says Twitter. *Mediabistro*. Retrieved November 2, 2011 from: http://www.mediabistro.com/alltwitter/twitter-ad-program-commitment_b7837.

Dyer, J. H., & Singh, H. (1998). The relational view: cooperative strategies and sources of interorganizational competitive advantage. *Academy of Management Review*, *23*(4), 660–679.

Eisenhardt, K. M. (1989) Building theories from case study research. *Academy of Management Review*, *14*(4): 532–550.

Eisenmann, T. (2002). *Internet business models: Texts and cases*. New York: McGraw-Hill/Irwin.

Enders, A., Hungenberg, H., Denker, H.-P., & Mauch, S. (2008). The long tail of social networking: Revenue models of social networking sites. *European Management Journal* *26*(3), 199–211.

Facebook. (2011). Facebook statistics. Retrieved October 20, 2011 from: http://www.facebook.com/press/info.php?statistics.

Facebook Press Release. (2011). Facebook pressroom. Retrieved March 24, 2011 from: http://www.facebook.com/press/info.php?statistics.

Feagin, J., Orum, A., & Sjoberg, G. (Eds.). (1991). *A case for case study*. Chapel Hill: University of North Carolina Press.

Gahran, A. (2011, March 22). More apps may be coming for feature phones, too. *CNN*. Retrieved from: http://edition.cnn.com/2011/TECH/mobile/03/21/facebook.snaptu.gahran/.

Graham, J. (2008, July 21). Twitter took off from simple to tweet success. *USA Today*. Retrieved March 5, 2011 from: http://www.usatoday.com/tech/products/2008-07-20-twitter-tweet-social-network_N.htm.

Gulati, R., Nohria, N., & Zaheer, A. (2000). Strategic networks. *Strategic Management Journal*, *21*, 203–215.

Gustafson, K. L. (2011, February 26). How Facebook invaded MySpace's space. Timesunion.com. Retrieved March 5, 2011 from: http://www.timesunion.com/business/article/How-Facebook-invaded-Myspace-s-space-1031286.php.

Ha, L., & Ganahl, R. (2009). Webcasting business models of clicks-and-bricks and pure-play media: A comparative study of leading webcasters in South Korea and the United States. *International Journal on Media Management*, *6*(1&2), 74–87.

Hachman, M. (2011a, January 24). Twitter's ad revenue predicted to pass MySpace. *PC Magazine*. Retrieved from: http://www.pcmag.com/article2/0,2817,2376180,00.asp.

Hachman, M. (2011b, September 8). Twitter continues to soar in popularity, site's numbers reveal. *PC Magazine*. Retrieved September 15, 2011 from: http://www.pcmag.com/article2/0,2817,2392658,00.asp.

Hawkins, L. (2011, November 7). Austin-based Mass Relevance strikes deal with Twitter. Statesman.com. Retrieved November 9, 2011 from: http://www.statesman.com/blogs/content/shared-gen/blogs/austin/startups/entries/2011/11/07/austinbased_mass_relevance.html.

Hedman, J., & Kalling, T. (2003). The business model concept: Theoretical underpinnings and empirical illustrations. *European Journal of Information Systems*, *12*(1): 49–59.

Helft, M. (2010, September 22). Facebook hopes credits make dollars. Retrieved from: http://www.nytimes.com/2010/09/23/technology/23facebook.html.

Hempel, J. (2010, March 25). How LinkedIn will fire up your career. *Fortune*. Retrieved from: http://money.cnn.com/2010/03/24/technology/linkedin_social_networking.fortune/.

Hernandez, B. (2011, December 6). Will Google buy Myspace? *NBC Bay Area*. Retrieved October 10, 2011 from: http://www.nbcbayarea.com/blogs/press-here/Could-Google-Buy-MySpace-112727014.htm.

Ho, Y.-C., Fang, H.-C., & Lin, J.-F. (2010). Value co-creation in business models: Evidence from three cases analysis in Taiwan. *The Business Review*, *15*(2), 171–177.

Hoepfl, M. C. (1997). Choosing qualitative research: A primer for technology education researchers. *Journal of Technology Education*, *9*, 47–63.

Hollifield, C. A. (2001). Crossing borders: Media management research in a transnational market environment. *Journal of Media Economics*, *14*, 133–146.

Hoque, F. (2002). *The alignment effect: How to get real business value out of technology*. Upper Saddle River, NJ: Financial Times/Prentice Hall.

Horn, L. (2011a, January 18). How Facebook earned $1.86 billion ad revenue in 2010. *PC Magazine*. Retrieved March 6, 2011 from: http://www.pcmag.com/article2/0,2817,2375926,00.asp.

Horn, L. (2011b, March 22). LinkedIn reaches 100 million users. *PC Magazine*. Retrieved March 24, 2011 from: http://www.pcmag.com/article2/0,2817,2382408,00.asp#.

Howell, C. (2007, June 12). LinkedIn versus Facebook: Success factors for social media. Retrieved March 5, 2011 from: http://www.educause.edu/blog/catherine/LinkedInVersusFacebookSuccessF/166981.

Jeffbullas.com. (2011). 11 New Twitter facts, figures and growth statistics plus. Retrieved November 5, 2011 from: http://www.jeffbullas.com/2011/09/21/11-new-twitter-facts-figures-and-growth-statistics-plus-infographic/.

Jelassi, T., & Enders, A. (2005). *Strategies for e-business: Creating value through electronic and mobile commerce*. London: Prentice-Hall.

Jennings, B. (2010, October 28). Fading Myspace tries new direction in social entertainment. Newsytype.com. Retrieved March 5, 2011 from: http://www.newsytype.com/3197-myspace-remodel-entertainment/.

Katz, M. L., & Shapiro, C. (1985). Network externalities, competition, and compatibility. *The American Economic Review*, *75*(3), 424–440.

Khalil, L. (2010, September 27). Promoted Tweets selling for upwards of $100,000. *Digital Trends*. Retrieved March 25, 2011 from: http://www.digitaltrends.com/trash/promoted-tweets-selling-for-upwards-of-100000/

Kim, M., & Cha, J. (2011, August). A winner takes all? Examining relative importance of motives and network effects in social networking site use. Paper presented at the 2011 annual convention of the Association for Education in Journalism & Mass Communication, St. Louis, MO.

Kim, W. C., & Mauborgne, R. E. (2000). Knowing a winning business idea when you see one. *Harvard Business Review*, *78*(5), 129–138.

Kiss, J. (2008, January 24). LinkedIn signals European expansion. *Guardian*. Retrieved March 24, 2011 from: http://www.guardian.co.uk/media/2008/jan/24/digitalmedia.web20.

Krazit, T. (2010, October 13). Microsoft, Facebook unveil deeper social search on Bing. Retrieved February 14, 2012 from: http://news.cnet.com/8301-30684_3-20019508-265.html.

Laudon, K. C., & Traver, C. G. (2007). *E-commerce: Business, technology, society*. Upper Saddle River, NJ: Pearson Prentice Hall.

Learmonth, M. (2011, September 20). Facebook credits revenue now growing faster than its ads. *Advertising Age*. Retrieved November 1, 2011 from: http://adage.com/article/digital/facebook-credits-revenue-growing-faster-ads/229874/.

Lee, A. (2011, June 13). Facebook users drop in U.S.: Millions left the social network in May 2011. *The Huffington Post*. Retrieved October 3, 2011 from: http://www.huffingtonpost.com/2011/06/13/facebook-users-members-us-growth-drops-may-2011_n_875810.html.

Lee, E. (2011, January 17). Facebook books $1.86b in advertising; muscles in on Google turf. *Advertising Age*. Retrieved February 11, 2011 from: http://adage.com/digital/article?article_id=148236.

Lee, Y., & O'Connor, G. C. (2003). New product launch strategy for network effects products. *Journal of the Academy of Marketing Science*, *31*(3), 241–255.

LinkedIn. (2011). About us. Retrieved November 5, 2011 from: http://press.linkedin.com/about.

Liu, H. (2008). Social network profiles as taste performances. *Journal of Computer-Mediated Communication*, 13. Retrieved March 15, 2011 from: http://jcmc.indiana.edu/vol13/issue1/liu.html.

Locke, L. (2008, April 17). MySpace music sees major money in free tunes. *Wired*. Retrieved February 10, 2011 from: http://www.wired.com/entertainment/music/news/2008/04/myspace_music.

Magretta, J. (2002). Why business models matter. *Harvard Business Review*, *80*(5), 86–92.

Maloney, P. (2011, February 9). Rain 2/9: TargetSpot serving audio ads to Myspace music. *Rain*. Retrieved October 10, 2011 from: http://textpattern.kurthanson.com/articles/882/rain-29-targetspot-serving-audio-ads-to-myspace-music.

McHugh, M. (2011, January 24). Twitter advertising revenue swiftly challenging MySpace. *Digital Trends*. Retrieved March 15, 2011 from: http://www.digitaltrends.com/computing/twitter-advertising-revenue-swiftly-challenging-myspace/.

Microsoft News Center. (2007, October 24). Facebook and Microsoft expand strategic alliance. Retrieved February 11, 2011 from: http://www.microsoft.com/presspass/press/2007/oct07/10-24facebookpr.mspx.

Miller, C. C. (2010, April 12). Twitter unveils plans to draw money from ads. *New York Times*. Retrieved March 25, 2011 from: http://www.nytimes.com/2010/04/13/technology/internet/13twitter.html?_r=1.

Morris, M., Schindehutte, M., & Allen, J. (2005). The entrepreneur's business model: Toward a unified perspective. *Journal of Business Research*, *58*(6), 726–735.

Myspace. (2011). About us. Retrieved October, 3, 2011 from: http://www.myspace.com/Help/AboutUs.

Noyes, J. (2011, January 27). Linkedin IPO reveals it's a job search powerhouse. *Eloqua*. Retrieved March 15, 2011 from: http://blog.eloqua.com/what-linkedin-ipo-reveals/.

O'Dell, J. (2011, September 29). Twitter's revenue tripled since last year, and its valuation doubled. *SocialBeat*. Retrieved October 15, 2011 from: http://venturebeat.com/2011/09/29/twitter-financials/.

Oreskovic, A. (2010, June 18). Facebook '09 revenue neared $800 million. *Reuters*. Retrieved March, 25, 2011 from: http://www.reuters.com/article/2010/06/18/us-facebook idUSTRE65H01W20100618?pageNumber=1.

Petrovic, O., Kittl, C., & Teksen, R. D. (2001). Developing business models for e-business. Paper presented at the International Conference on Electronic Commerce. Vienna, Austria.

Porter, M. E. (1985). *Competitive advantage*. New York: Free Press.

Porter, M. E. (1996). What is strategy? *Harvard Business Review*, *74*(6): 61–78.

Quan-Haase, A., & Young, A.L. (2010). Uses and gratifications of social media: A comparison of Facebook and instant messaging. *Bulletin of Science Technology and Society*, *30*(5), 350–361.

Quantcast (2011). Quantcast. Retrieved January 2, 2011 from: http://www.quantcast.com/.

Rao, L. (2009, June 23). Myspace layoffs coming to countries where it is getting trounced by Facebook. *Tech Crunch*. Retrieved February 14, 2012 from: http://techcrunch.com/2009/06/23/myspace-layoffs-coming-to-countries-where-it-is-getting-trounced-by-facebook/.

Reuters. (2009, October 8). Twitter in Google, Microsoft licensing talks: Report. Retrieved March 25, 2011 from: http://www.reuters.com/article/2009/10/08/us-twitter-sb-idUSTRE5975BR20091008.

Saba, J. (2011, June 26). News Corp. sells Myspace, ending six-year saga. *Reuters*. Retrieved September 4, 2011 from: http://www.reuters.com/article/2011/06/29/us-newscorp-myspace-idUSTRE75S6D720110629.

Schroeder, S. (2011, January 24). Twitter ad revenue may reach $150 million this year. *Mashable.com*. Retrieved March 24, 2011 from: http://mashable.com/2011/01/24/twitter-revenue-150-million/.

Schrum, R. (2010, August 23). The 3 main income streams for LinkedIn: How Linkedin makes money. *My Corporate Media*. Retrieved March 10, 2011 from: http://mycorporatemedia.com/tag/linkedin-revenue/.

Sec.gov. (2011, January 27). Linkedin Corporation. United States Securities and Exchange Commission. Retrieved March 6, 2011 from: http://www.sec.gov/Archives/edgar/data/1271024/000119312511016022/ds1.htm.

Stewart, D. W., & Zhao, Q. (2000). Internet marketing, business models, and public policy. *Journal of Public Policy & Marketing*, *19*(2), 287–296.

Tartakoff, J. (2010). Facebook, Microsoft scale back ad relationship. *Paidcontent.org*. Retrieved March 24, 2011 from: http://paidcontent.org/article/419-facebook-microsoft-scaling-back-ad-relationship/.

Taylor, C. (2011a). Facebook's new acqui-hire: HTML5 mobile app startup Strobe. *Gigaom*. Retrieved March 15, 2011 from: http://gigaom.com/2011/11/08/facebook-acquires-strobe-sproutcore/.

Taylor, C. P. (2011b). Promoted trends look like a hit on Twitter; promoted Tweets, not so much. *Bnet*. Retrieved February 13, 2011 from: http://www.bnet.com/blog/new-media/promoted-trends-look-like-a-hit-on-twitter-promoted-tweets-not-so-much/7260.

Teagarden, M. B., von Glinow, M. A., Bowen, D., Frayne, C. A., Nason, S., Huo, Y. P., Milliman, J., Arias, M. E., Butler, M. C., Geringer, J. M., Kim, N.-H., Scullion, H., Lowe, K. B., & Drost, E. A. (1995). Toward a theory of comparative management research: An idiographic case study of the best international human resources management project. *Academy of Management Journal*, *38*(5), 1261–1297.

Thomases, H. (2010, July 27). Why LinkedIn's advertising business is booming. *ClickZ*. Retrieved February 11, 2011 from: http://www.clickz.com/clickz/column/1724490/why-linkedins-advertising-business-is-booming.

Timmers, P. (1998). Business models for electronic markets. *Electronic Markets*, *8*(2): 3–8.

Twitter Blog. (2010, April 8). Growing around the world. Retrieved October 10, 2011 from: http://blog.twitter.com/2010/04/growing-around-world.html.

Vivekavonrosen. (2011, August 20). The latest LinkedIn statistics. *Linked Into Business*. Retrieved February 11, 2011 from: http://linkedintobusiness.com/2011/08/the-latest-linkedin-statistics/.

Warman, M. (2011, November 22). Facebook phone 'coming next year' from HTC. *The Telegraph*. Retrieved November 26, 2011 from: http://www.telegraph.co.uk/technology/facebook/8906119/Facebook-phone-coming-next-year-from-HTC.html.

Watters, A. (2010, April 21). Facebook consolidates its virtual currency with Facebook credits. *Read Write Web*. Retrieved February 11, 2011 from: http://www.readwriteweb.com/archives/facebook_consolidates_its_virtual_currency_with_facebook_credits.php.

West, J. (2007). Value capture and value networks in open source vendor strategies. In *Proceedings of the 40th Hawaii International Conference on System Sciences*.

Womack, B. (2011, September 20). Facebook revenue will reach $4.27 billion E-marketer says. *Bloomberg*. Retrieved January 5, 2011 from: http://www.bloomberg.com/news/2011-09-20/facebook-revenue-will-reach-4-27-billion-emarketer-says-1-.html.

Yin, R. (2003). *Case study research: Design and methods* (3rd ed.). Thousand Oaks, CA: Sage.

Zeng, M., & Reinartz, W. (2003). Beyond online search: The road to profitability. *California Management Review*, *45*(2), 107–130.

Zhang, S. I. (2010). Chinese newspaper ownership, corporate strategies, and business models in a globalizing world. *International Journal on Media Management*, *12*(3), 205–230.

5

SOCIAL MEDIA MARKETING

Paige Miller

Marketing Social Media

Social media are the latest Internet sensations to capture the interest of millions of people. They join personal computers, the Internet, websites, email, cell phones and portable music players on the list of disruptive technologies that have changed the way people live, work and communicate.

The number of people using social media in 2011 is staggering in comparison to users of other communication media. Some 800 million people use Facebook (Facebook, 2011), 200 million use Twitter (Shiels, 2011), and 135 million use LinkedIn (LinkedIn, 2011). YouTube streams over 10 billion videos a month (NielsenWire, 2011).

With such large audiences readily available, social media rival television, radio, magazines and newspapers as powerful channels of communication. Marketing professionals realize this, and many are carving out a role for social media in their marketing plans.

Social media sites are rapidly proving their abilities to sell products, provide insights into customers' needs, nurture sales leads, improve search engine rankings and build long-term relationships with prospects and customers. As a result, marketers expect the role of social media in marketing to continue to increase for the near future.

Social Media Defined

The term social media differs in meaning from profession to profession. To a computer programmer, social media are Web 2.0 applications, applications written after 2005 when the focus of computer programming shifted from providing websites for static information to making the Internet more usable by non-programmers (Singel, 2005). No one set out to develop social media. Rather, social media applications resulted from new programming capabilities that gave people new ways of communicating.

To website developers, social media applications let users create, tag and share content spontaneously without programmer intervention. Communications can be verbal, graphic or text-based and can be displayed on a wide range of digital devices.

To a marketing professional, social media (new media or interactive media, as some call it) are ways of communicating with people online. Marketers often extend the term to include earlier forms of two-way Internet communications, such as email, e-newsletters, web-based presentations (webinars) and instant messaging.

A social media application can be any of the following: (1) a website, like Facebook, (2) an application embedded in a website, such as a news site that permits commenting on news items, or (3) an applet or widget that resides on a mobile phone or tablet, like the Angry Birds® game.[1] While Facebook, Twitter, LinkedIn and YouTube are the top four social media tools (Alexa, n.d.), dozens of other sites exist in the U.S. and around the world (Traffikd, n.d.).

Social Media Marketing Advantages

Social media changed marketing more between 2005 and today than marketing changed between the 1950s (when television became a mainstream medium) and the start of the 21st Century (Meeker, 2011). Social media is ushering in a new era of marketing with new ways of reaching people, different venues for presenting information, and more opportunities to send the right message to the right person at the right time. Foremost among social media advantages are:

- *Numerous channels and functions.* Social media provide an overwhelming array of channels and an ever-growing set of activities. From a marketing perspective, social media activities fall into the following categories:
  - *Networking*, where company representatives build relationships with future prospects (or suspects), share industry insights and present product information. Networking sites enable companies to hear customers' ideas, insights and experiences, along with questions, complaints and suggestions. Nearly 1.5 million businesses have Facebook pages (SocialBakers, n.d.), with the two largest fan-based pages reported to be Coca-Cola, with 29 million fans, and Disney, with 24 million fans (Facebook, n.d.).
  - *Information sharing*, where marketing or sales people exchange content and information with customers and prospects via text, presentations, videos, slide shows and collaboration. The most notable services are WebEx for webinars, Vimeo for videos, SlideShare for slide shows and presentations, Huddle and Adobe Connect for real-time collaboration using video, text and voice simultaneously.

    Information sharing also includes commenting on e-zines (online magazines) and clicking icons (like Twitter's retweet icon, Facebook's "Like" icon or Del.icio.us's bookmark icon) to share a webpage with other people. These expand the awareness of a brand without additional cost to the company and, for better or worse, without control or censorship by the company.

- *Viral communication*, where content is quickly emailed from person to person to spread the word. Blendtec, an appliance company, gained national recognition when its video, Will It Blend?, in which an iPhone is chewed to pieces in a Blendtec blender, went viral (Borges, 2008).

- *Commenting and reporting*, where company marketers and subject-matter experts blog (write online Web logs) about topics of interest to customers and prospects. An estimated 39% of all companies use blogs to call attention to a product, present views on industry activities and trends, and solicit prospects' and customers' views (eMarketer). Chris Brogan, Seth Godin and Guy Kawasaki are top bloggers in marketing, and Mashable, which started as a site for social media updates, now covers technology, business and general news and is the second-most-followed blog on the Internet (Technorati, n.d.).

- *Polling and surveying*, where marketers use a poll on a website, within a newsletter, or in email to solicit opinions of customers and prospects. Polls provide quick and valuable insights to marketers. In a sense, Twitter is a polling channel. Its hashtag-designated keywords (like #iPhone4s), let large numbers of people comment on a topic. While it is not a scientific measure, like a man-on-the-street poll, it indicates the scope and depth of opinions on a topic. Survey Crafter and StatPac are two sophisticated survey research applications, while Zoomerang and Survey Monkey offer economical means of conducting opinion polls and inquiries.

- *Rating and reviewing*, where people vote, rank, review, rate or assign a level of satisfaction to an idea, person or product. Sites like Yelp, Citysearch and TripAdvisor store ratings and comments on a wide range of businesses. People rate everything from companies to colleges, apartment buildings, movies, cars and computers online. Marketers follow rating sites to see how their company and its products are faring in the uncensored arena of public opinion, and they work diligently to defuse or push down negative comments.

- *Gathering*, where people meet for social interaction, as when a business uses Twitter to invite people to its grand opening. In 2009, Mashable held meet-ups in many U.S. cities to gather social media marketers together. By 2011, some 1500 Mashable communities, with 27,000 members across the U.S. met every two weeks (Mashable, n.d.).

- *Checking-in*, where a business encourages people to tell their friends they are patronizing the business. Marketers use check-in applications, like Foursquare, to build customer loyalty. Retail stores and, especially, restaurants use check-in services to offer coupons or other rewards to their most frequent customers, while brands use it judiciously to post messages to their followers.

- *Mobilizing*, where a business organizes people to act individually or as a group. While Twitter is famous for supporting political dissidents during the Arab Spring of 2011, marketers use it like a public address system to direct attendees to conference sessions and as a bulletin board where attendees post comments about sessions (Bruff, 2011). Similarly, small business owners use it as a private radio station to broadcast the location of their mobile businesses, as when a cupcake truck or sandwich cart announces it is outside an office building.

- *Crowd-sourcing*, where a business solicits input and answers by tapping the collective wisdom of disparate people. Marketers can conduct crowd-sourcing exercises on any social media site or can set up a wiki webpage, a Hawaiian word for fast, to let a group of people collaborate on a project. Wikipedia is a crowd-sourced encyclopedia, and Ning, SocialGo and Boonex are examples of sites that host wikis. Bookmarking sites, such as Digg, Del.icio.us, and Reddit use crowd-sourcing to determine the most popular news items each day.

- *Group deals*, where a business offers a discount to a group of people if a certain number of purchases are made. Businesses use the services of Groupon and LivingSocial among others, to distribute their offers regionally or nationally. Through LivingSocial, Whole Foods offered a $20 coupon for $10 to acquire new customers. They sold one million coupons (LivingSocial, n.d.).

- *Entertaining*, where a business provides a game, widget or application that entertains the prospects in some way and helps keep the business's name top-of-mind. Second Life, a virtual-world networking site, lets businesses build virtual stores to advertise their products, as Bank of America does. Facebook enables friends to send friends virtual gifts, like a Budweiser beer, and solicit virtual livestock for their Farmville farms.

Social media provides many more channels for engaging prospects and customers than do traditional media, which is precipitating major changes in marketing. However, other social media attributes also are disrupting traditional marketing strategies, plans and activities, including:

- *Relationship building.* As prospects and customers interact with company spokespersons, they witness the expertise, experience and professionalism of a company and gain confidence in the company's ability to deliver. As a result, a relationship forms. In time, a certain percentage of these relationships turn into sales. It is marketing's job to determine if that percentage is acceptable or whether other media—social or traditional—could garner more sales.

- *Earned exposure.* As relationships and trust build, customers often relay their positive experiences to their colleagues via social media sites for reviews and ratings. Marketers call this type of unrequested endorsement earned exposure.

Like word-of-mouth endorsements, earned exposure is harder to obtain and, thus, marketers believe it to be more effective than paid exposure, such as advertising and direct mail, and owned exposure, such as the company's website or Facebook page.

- *Authentic insight.* Social media sites offer exceptionally valuable input because of the authentic comments they elicit from the public. On most sites, all are welcome to join the conversation, discussions are free flowing and uncensored, and participants are mostly anonymous (a person's email address is known, but not his or her name or home address). These attributes encourage a more inclusive group of participants than might be available for face-to-face conversations, focus groups, or surveys. They also encourage truthfulness and, often, brutal honesty. The diverse personalities, experience, behaviors and thoughts of the participants provide an endless stream of fresh insights for marketers.
- *Search engine visibility.* Blog entries, posts on social media sites, tweets, and comments on news items add value to a company's website. Search engines, like Google, Bing, and Yahoo, include social media interactions in their algorithms for ranking websites. Over time, social media raise the ranking of a website and the value of the company's brand, or goodwill, as an accountant would label it if the company were for sale.
- *Cost savings.* Social media activity is not free. Social media require significant time to develop a strategy, create and monitor content, engage prospects and clients, measure results, and adjust tactics. Nevertheless, in comparison to traditional media such as TV, radio, newspapers, magazines, and billboards, social media is a fraction of the cost. In a few hours a day, a marketing person can build a substantial presence on the Web.
- *Trackable results.* Quick feedback and trackable results are potent attributes of social media. Social media provide the data that marketers need to fine-tune their programs. Historically, companies have paid fees to monitoring services, like Nielsen, for TV viewership data and membership dues to auditing organizations, like Audit Bureau of Circulations, for magazine circulation data. Google Analytics provides data about website traffic for free.

Cookies, small files automatically downloaded to the computers of website visitors, enable marketers to follow the path of people across corporate websites and social media sites. Web analytic applications, like Google Analytics, capture the behavior of visitors on the site, that is, the pages viewed, the page where the viewer abandoned the site, the amount of time the viewer spent on the site, and often the website referring the visitor, among other details. Some applications combine that behavior data with the social media information provided by visitors themselves on their Facebook page or other social media site (Gartner, 2011). With these rich behavioral and demographic descriptions of visitors, marketers construct buyer personas and develop marketing campaigns targeted at each type of persona.

Companies with low social media activity and few followers can track prospects manually using spreadsheets and free tools, like Google Analytics. Other tools let marketers track comments and trends, like Google Discussion, Google Alerts, Twitter's own tracking feature, TweetDeck, Twilert, HootSuite, Pulse of the Tweeter, Trendrr, and MentionMap, among many others.

However, companies with active social media programs require automation that is more robust. Social customer relationship management systems (Social CRM or sCRM, as they are called) track social media activities automatically. Major software applications include IBM's Coremetrics, Google™ Analytics Premium and Adobe's® Omniture®. Other vendors are making names for themselves, including SalesForce.com with Chatter® (formerly Radian6®) and, for smaller companies, HubSpot, Nimble, Eloqua and Marketo.

Social CRM is an emerging area, but the number of activities it tracks is already impressive. Capabilities include:

- Capturing customers' social media profiles.
- Capturing customers' interactions (i.e., history of relevant posts, tweets, check-ins, etc.).
- Scheduling the posting of messages to different social media sites.
- Managing email campaigns.
- Ranking fans and followers by influence and clout (based on an undisclosed algorithm created by the vendor).
- Listening to online comments across the Web (actually, capturing them) and evaluating their sentiments (positive and negative).
- Reminding Marketing or Sales to contact a prospect (e.g., end of trial usage).
- Analyzing website behaviors, referring sites, visitor statistics and interactions with fans and followers.
- Scoring leads.
- Sending leads to a sales management system.
- Providing closed-loop reporting and analysis, which combines social media, marketing and sales contact with a prospect with the revenue generated by that prospect to provide a fuller understanding of the time, intensity and cost of a sale.

No product supports everything, and different vendors support different functions at different levels of sophistication. Consequently, it is sometimes necessary to use multiple applications to cover all the functions.

Social Media Marketing Requirements

In return for multiple marketing channels, engagement, authentic insight, cost savings, trackable results and closed-loop reporting, prospects and customers expect a few things in return. Here are a few examples:

- *Content.* Compelling content attracts and retains prospects and cultivates them into customers. Prospects require a consistent stream of information, whether on a daily, weekly or monthly frequency, to keep them returning to a site.
- *Conversation.* The basis of social media is informal conversation. Prospects want to be involved in a dialogue, not subjected to a stream of sales pitches. Even when no back-and-forth conversation is taking place, a company's posts need to sound like human speech.
- *Integrity.* If a company is to earn the trust and respect of prospects, it must act with the highest level of integrity. Prospects quickly and loudly denounce marketing hype, falsehoods and deceptive statements online and often cause a firestorm of consequences. The old saying "all publicity is good publicity, even bad publicity" no longer works. Bad publicity can hurt a company badly on the Web. Just ask Netflix, which lost 800,000 customers in 2011 as word of its 100% price hike spread across the Web (Gilbert, 2011).
- *Unfettered discussion.* A company cannot control the online comments or discussion about its products, employees and practices. Rather, it must earn the respect of its prospects and customers and trust them to ferret out the truth in a disgruntled comment and to counter false claims with positive infor-mation.
- *Performance.* Social media make it difficult for companies to hoist inferior products onto unsuspecting buyers. The saying "there's a sucker born every day" loses traction in a world where customers can announce a product's deficiencies online in product reviews and rating.

Social Media Impact on the Selling Process

To understand the significance of the impact of social media on marketing and selling of products today, a marketer needs an understanding of the sales cycle used over the past half century. Figure 5.1 presents a brief overview of the traditional sales process.

The Traditional Selling Process

The following presents a general overview of the steps involved in traditional business-to-business selling (B2B). While retail selling is familiar to all of us as consumers, B2B selling is often a longer sales process, involving more people, more specific requirements, a longer decision-making cycle and strenuous negotiations. The process begins in the marketing department.

1   *Generate leads.* Prior to selling, the Marketing department develops sales collaterals, ads, public relations and promotional materials; buys media time and/or space to advertise the product, and executes marketing activities such as telemarketing, trade shows, direct mail campaigns and print, TV and radio

FIGURE 5.1   The traditional sales process

advertising. Marketers call the people responding to marketing materials leads, which they send to the sales department for follow-up.

2   *Qualify leads.* Salespeople contact the leads and, if the level of interest is adequate, they schedule an appointment with the prospect. They prepare for the meeting by setting objectives and by learning as much as possible about a prospect.

3   *Meet with prospect.* During the initial meeting, the salesperson learns more about the prospect's needs and identifies the ultimate decision-maker, the time frame, the budget and the decision-making process. He or she also works to pique the prospect's interest, build the prospect's confidence in the product and company, and move the prospect toward action. The salesperson may need several meetings to understand the prospect's needs fully.

4   *Submit proposal.* The salesperson prepares a proposal outlining the services recommended for the prospect. For very large purchases, prospects often require the salesperson to respond to a request for proposal (RFP), which lists questions about the product and the company. The salesperson may include a pricing quote or may submit it later in a face-to-face meeting.

5   *Wait.* Typically, the salesperson waits while the prospect reviews proposals (or RFPs) from all the vendors under consideration.

6   *Present information and negotiate.* The prospect invites the vendors of the two or three best-fitting products to compete for the business. Each salesperson presents company credentials, product information, product benefits, features, advantages, auxiliary services and pricing scenarios. The prospect negotiates with all the vendors before selecting a product.

7   *Win or lose the deal.* The prospect notifies the salesperson of the winning vendor. Salespeople for the losing vendors usually request feedback about the winning product and the reason(s) their products lost. The salespeople share the feedback with their sales colleagues and with the marketing department to gain insights to improve future outcomes.

Weaknesses in the Traditional Selling Process

The traditional selling process is weak in that marketing and sales often disagree about the definition of a lead. Marketers define a lead as anyone responding to one of its advertising programs, while salespeople define a lead as someone looking to purchase the product in the near term. Consequently, salespeople have shelved many leads attracted by marketing because they are soft leads, not sales-ready.

Few marketing departments have the resources or programs to nurture soft leads and, as a result, future prospects in the planning, research or budgeting stage of decision-making get little attention from salespeople, often less than a phone call every six months.

A second weakness of the traditional selling process is the length of time it takes a salesperson to close a sale. Often the salesperson must educate and cultivate a prospect for a long period before he or she makes (or loses) a sale. The longer a sale takes, the more expensive it is and the more salespeople it takes to meet a company's revenue goals.

The traditional sales cycle will continue to exist for many years to come, especially for expensive and complicated products. However, social media now play a significant role in the marketing and selling of more and more products and, as a result, they are changing the process.

The New Sales Process Using Social Media

The marketing and sales process is changing primarily because of three factors. First, new technologies give prospects the ability to block or ignore marketing messages. For example, cell phones and caller ID thwart telemarketing calls; DVDs thwart TV commercials; Internet, satellite radio and iPods® thwart radio advertising; news websites thwart newspaper advertising; spam filters thwart email, and direct mail often does not make it past the wastebasket.

Second, prospects use the Internet to find vendors, identify products, vet solutions and compare prices before ever contacting a company's sales representative to discuss their needs. This process is especially prominent in retail, or business-to-consumer (B2C) selling, but it is also becoming more usual in manufacturing, technology and other industries that sell wholesale, or business-to-business (B2B).

Finally, Google, Bing and Yahoo drive prospects to the sites where the highest ranked content resides. Those sites could be social media sites (often blogs) just as easily as websites. As a result, social media sites play an important role in improving a company's search engine ranking.

A new selling process is evolving because of these trends. The new process makes use of social media as a means of attracting and nurturing prospects until they are sales-ready. In effect, the new process elongates the marketing period and, sometimes, shortens the selling steps. Often, the cost of the social media tools is more than offset by a decrease in sales time and travel. Figure 5.2 illustrates the basic steps, and the following outlines the steps in more detail.

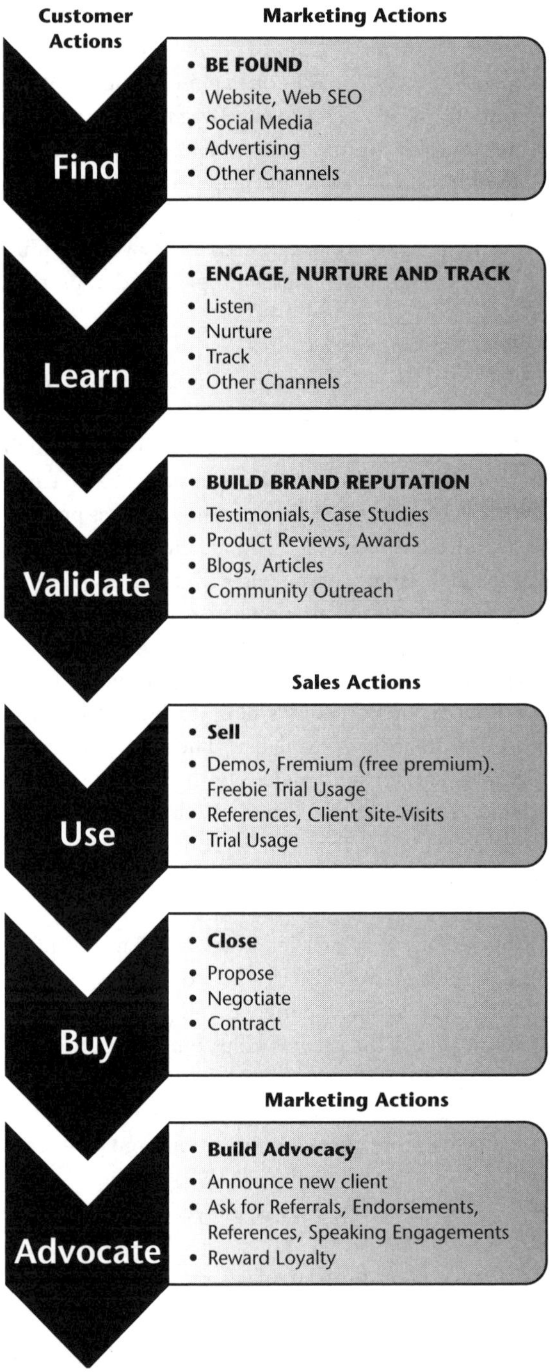

Customer Actions

Marketing Actions

Find

- **BE FOUND**
- Website, Web SEO
- Social Media
- Advertising
- Other Channels

Learn

- **ENGAGE, NURTURE AND TRACK**
- Listen
- Nurture
- Track
- Other Channels

Validate

- **BUILD BRAND REPUTATION**
- Testimonials, Case Studies
- Product Reviews, Awards
- Blogs, Articles
- Community Outreach

Sales Actions

Use

- **Sell**
- Demos, Fremium (free premium). Freebie Trial Usage
- References, Client Site-Visits
- Trial Usage

Buy

- **Close**
- Propose
- Negotiate
- Contract

Marketing Actions

Advocate

- **Build Advocacy**
- Announce new client
- Ask for Referrals, Endorsements, References, Speaking Engagements
- Reward Loyalty

FIGURE 5.2 The news sales process

1   *Be found.* Because the first step in the prospect's buying scenario is to find vendors, a presence on the Web is essential. Some 17.1 billion searches take place online every month (comScore, 2011). Without a presence on the Web, a company misses that continuous parade of prospects. Blog items, comments on social media sites and website optimization (called search engine optimization or SEO) improve website rankings and help companies be found by the search engines (Google, 2010). SEO involves embedding keywords in the website's content and using programming tags to add keywords within the website code to help Google categorize a website properly and, thus, rank it higher.

    A new research step associated with social media is listening. Listening software helps marketers find social media sites where prospects gather, identify topics of interest and meet people with influence. However, marketers can listen without special software. SocialMention is a free online search engine especially for social media research, and Google Alerts™ is a free application that emails the marketer when certain keywords, such as product names, appear in a social comment. Several vendors mentioned in the previous CRM discussion include listening modules in their product offerings.

2   *Engage/nurture/track.* Engaging prospects means interacting with customers in fruitful exchanges of information and ideas. To begin the conversation, marketers or in-house experts ask questions on a blog or respond to an article online, including a link to the company's blog, website, Facebook fan page, etc., where more information is available. The huge and ever-increasing numbers of searches performed each month on the Internet confirm that people interested in a product look to the Web to find vendors. To entice that traffic to a company's website, new content must appear often. Statistically, the more frequently new content appears, the more traffic a website gets (Mershon, 2011).

    The goal of the nurturing process is to provide a steady stream of information that draws prospects and customers to the company's website repeatedly to demonstrate the expertise, experience and integrity of the company's products and employees. This process helps build a relationship between the prospect and the company.

    The best nurturing programs use a series of progressively in-depth marketing materials, each requiring more contact information from prospects. For example:

- Some resources are free (brochures, case studies, conversations on forum or social media sites).
- Some resources require the identification of an email address (e.g., newsletters, white papers, e-books, etc.).
- Some resources require a response to a few questions, such as the buying timeframe or most pressing need (e.g., trial usage, webinars, virtual trade show, survey results).

– Some resources require attendance at an event and interaction with a salesperson (e.g., training session, customized demo).

MetaVis Technologies, a utility software company based in Philadelphia, relies exclusively on the above tactics. In three years, this start-up grew to 700 clients, 26 employees and over $5 million in annual revenues, according to Peter Senescu, president (pers. comm., November 18, 2011).

Nurturing materials refer the prospect to the company's dominant social media site (usually the company's website but sometimes a Facebook page or blog), where the prospect reads, compares, questions and, ultimately, buys. Social media apps, such as online chat, a forum, a blog, videos and sharing icons, make communicating with prospects and selling easier.

Nurturing also enables marketers to continually interact with prospects and stay at the forefront of emerging trends, needs, concerns, problems, product advantages and use cases (case studies). In effect, social media enables marketing and sales departments to validate their understandings of the market and agree on the best messaging to use in collaterals and sales presentations.

A lead nurturing program is incomplete without some way to capture and track prospects' interactions. A history of prospects' interactions with company employees makes it easy to score and qualify leads. With that information— whether collected manually or by an sCRM system—the marketing and sales departments, jointly, can determine the number or types of interactions that distinguish a sales-ready lead.

3 *Build brand reputation.* Most prospects search and review many websites for information about a vendor before buying. Thus, online reputation management is an important, though relatively new, marketing function. Marketers use the same listening software to monitor the company's reputation as they use to find audiences. Listening for comments made by others on their blogs, Facebook, Twitter, Tumblr, etc., and responding to those comments are important components of reputation management.

In addition to monitoring the company's reputation, marketing depart- ments must proactively build the company's reputation. This is done by building positive offsite (meaning sites other than the company's website) information using traditional marketing tactics, such as press releases, product reviews, articles in trade publications and community outreach, as well as the social media capabilities listed previously.

Similarly, marketing departments ensure the company website advances the company's reputation through testimonials, customer success stories and information that shows the company's thought leadership (i.e., a public display of the company's understanding of industry trends and future innovations).

4 *Sell.* Once a prospect achieves a sales-ready score, a salesperson takes responsibility for bringing the sale to fruition. Salespeople, too, use social media, such as webinars, online collaboration and, increasingly, trial usage or free usage of the product, to engage the prospect.

Because of the nurturing program, a prospect has answers to basic questions and a great deal of information about the product. Logically, fewer sales obstacles should arise during the selling process, which lets the salesperson focus on orchestrating in-depth meetings between the prospect and in-house experts, providing customer references, arranging prospect visits with "show-case clients," and negotiating the pricing package. If that is not the case, sales and marketing need to determine why. Perhaps, the lead-scoring algorithm may be inadequate or the prospect may need different information or a different level of information.

5   *Close.* The salesperson is responsible for preparing the final proposal for the client and negotiating the final price and contract terms. For large complex products where negotiations may take months, a specialist may handle the final negotiations to free the salesperson to pursue the next sales opportunity.

6   *Build advocacy.* Once a prospect becomes a client, the marketing department steps in again to grow that customer into an advocate—someone who recommends or endorses the product through word of mouth among his or her colleagues. A press release, an announcement on the company website and a mention in a customer newsletter are the first steps in cultivating the client. For large or highly competitive sales, a celebration dinner may take place. Over time, marketing can invite the customer to be a guest blogger, the subject of a case study, a presenter at a conference, or recipient of special discounts to further the relationship.

To summarize, social media expands the role of the marketing department by providing tools to nurture prospects toward sales-readiness. The nurturing process enables the prospect to gain confidence in the company, its product and its employees. It also helps align the perspectives and working relationship between marketing and sales, and helps marketers to maintain close relationships with potential buyers, which keeps their understanding of the market, buying criteria and value proposition fresh, rich and on target.

Social Media Success Stories

The revised sales process did not spring into being when Facebook opened to the public in 2005. Instead, it evolved over time as experiences and stories of successful social media activities took place. Not surprisingly, marketers learned about social media by using it themselves. The following social media success stories are legendary:

*   *Kiva.* In 2005, Kiva, a non-profit organization that enables people to provide micro-loans to fledging entrepreneurs in developing countries, was mentioned by founder Chris Kulczycki in his diary on Daily Kos, an online activist

community. To date, over 600,000 people have loaned $248 million to over 600,000 entrepreneurs (Kiva, n.d.).

- *Blendtec.* Blendtec, a relatively unknown maker of food blenders since 1975, gained a five-fold increase in sales in 2006 as the result of a low cost YouTube video that asked, "I love my iPhone, but will it blend?" In five days, six million people watched it (Mashable, 2008).
- *Dell.* In 2008, Dell announced they had received $1 million in sales during the previous 18 months through Twitter. Today Dell runs multiple Twitter sites and multiple Facebook pages, including one devoted exclusively to using social media for marketing (Mashable, 2009).
- *HubSpot.* Co-founders Brian Halligan and Dharmesh Shah started HubSpot, an inbound marketing software company, after they realized Shah's blog garnered more attention than the advertising of many well-capitalized, larger companies. Using their own software to support their social media activities, HubSpot grew to $15.6 million with 3500 small business customers in 34 countries in three years (Inc. 500, 2011). The Inbound Marketing University they started is an excellent source of social media classes, information and case studies.
- *Starbucks.* Starbucks' extensive use of social media resulted in a #1 rating in online engagement, #1 on Facebook with 25 million fans, and recognition as the most tweeted brand on Twitter during much of 2010 (Digital Buzz, 2010).
- *EMC Corporation.* EMC, an information technology services provider, began its social media program in 2007 when Chuck Hollis, Global Marketing CTO, started building an online community where prospects and clients could share ideas about housing, indexing, sharing, protecting and managing documents. For two years, Hollis blogged about his journey on Chucksblog. emc.com, providing a real-life view of social media marketing. Now EMC has 15,000 registered users across the 160 communities they operate. Each month their social media sites draw 27,000 unique visitors and 4.6 million page views (Pappas, 2010).[2]

Social Media Results

In December 2010, a survey by McKinsey & Company, a management consulting firm, of 3249 executives from a mix of industries, regions and functional specialties showed 69% of the surveyed companies gained measureable benefits from the use of social media with their customers and business partners (i.e., re-sellers, distributors, suppliers, etc.) (McKinsey Quarterly A, 2010). As Table 5.1 shows, the marketers believed costs decreased and revenues increased because of social media usage.

TABLE 5.1 Improvements in partner and customer relationship using social media

Category	Average Improvement with partners	Average Improvement with customers
Decreased communications costs	15	45
Decreased product development costs	15	
Increased speed of access to experts	25	
Increased partner/customer satisfaction	20	50
Increased speed to access knowledge	20	
Increased innovations	15	24
Increasing revenues	11	24
Increasing effectiveness of marketing		63
Reduced supply chain costs	10	
Reduced time-to-market	15	15
Reduced travel cost	20	29
Reduced customer support costs		35

Social Media Impact on Market Budgets

Social media are forcing marketing allocations to change. In June 2010, MarketingSherpa, an industry analysis firm, surveyed 935 marketers to determine the budget allocation, on average, for various marketing channels (Marketing Sherpa A, 2012). As Figure 5.3 shows, tradeshows are the only traditional medium increasing in budget. Predictably, tradeshows hold the top spot because of the high cost of such shows and because they are rebounding from severe budget cuts over the last few years.

Similarly, the December 2010 McKinsey & Company study mentioned previously reported 63% of respondents expect to increase their Web 2.0 budgets

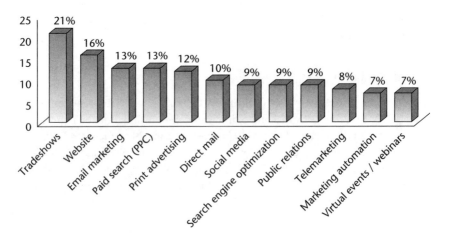

FIGURE 5.3 Average B2B budget allocations

between 2011 and 2014. Finally, a February 2011 survey of over 400 chief marketing officers by Duke University's Fuqua School of Business projected social media spending to grow from 7.1% of the total marketing budget in 2011 to 10.1% in 2012, with projections of 17.5% by 2017 (Moorman, 2011).

Additional evidence of the growing importance of social media comes from Distribion, a marketing software company, which asked 190 marketing managers in June 2011, "Do you expect your budget for the following marketing communications channels to remain the same, increase, or decrease in 2012?" Figure 5.4 shows the averages for each category. Some 55% of the marketers expect to increase mobile communications (i.e., downloaded social media programs) and social media. Conversely, 40% of the marketers expect to see direct mail and printing to experience serious decreases in budget. The results were consistent across the B2B and B2C companies and across large and small to mid-sized companies (Distribion, 2011).

Social Media Return on Investment

Even as social media take a larger role in marketing, they must continue to prove their worth. Because so many variables play into a successful sale, identifying the marketing or sales activities that drive a sale is difficult. However, identifying the channels that foster the most sales is necessary to optimize the marketing budget.

One way to determine the value of a marketing channel is to compare the yearly sales forecast with actual sales for the year. The sales forecast is based on the salespeoples' expectations that prospects in the pipeline (prospects already contacted by a salesperson) will buy within the next 12 months. If sales occurred

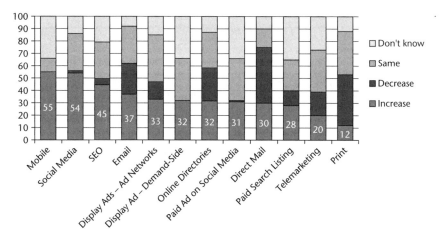

FIGURE 5.4 Expected marketing budget allocation increases for 2012 (by percentage per channel)

that were not forecast, it is reasonable to assume marketing played a role, and the marketing department should trace the interactions with those customers to see when and where they entered the sales funnel. This analysis is easier if an sCRM or CRM system exists. Often, the analysis does not result in definitive, clear-cut answers because customers used multiple channels to find, research, review or buy a product.

Many marketers are leery of changing the marketing mix for fear of damaging what worked in the past. To compensate, some allocate a percentage of their budgets for experimentation to see which new channel shows promise, while others ignore new channels until the channel is proven by others in the industry.

Marketers in some billion dollar companies have access to modeling software to forecast the results of different allocations based on customer behaviors. Marketing mix modeling software, pioneered in the 1990s, is evolving to include social media channels, enabling marketers to run what-if scenarios against huge databases of consumer behavior and buying habits data (Forrester, 2011). Software by MarketShare, Marketing Management Analytics, and ThinkVine earned the highest rating from Forrester.

Conclusion

Social media are exciting new marketing channels deserving serious experimentation and analysis for integration into marketing programs. They provide hundreds of channels for networking and building relationships with prospects, earning their accolades and recommendations, and obtaining their insights. Furthermore, they are easy to use and lower in cost than most traditional media. Finally, social media posts and comments improve search engine rankings, which can drive more traffic to a company's website and provide quick, measurable feedback that is invaluable in fine-tuning a marketing campaign.

In return for their participation, prospects and customers demand informative and accurate content presented in a conversational manner without underlying sales motives. The conversation must be unfettered, without the company trying to control it. The company must respond honestly to complaints or criticism and trust its customers to distinguish unfair comments from fact.

Social media has changed the sales process by giving prospects access to information, ratings, reviews and comments from customers and other prospects. Conversely, social media have changed the sales process by giving marketers tools to nurture prospects through the research and validation phases, toward a state of sales-readiness. The nurturing process also keeps marketers in close contact with their markets, which results in more relevant and effective messaging, and provides access to customers who can become advocates.

Many companies gain measurable benefits from the use of social media. Consequently, marketing budgets are changing to allocate more money to social media channels. Marketers must determine which social media channels work best for their particular industry, company and product, since solid research and data are scarce. Subsequently, they must refine their budgets to promote the channels that offer the best return on investment.

Notes

1 Angry Birds is a trademark of Rovio Mobile Ltd.
2 For more case studies, visit A Wiki of Social Media Marketing Examples at http://wiki.beingpeterkim.com, and *BtoB Magazine*'s 2011 B2B Social Media Winners at http://socialmediab2b.com/2011/04/b2b-social-media-winners/#ixzz1dw3qg9bw.

References

Alexa. (n.d.). Top Sites in United States. Retrieved on April 11 2011 from: http://www.alexa.com/topsites.

Borges, B. (2008, November 13). Viral video pays big for Blendtec. [web log comment]. Retrieved on April 11 2011 from: http://www.findandconvert.com/blog/2008/viral-video-pays-big-at-blendtec/.

Bruff, D. (2011). Encouraging a conference backchannel on Twitter. *Chronicle of Higher Education*. Retrieved on April 11 2011 from: http://chronicle.com/blogs/profhacker/encouraging-a-conference-backchannel-on-twitter/30612.

comScore. (2011, October 11). comScore releases September 2011 U.S. search engine rankings. Retrieved on April 11 2011 from: http://www.comscore.com/Press_Events/Press_Releases/2011/10/comScore_Releases_September_2011_U.S._Search_Engine_Rankings.

Digital Buzz. (2010, July 26). Starbucks social strategy keynote. Retrieved on April 11 2011 from: http://www.digitalbuzzblog.com/starbucks-social-strategy-keynote/.

Distribion. (2011, July 25). 2012 budget survey results: Spending plans shift toward social, mobile. *The Distributed Marketing Blog*. Retrieved on April 11 2011 from: http://distributedmarketing.org/2011/07/25/2012-budget-survey-results-spending-plans-shift-toward-social-mobile.

eMarketer. (2011, October 20). Corporate blogging goes mainstream. Retrieved on April 11 2011 from: http://www.emarketer.com/Article.aspx?R=1007996.

Facebook. (November 4, 2011). Statistics. Retrieved on April 11 2011 from: https://www.facebook.com/press/info.php?statistics.

Facebook. (n.d.). Statistics: Top 100 most popular Facebook pages in the world 2011. Retrieved on April 11 2011 from: https://www.facebook.com/pages/Top-100-Most-Popular-Fac%E1%BA%BBbook-Pages-In-The-World-2011/165408200173753.

Forrester. (2011, September 21). The Forrester Wave™: Marketing mix modeling, Q3 2011. Retrieved on April 11 2011 from: http://www.brandchannel.com/search_result.asp?cx=000980657010496705841%3Avvjr5rsv4ws&cof=FORID%3A10&ie=UTF-8&q=The+Forrester+Wave%E2%84%A2%3A+Marketing+Mix+Modeling%2C+Q3+2011&sa=Search.

Gartner, Inc. (2011, July 25). Magic quadrant for Social CRM. Retrieved on April 11 2011 from: https://secure.sfdcstatic.com/assets/pdf/misc/Gartner_2011_socCRM_MQ.pdf.

Gilbert, J.O. (2011, October 24). Netflix account losses much higher than expected after pricing backlash. *The Huffington Post*. Retrieved on April 11 2011 from: http://www.huffingtonpost.com/2011/10/24/netflix-account-losses-q3-2011_n_1029269.html.

Google. (2010). Search engine optimization starter guide. Retrieved on April 11 2011 from: http://static.googleusercontent.com/external_content/untrusted_dlcp/www.google.com/en/us/webmasters/docs/search-engine-optimization-starter-guide.pdf.

Inc. 500. (2011). Ranking: #33 Hubspot. Retrieved on April 11 2011 from: http://www.inc.com/inc5000/profile/hubspot.

Kiva. (n.d.). About us. Retrieved on 11/16/11 from: http://www.kiva.org/about.

LinkedIn. (2011, November 3). About us. Retrieved on April 11 2011 from: http://press.linkedin.com/about.

LivingSocial. (n.d.). Whole Foods market. Retrieved on April 11 2011 from: http://livingsocial.com/deals/123805-20-to-spend-on-groceries?msdc_id=27.

MarketingSherpa (2012, August). 2012 B2B marketing benchmark survey, page 6. Retrieved on April 11 2011 from: http://ftp.marketingsherpa.com/Marketing%20Files/PDF%27s/Executive%20Summary/2012B2BBRMExcerpt.pdf.

Mashable (n.d.) About Mashable Meetups everywhere. Retrieved on April 11 2011 from: http://www.meetup.com/Mashable/.

Mashable. (2008, May 22). Social media marketing primer: How Blendtec got its face on. Retrieved on April 11 2011 from: http://mashable.com/2008/05/22/social-media-marketing-primer/.

Mashable. (2009, June 11). Making millions via Twitter: @DellOutlet surpasses $2 million in sales. Retrieved on April 11 2011 from: http://mashable.com/2009/06/11/delloutlet-two-million/.

McKinsey Quarterly. (2010, December). Business and Web 2.0: An interactive feature. Retrieved on April 11 2011 from: https://www.mckinseyquarterly.com/Business_and_Web_20_An_Interactive_Feature_2431.

Meeker, M. (2011). *Internet Trends 2011* [PowerPoint slides, slide 11]. Retrieved on April 11 2011 from: http://www.kpcb.com/insights/internet-trends-2011.

Mershon, P. (2011, July 14). How to grow social media leads: new research. *Social Media Examiner*. Retrieved on April 11 2011 from: http://www.socialmediaexaminer.com/how-to-grow-social-media-leads-new-research/.

Moorman, C. (2011, September 6). CMO survey: marketers to significantly increase their investment in social media. Retrieved on April 11 2011 from: http://www.fuqua.duke.edu/news_events/releases/cmo-survey-sep-11/#.Ttbw8_IZ-dk.

NielsenWire. (2011, November 3). September 2011: Top U.S. online destinations for video. Retrieved from: http://blog.nielsen.com/nielsenwire/online_mobile/september-2011-top-u-s-online-destinations-for-video/.

Pappas, J. (2010). EMC Enterprise 2.0 case study webinar for the 2.0 Adoption Council & Newsgator. [PowerPoint slides]. Retrieved on April 11 2011 from: http://www.slideshare.net/JamiePappas/emc-enterprise-20-case-study-webinar-for-the-20-adoption-council-newsgator.

Shiels, M. (March 28, 2011). Twitter co-founder Jack Dorsey rejoins company. *BBC News*. Retrieved on April 11 2011 from: http://www.bbc.co.uk/news/business-12889048.

Singel, R. (October 6, 2005). Are you ready for Web 2.0? *Wired*. Retrieved on April 11 2011 from: http://www.wired.com/science/discoveries/news/2005/10/69114.

SocialBakers. (n.d.). Facebook pages statistics. Retrieved on 11/29/11 from: http://www.socialbakers.com/facebook-pages/.

Technorati. (n.d.). Top 100. Retrieved on April 11 2011 from: http://technorati.com/blogs/top100/.

Traffikd. (n.d.). List of social media and social networking sites. Retrieved April 11 2011 from: http://traffikd.com/social-media-websites/#link.

6

SOCIAL MEDIA CONTENT

Daniel Schackman

Introduction

This chapter investigates how social media offers content (traditional media content as well as professional and user-generated content produced for the Web) to ever more segmented audiences who are also acting as gatekeepers by curating and aggregating the content that they consume.

Media content has always been social. Radio and television shows, movies, and recorded music have brought people together, sharing common values, and have sparked debate as audiences try to discern their meaning and relate to them as expressions of their own lives or see in them what they aspire to be. In the 20th Century, mainstream media industries broadcast content to a wide cross-section of the American population who engaged in national conversations, actively participating in decoding the content (Hall, 1973) together as a shared experience. In the 1950s, the exploits of Lucy were shared by over 50% of the viewing public watching on CBS on Monday nights at 8:00 PM, to be recounted the next day around kitchen tables and office watercoolers. In the 1970s, *All in the Family* brought controversial issues into television viewers' homes, igniting or fanning the flames of intense debate on major social, cultural, and political themes. The increased diffusion of cable television in the 1980s and 1990s brought new specialized television networks, with increasing segmentation and fragmentation of content consumption. The arrival of VCRs in the 1970s, personal computers in the 1980s, and the World Wide Web in the 1990s has catalyzed the consumption of content in even more specialized and individualized ways.

Busy families spent less time together watching or listening to content and talking about it as a shared experience. The image of a nuclear family gathered around the living room television set to watch *The Ed Sullivan Show* was replaced in the popular culture by an image of family members each on their own personal computers or other devices, in separate rooms or even in the same room, all consuming different content.

However, the early 21st Century has witnessed the exponential growth of Web 2.0 social media, allowing for virtual shared experiences of content. The Web has facilitated global conversations about content that spread their reach to worldwide audiences. Now, the Internet has become the new watercooler, particularly around live events such as entertainment awards shows like the Golden Globes, sports competitions like the Super Bowl and Winter Olympics (Stelter, 2010), and reality competition series. Audiences participate in these conversations both in real time and with time delay. Media content producers and distributors are increasingly embracing and developing these communities of fans. CBS CEO Les Moonves said, "The Internet is our friend, not our enemy . . . People want to be attached to each other" (Stelter, 2010).

Moreover, some of the content is coming from the independent media sector and from non-professional media makers vying for audiences in open, collaborative, social media platforms that have disrupted the classic models of mass communications and have brought a new band of "prosumers"—producer-consumers of content (Bruns, 2008)—to the forefront as they not only engage in the active decoding of texts, but also encode texts that they create themselves, from *Star Trek* fan-produced Web series to YouTube videos of their cat playing the piano.

In the golden age of broadcasting, programmers acted as gatekeepers, pushing content through the distribution pipeline from producer to consumer, with limited opportunities for feedback or any other participation by listeners and viewers. Utilizing a linear distribution model, television and radio stations would provide limited right to reply segments on the air for audience members to express their opinions about the programming or news reporting. The newspaper industry followed a similar model, with letters to the editor published on the opinion-editorial pages, providing limited space for readers to share their opinions. In more recent decades, cable television and VCRs brought about a shift from appointment viewing to consumers having more control of their choices, no longer bound by the limitations of network program scheduling.

In the current media climate of digital content distributed online and viewed at all hours of the day on various media players and devices, the traditional linear communication model has given way to an interactive "prosumer" process in which consumers of content also act as producers of content in an ongoing feedback loop (Bruns, 2008). The content itself may be produced by traditional media industries, alternative and independent media makers, or non-professionals posting blogs, podcasts, or videos on their own websites or on content aggregation portals such as Wordpress, podcast Alley, or YouTube. The portals include feedback opportunities for consumers to respond, sometimes in the form of their own original creative content such as a video. Furthermore, social networking applications provide opportunities for professional and amateur content creators to distribute and exhibit their work, as well as the content of other media makers both legally and illegally. Beyond being prosumers, these applications are providing media content consumers the opportunity to take on gatekeeping functions.

Search engines, RSS feeds, content aggregators, crowdsourcing, and social networking have superseded the traditional role of media gatekeeping in the digital age. YouTube channels, MySpace pages, Facebook fan sites, and independent websites contain embedded and linked content, often with recommendations. Sites such as YouTube, Netflix, and Amazon use data from individual users to push content that the sites think the consumer will like. YouTube invites viewers to comment on what they have watched in a global conversation, and to make their own video responses as well; numbers of views and comments are an indication of the appeal of the content. Facebook friends and Twitter users make recommendations of specific content, hoping to embellish their personal reputations when their friends thank them for the referral. StumbleUpon enables members to view random content, rate it, and have other "stumblers" access their viewed content pages.

In the following sections, we will consider the development of social media content by first looking back at the history of broadcast programming, how broadcasting evolved into narrowcasting, the role of gatekeepers, the origins of social media, how the Internet is now a primary outlet for content and distribution, and the role of broadcatching in this new environment.

A Brief History of Broadcast Programming

The concept of programming has its roots in the vaudeville circuits that had their heyday from the 1860s–1930s. These performance "wheels" sent out to theaters around the country a variety of different acts programmed on the bill, from comedians to singers to novelty acts. In the early days of radio, small-time radio operators competed with corporations that started or acquired local stations such as AT&T, GE, Westinghouse, and RCA. Some early operators viewed radio as a hobby, in which the owners had control over the content. Eventually the radio industry would develop into a more professional system. Stations began to affiliate with networks that emerged to link them together and create a national broadcasting system. The Radio Act of 1927 solidified the shift from independent operators to centralized control through the assignment of airwaves with terms favorable to larger companies based on their popularity and technological superiority.

Network radio, which appropriated a number of vaudeville performers to broadcast their own shows starting in the 1920s, adapted the vaudeville circuit format, offering various kinds of content to their listeners, developing schedules that fitted the needs of the audiences (for example, soap operas in the daytime for women working at home). In the Golden Age of Radio (late 1920s–1930s), programming genres included variety (a direct link to vaudeville), drama, mystery, westerns, comedy, music, sports and news.

After World War II, television broadcasting began in earnest, largely controlled by the radio network parent corporations NBC and CBS. Early TV was mostly produced in New York, and served Northeastern, wealthy, educated audiences who were the early adopters of this new technology. Most television was live, in a studio, and cheap to produce—there would be no post-production editing, and few exterior shots where taping conditions were variable. Television was less like the movies, and more like live performances (highbrow and middlebrow). Variety series including *Texaco Star Theater* and *Your Show of Shows* were particularly popular with audiences of all ages, and continued to be well into the 1970s, with a revival in the reality competition format in the 2000s. By 1953, over 50% of American homes had a television set. By end of decade, that percentage had jumped to nearly 90%, and the medium was firmly established as the preeminent form of media in the U.S. As television sets became less expensive to mass produce and for consumers to buy, television content became even more popular and most of the programming was produced in movie studios in Los Angeles.

Broadcasting to Narrowcasting

The rapid growth of cable television in the 1970s would lead to the demise of network television's leadership position as a variety of new channels were introduced to audiences, creating strong interest and demand for adopting cable. Perhaps more than any other channel, the premium service Home Box Office (HBO) offered households a wide variety of movies, live sports, and comedy specials—and over the years added original award-winning content in the form of series (e.g., *The Sopranos*, *Sex in the City*).

HBO changed the way audiences watched media content. HBO paved the way for the development of the home video market, and influenced the introduction of pay-per-view (PPV) for movies and special events. With multiple broadcasts of movies and specials, HBO moved audiences away from the appointment television model demanded by network television. If you missed a movie, you could be sure it would be shown again later in the week.

But HBO was not the only channel that drove the growth of cable television. CNN offered 24-hour news. ESPN became an early leader for sports journalism. MTV and Nickelodeon appealed to younger audiences. These early innovations led to cable television networks more directly serving narrower, specific niche audiences, and today newer digital cable networks are allowing for even more segmentation. There are now over 550 cable or satellite television networks, according to the National Cable & Telecommunications Association (www.ncta.com).

It is important to recognize that cable and satellite content is not regulated by the Federal Communications Commission (FCC). In the 1979 Midwest Video case, the Supreme Court defined cable systems as electronic publishers, not common carriers. The result of this ruling allowed cable and satellite service to offer programming that is edgier than broadcast TV, meaning channels are free to air programs that stretch the traditional boundaries in terms of language, sexual situations, and nudity. This gives writers, producers, and directors more freedom over the content they create, and allows them to operate without the gatekeeping restrictions imposed by broadcast media.

The end result of these changes has been a narrowcast environment for television. The broadcast networks have had to respond to changing economic conditions and audience erosion by offering more reality television and live series competitions (e.g., *Dancing with the Stars*, *American Idol*, *America's Got Talent*) and less episodic television. One can still find situation comedies and dramas on broadcast network schedules, but each season results in fewer programs with high production costs.

Audiences now know that more cutting-edge content with higher production costs is found on cable and satellite channels. The popularity of series like *Mad Men* and *Breaking Bad* on AMC, and *Rescue Me* and *The Shield* on FX, and *Dexter* (Showtime) and *The Sopranos* (HBO) on pay cable are examples of these shifts. Even mini-series, once the mainstay of broadcast networks, have emerged on cable, evidenced by the 2012 rating success of the three-part *Hatfields and McCoys* premiering on the History Channel.

Programming and Gatekeeping

The function of programmers in the broadcast and cable television industries in the U.S. has been to filter and organize content to attract specific audiences, and, in the case of broadcast television, to work within the boundaries of decency enforced by the Federal Communications Commission. Shoemaker and Vos (2009) described how media managers become gatekeepers of content moving through their channels, working from David Manning White's seminal research on "Mr. Gates" (1950) in which a variety of factors played a part in the acceptance or rejection of content to be disseminated to an audience. Shoemaker and Reese (1996) identified five levels of influence on media content: (1) influence on content from individual media workers; (2) influence of media routines; (3) organizational influences on content; (4) influences on content from outside of media organizations; and (5) the influence of ideology.

In the era of broadcast and cable television, broadcast radio, and print media, programmers and editors acted as gatekeepers for content in the traditional linear model of mass communication, from producer to consumer. In the current media climate of digital television, radio, and text content distributed and exhibited online via many platforms, the traditional model has given way to an interactive "prosumer" process in which consumers of content also act as producers of content in an ongoing feedback loop. No longer bound by the limitations of TV schedules or particular networks, search engines, content aggregators, crowdsourcing, and social networking have superseded traditional media gatekeeping.

When there are fewer media workers, less standardized media routines, and no organization to influence the content, there is less mediation of messages. Furthermore, with the Internet unregulated by the FCC, who is performing the role of gatekeeper? This is a matter of some controversy with the net neutrality movement being largely opposed by Internet Service Providers (ISP) that want to be able to decide what content they push out to their subscribers at what rate of speed and ease of access, based on the ability of subscribers and content producers to pay for tiers of service; net neutrality activists fear that the ISPs also intend to act as gatekeepers of content based on influences other than concerns about revenue, particularly as content is increasingly concentrated among a few media conglomerates (Media and democracy in America, 2008).

In terms of other issues, it has become much easier for people to bypass traditional revenue models by downloading and sharing content for free without regard to copyrights. Further, limitations of geographic boundaries of broadcast media have been diminished, with local content shared nationally and internationally (for example, a tornado report in Oklahoma gets posted on YouTube) and international content clips both allowed and illicit appearing on the Web (e.g., Susan Boyle's performance on *Britain's Got Talent* in 2009 watched over 100 million times on YouTube) regardless of licensing deals and distribution through official channels. One key question to consider is the value of and role for content programmers and editors in this new era. Is it possible to quantify this value in some way?

Certainly reputation would play a role. In the 21st Century, many media professionals are moving to digital platforms to create new channels and content, away from the traditional network model. Here are a few examples (Jurgensen, 2012):

- Kiefer Sutherland is starring in a new online series *The Confessional*.
- Netflix is debuting two original series; *House of Cards* starring Kevin Spacey, and *Lilliehammer* starring Steven Van Zandt.
- Netflix is also bringing back new episodes of *Arrested Development*.
- Madonna is producing *DanceOn*, a YouTube channel, and TV star Amy Pehler is involved in *Smart Girls at the Party*, another YouTube channel.

The content options are quite staggering, ranging from network-driven sites and applications to new channels and sites entering the marketplace. All of the networks have websites that offer programming, along with apps developed for mobile devices to access content. Hulu Plus, Netflix, Amazon Prime, and Blockbuster offer subscription services to users, while Vudu offers an online pay-per-view type model of HD movies with no monthly fees.

No doubt, there is a lot of content to sort out and even more will be created going forward. One method to sort through the plethora of content is to consider recommendations made by key opinion leaders who are experts in their areas. YouTube, Viemo and other video sites post comments and sort content by popularity. Audience members may examine their Facebook friends to see what their peers "like" and comment on. Twitter is also a useful tool, especially through the use of hashtags to quickly identify comments on a particular type of content. Social media imposes an obligation on the user to check their Facebook and

Twitter links regularly in order to stay connected and aware. Some audience members might seek out background information and detail from a service like Wikipedia.

Social media can also disrupt traditional patterns of programming by its ability to leak plots and themes and share feedback among users. Consider the case of the popular U.K. TV program *Doctor Who*. When new episodes of that long-running BBC science-fiction drama were broadcast in Britain in 2011, executives at the BBC America channel observed a major spike in illegal file sharing of the show in the United States. Some Stateside fans, it seemed, were unwilling to wait the two weeks between the British and American premieres. Fans waiting on the new episodes were frustrated by online spoilers on blogs and Twitter. The BBC's solution was to compress time and space. Taking a page from the same-day worldwide premieres of blockbuster films, the new season of *Doctor Who* started on a Saturday, not just in Britain, but in the United States and Canada as well (Stelter, 2011).

Bloggers and critics are thus another source for comment and criticism of content. Film critics like Austin's Harry Knowles have carved a niche online that would not be possible through traditional media. In the era of social media, the roles of critics and programmers seem to be merging, so one can be a sort of archivist or curator in the sense of creating catalogs to help categorize content. In this sense, the personal touch, based on the track record of recommendations and how people may know you or think of you, is perceived as being better than a computer aggregating rating data through a service like Netflix that is tied to more mainstream popularity. Social media allows each individual to participate, exhibiting their own personal, quirky, human touch.

Social media has emerged to take on a new role in this gatekeeping process, one that is more open and participatory than previous models. In one sense, social media is an extension of previous efforts to unite audiences via technology. These ideas are explored in the next section.

Origins of Social Media

The introduction of the Internet brought with it the opportunity to bring people together who share common interests. While the original Internet was designed with research as its focus, the new medium also allowed people to connect with others who shared the same interests. The Internet made these communities of interest possible, especially for "social" interests. These online intentional communities based on interests rather than proximity (such as local clubs/ organizations) formed the early roots for social media as we know it today.

The terms "friends" and "followers" were not used in these early efforts to unite people with common interests, but easily could have been used. What is interesting is to remind ourselves that the Web at that time was all text-based—no graphics, audio or video material that we take for granted today. Here are a few examples of these early efforts to utilize the Internet to bring interest communities together:

- SF-LOVERS appeared in the late 1970s on the ARPANET listserv for Science Fiction fans.
- 1978 BBS (Bulletin Board System) debuted.
- 1979 debut of Usenet.
- 1980 MUD (Multi-User Dungeon).
- 1985 the WELL debuts.

The WELL (Whole Earth 'Lectronic Link) was a pioneering virtual community bulletin board system inspired by counterculture (see "Learn about the WELL"). Founded by Whole Earth editor Stewart Brand, the WELL was designed to be a vehicle for social change using a decentralized management model, with little top-down control of content or networking. The WELL would eventually be acquired by Salon.com in later years, but is widely recognized for its role as one of the first virtual online communities.

In addition to online communities, computer users began to form clubs and interest communities that functioned both online and offline. The Homebrew Computer Club, first organized on the West Coast in 1975, was one of the most influential clubs to help shape the growing personal computer revolution.

Open source software was also a critical development in the growth of the Internet and ultimately social media, thanks in large part to scientist and innovator Tim Berners-Lee and his work through CERN (The European Organization for Nuclear Research) in Switzerland. Berners-Lee envisioned the Web to be collaborative, interactive, and open, and his ideas ultimately led to the development of the World Wide Web and html language in 1989. Lee's early software code helped people search for information more easily, and brought a graphic interface to the Internet.

The growth of the Internet and its various digital platforms brought about a new form of media convergence, and ushered in what Jenkins (2006) refers to as transmedia. Transmedia involves storytelling across multiple platforms, with each medium adding its own distinct contributions to an understanding of our world. Jenkins refers to this phenomenon as "additive comprehension," where an expansion of interpretive possibility occurs when fictional franchises are extended across multiple media texts and media outlets. This new era of transmedia established a clear role for the development of original Web content and new opportunities for distribution.

Web Content's Creation and Distribution

The explosive popularity of the World Wide Web in the 1990s brought about a paradigm shift in media content. It became inexpensive and easy for anyone with access to the technology to create and distribute content in this new environment. The first efforts to create content for the Web were text-based, established by blogging and wikis.

Blogging (Web logs) emerged as one of the first content forms to gain popularity on the Internet. The number of blogs on the Web changes by the hour; well over 150 million were estimated to be in existence in 2012. Blogs are often short-lived, in that 80% of blogs are abandoned in the first month.

In the United States, bloggers are more or less evenly split among gender groups, and about three-quarters are college-educated. There are many tools to develop a blog. Among the more popular are Wordpress.com, LiveJournal.com, TypePad.com, and Blogspot.com. Twitter is considered a micro-blogging tool, and one can find tweets linked to blogs offering original content.

Wikis allow users to share in the writing and editing of multiple versions of content. Wikipedia, the virtual online encyclopedia, is the best-known wiki. Wikipedia was first established as Nupedia, utilizing a traditional encyclopedia format with expert editors and writers who provided a rigorous review of content, but this model proved to be very inefficient and unsustainable.

An interesting paradox exists with Wikipedia. Anyone can use the site, but elite experts have created a small community of editors/writers who in effect run the site. There are also concerns about the accuracy of many of the entries on Wikipedia, and usually disclaimers are found on entries where more validation and research are needed.

The growth of social media networking sites like Facebook, Myspace, and YouTube established more outlets for sharing original content. While originally limited to user-generated content, eventually corporate entities would create their own pages and channels on which to offer content and promote their own programming.

The introduction of smart phones and the companion application markets quickly fueled interest in mobile platforms that offered new ways to consume content. Along with the establishment of tablet technology, the applications market continues to explode. Companies followed suit, with Netflix, Hulu, YouTube and virtually all the major broadcast and cable networks creating applications to deliver content in the mobile world. These efforts have led to a new form of gatekeeping called broadcatching.

Broadcatching

One popular way in which content is distributed on the Web has been mechanized by cutting out the gatekeeping role of programmers, through broadcatching:

> To understand the concept described by this term, first take a look at traditional *broadcast* media (such as radio, TV, magazines and newspapers) and note that they generally consist of a *one publisher to many consumers* flow of information, and as such rely upon common opinions and beliefs, as each published issue is targeted for a mass audience.

On the other hand, *Broadcatch* connotes a *many to one* gathering of information, using a network of personalized agents to ideally sift through all
available information and return just that which is of possible current interest
from trusted, authenticable sources and in a form and style amenable to the
user. Broadcatch is designed to thrive in a diversity of opinions and provide
a mechanism that *effectively automates word of mouth.*

(*Broadcatch defined*, 2007)

One of the more popular formats of broadcatching is RSS feeds that syndicate
(note that this is another term appropriated from broadcasting) content according
to user preferences. *PC Magazine Encyclopedia* (2011) defines RSS as **R**eally **S**imple
Syndication, a syndication format that was developed by Netscape in 1999 and
became very popular for aggregating updates to blogs and news sites. RSS also
stood for "Rich Site Summary" and "RDF Site Summary."

RSS allows Web users to act as their own content programmers, filtering
for themselves only the content that they are most interested in consuming.
Broadcatching has become for some mainstream media companies a strategic way
for them to control the feedback.

With the development of social and participatory media applications, and as
broadcatching applications continue to be used, the personalization of content
distribution once again has a human element while also utilizing the technologies
of content aggregation. In this iteration, content distributors use their own filtered
content choices to push out content to their subscribers or visitors, using broadcatching technologies and/or their own editorial recommendations. Individual
website owners and bloggers can take on this task, and some have turned these
formats into businesses such as *Technorati* and *The Huffington Post.*

Social bookmarking sites such as Del.icio.us and Digg use the participatory
format to monitor members' ratings of content to prioritize its presentation.
StumbleUpon also uses this kind of functionality, in a way that gives users a chance
to find some content that they may not otherwise find through their own searches
or through bookmarking and recommendations of others. StumbleUpon enables
members to view random content, rate it, and have other "Stumblers" access their
viewed content pages. Helft (2007) described this unique website in terminology
that recalls that of television programming: "You tell the service about your
professional interests or your hobbies, and it serves up sites to match them. As you
'stumble' from site to site, you will feel as if you are channel-surfing the Internet,
or rather, a corner of the Internet that is most relevant to you." Moreover, the site
picks are based on user ratings. This form of crowdsourcing puts the programming
into the hands of the users themselves. YouTube also has a rating system function,
and users not only can rate and post comments about the content in a conversation
with other viewers, but they can also post their own video responses. YouTube
channels also give people a chance to present their own user-generated content
(UGC) and act as programmers of their own networks. Sites such as Netflix and

Amazon also use data from individual users and others to push content that the sites think the consumer will like.

Finally, social networking sites have also given a voice to users to act as programmers. Facebook friends and Twitter users make recommendations of specific content, hoping to embellish their personal reputations when their friends thank them for the referral. Twitter has taken on a role as an online "watercooler" by driving viewers to tune in to television. This is especially true for live sporting events, where tweets may spike as many as fifty times the normal traffic flow (Boorstein, 2011). Active social networkers can expect to spend at least a small part of each day following links provided by their friends, and doing the same for others. This is a much more intimate kind of gatekeeping, in which the channel programmers are not some distant executives deciding what content they will exhibit for mass audiences, but people we know and whose opinions and tastes we value, serving just their own network of friends and acquaintances. Facebook and Twitter posts can also be forms of media content for readers who are not actively participating.

Conclusion

Audiences in the digital era have a variety of choices of how to access content, from the old-style gatekeeping of broadcast media to personalized feeds to the recommendations of crowds and their friends. At what level they want their messages mediated, if at all, is up to them to decide. Media consumers become fans and followers, developing an emotional connection and sense of identification with and a sense of identity from the product or service, be it a television network or series, website, movie, or original content produced for digital media.

This also begs the question—can traditional media ever adapt to this environment? If so, traditional media must require links to non-owned content, and user-generated content (UGC). Such a move would counteract the tendency of corporate conglomerates to promote their own content ad nauseam, thereby limiting original content by constantly cross-promoting across platforms. This new environment would hopefully add variety and more choices for consumers.

This chapter has investigated how social media offers content (traditional media content as well as professional and user-generated content produced for the Web) to ever more segmented, fragmented, and individualized audiences who are also acting as gatekeepers by serving as curators and aggregators of the content that they consume. The traditional linear model of mass communications has undergone seismic shifts, as receivers of messages increasingly also act as producers of messages, actively provide feedback to messages, and also act as gatekeepers of channels that they control.

Editor's note

Dr. Dan Schackman died of a heart attack on November 20, 2011. He was 47 years old. A bright young scholar, Dan had agreed to participate in this project and completed a large draft of this chapter at the time of his passing. Some material was written by the Editor using notes from Dan's text as well as other sources to complete missing sections without changing the focus of the author's intent.

I am pleased to present this chapter in Dan's memory, and thank Professor Greg Bray at SUNY-New Paltz for his help in locating the chapter drafts written by Dan so his final work could be included posthumously in this volume.

References

About StumbleUpon. (2010). StumbleUpon.com. Retrieved from: http://www.stumble upon.com/aboutus/.

Boorstein, J. (2011, April 12). Can Twitter save live TV? Retrieved from: http://www.cnbc.com/id/42559646/Can_Twitter_Save_Live_TV.

Broadcatch defined. (2007). Broadcatch Technologies. Retrieved from: http://www.broadcatch.com/definition.shtml.

Bruns, A. (2008). *Blogs, Wikipedia, Second Life, and beyond: From production to produsage.* New York: Peter Lang.

Hall, S. (1973). *Encoding and decoding in the television discourse.* Birmingham: Centre for Cultural Studies, University of Birmingham.

Helft, M. (2007, October 7). A way to find your corner of the Internet sky. *New York Times.* Retrieved from: http://www.nytimes.com/2007/10/07/technology/circuits/07stream.html?_r=3&ref=business&oref=slogin&oref=login.

Jenkins, H. (2006). *Convergence culture: Where old and new media collide.* New York: NYU Press.

Jurgensen, J. (2012, February 17). Web TV's new lineup. *The Wall Street Journal*, D1-2.

Learn about the WELL. Retrieved from: http://www.well.com/aboutwell.html.

Media and democracy in America: A reform plan for a new administration. (August, 2008). *Common Cause.* Retrieved from http://www.commoncause.org/site/pp.asp?c=dk LNK1MQIwG&b=4773591.

PC Magazine Encyclopedia. (2011). RSS definition. Retrieved from: http://www.pc mag.com/encyclopedia_term/0,2542,t=RSS&i=50680,00.asp#fbid=x4QZbtfDOby.

Shoemaker, P. J., & Reese, S. D. (1996). *Mediating the message: Theories of influence on mass media content.* (2nd ed.). New York: Longman.

Shoemaker, P. J., & Vos, T. P. (2009). *Gatekeeping theory.* New York: Routledge.

Stelter, B. (2010, February 23). Water-cooler effect: Internet can be TV's friend. *New York Times.* Retrieved from: http://www.nytimes.com/2010/02/24/business/media/24 cooler.html?scp=1&sq=Watercooler%20effect%20of%20the%20Internet&st=cse.

Stelter, B. (2011, April 22). New time warp for 'Doctor Who'. *New York Times.* Retrieved from http://www.nytimes.com/2011/04/23/arts/television/doctor-who-us-premiere-will-not-be-delayed.html.

Stodart, E. (2008, December). Who watches the watchers? Toward an ethic of surveillance in a digital age. *Studies in Christian Ethics, 21*(3), 362–381.

White, D. M. (1950). The "gate-keeper": A case study in the selection of news. *Journalism Quarterly, 27*(4), 383–390.

7

SOCIAL MEDIA AND THE VALUE OF TRUTH

Navigating the Web of Morality

Berrin Beasley

Cute. Cuddly. Pink. Big brown eyes, a smile that never quits, and smells like straw-berries. That's Lots-o'-Huggin' bear, a new toy addition to Disney Pixar's *Toy Story* film trilogy that made its 2010 debut in a viral video uploaded to YouTube by MyCrazyCommercials. The video appears to be an early 1980s advertisement for the Lotso bear taken from an old VHS tape. Flickering images and distorted sound contribute to the ad's seeming authenticity. MyCrazyCommercials features other vintage television commercials that are legitimate, which lends credibility to the Lotso video as a real ad. And in *Toy Story 3*, the film in which audiences first meet Lotso, the bear is depicted as a 1980s toy, which supports the veracity of the viral video ad. By November 2012, the video had recorded nearly 1.4 million views (Lots-o'-Huggin' bear commercial, YouTube, 2011).

But as is common with popular viral videos, viewers quickly began to question the ad's authenticity. Some doubted because there was no brand logo shown or mentioned in the commercial. Others posted that the school bus steps shown in the video were inconsistent with the buses of the time and that the little girl's school lunch box was made post 1980s. They were right to doubt. John Lasseter, chief creative officer of Disney and Pixar Animation Studios, is shown in a different YouTube video, one by Disney Living, saying that Lotso was a character idea from the first *Toy Story* that finally made its way into the latest film. Therefore, the video couldn't possibly be authentic (Toy Story 3 drops in at toy fair, 2011).

Posting the Lotso video on a YouTube channel next to real retro TV ads but without any mention of *Toy Story 3* is part of a sophisticated viral video marketing campaign by Disney and Pixar. Lots-o'-Huggin' bear's viral video falls into an ethical gray area because while it never purports to represent a real product, it does present the product in such a way as to imply it is real. By using traditional advertising norms it blurs that line—intentionally—between Hollywood fiction and marketing reality. Contributing to the ethical gray zone is the fact that Disney Pixar wasn't trying to sell the Lotso toy, but promote the movie in which it appears. Creative marketing strategies happen around us all the time, so as a public we're not terribly surprised to learn that the Lotso video was fake. In fact, some YouTube users enjoy trying to determine the authenticity of videos, such as that of Kobe Bryant jumping over a moving Aston Martin. The video is shot to look like a personal camera is recording an impromptu challenge for Bryant to jump over an oncoming car, but it is really a viral video in which Nike's Hyperdunk Black Colorways sneakers are hawked without Bryant ever saying a word about them (Kobe Bryant jumps over an Aston Martin car, 2011).

Disney Pixar's and Nike's videos do more than just promote a product on YouTube. They take advantage of the unique characteristics of social media to engage viewers in conversation about the product, silently challenging them to uncover the truth of the video and consequently spurring the video's popularity on the web. Some see these kinds of videos as harmless fun, an entertaining way to spark interest in a product. Others are concerned they mislead viewers into thinking they are watching a truthful video, not a marketing one.

Changing Model of Communication

Ethical decision-making is a tricky business under the best of working conditions. At least with legacy media like newspapers, magazines, and television there have been more than 80 years of wrangling over the subject of ethics, resulting in a number of well thought out ethics codes and countless books on the ethical practice of the media. These codes were created under the media industry's business model of communicating from one to many with limited ways in which the public could contribute to the information-making process. But social media are different; they are an extension of the Internet construction of communicating from one-to-many or one-to-several or one-to-one, depending on user intent.

Because so many of the legacy media's ethical codes applied to the Internet, media practitioners at first considered social media little more than a sophisticated version of traditional communication modes. In the early days of the Internet, traditional media posted for free content that was already published in newspapers and broadcast on the news. Banner ads accompanied the content in the hope users would notice them and click through to the product or service advertised. Over time, information presentation and data collection evolved and a new Internet-based communication form emerged. As a result, social media forced news and advertising content producers to rethink a centuries-old communication method, and the ethical practices that go with it.

Social media are generally defined as mobile and web-based technologies that facilitate interactive dialogue, allowing users to create and exchange their own content. The best-known of these are YouTube, Twitter, and Facebook. Social media technologies are easily accessible and scalable, permitting the expansion and contraction of users and content as dictated by user interest. Skilled media industry practitioners recognize these basic elements of social media and make use of them accordingly. The key difference between social media and other forms of communication on the Internet is the concept of authoritative user-generated content, the ability of users not just to respond to information presented by the media industry, but to usurp its role as authority on the dissemination of information and persuasion content. This difference requires industry professionals to compete with other information outlets, which is not really a new challenge, except that this time the competitor communicates with audiences tied together by conversation, personal relationships, and the sharing of knowledge in an intimate manner, even if shared with millions (Kietzmann, Hermkens, McCarthy, & Silvestre, 2011).

The Marketplace of Ideas

More than four centuries ago, poet John Milton, followed by John Stuart Mill, Thomas Jefferson, and U.S. Supreme Court Justice William Brennan, among others, championed the First Amendment need for a free and open marketplace of ideas, where truth and falsity compete for attention, but where truth always emerges victorious. In her book on the application of the marketplace of ideas philosophy to the practice of public relations, Kathy Fitzpatrick identifies four foundations of the Marketplace of Ideas: access, process, truth, and disclosure (Fitzpatrick & Bronstein, 2006). The extension of Fitzpatrick's model to include social media can provide a framework through which to view the ethical use of such by media practitioners. The legal interpretation of the marketplace of ideas concept originated with U.S. Supreme Court Justice Oliver Wendell Holmes in 1918 when Holmes wrote that "the free trade of ideas" was necessary for the good of the people (*Abrams v. United States, 1919*). His decision supports previous philosophical postulations that people have a right to freely speak information and hear information and that they can deduce the truth in a rational manner because there is one objective truth to be divined (Fitzpatrick & Bronstein, 2006).

Alexander Meiklejohn (1948) valued speech in a hierarchy in which political speech is classified as the most valuable, and commercial speech the least valuable. Even when it comes to false information, political speech (*NYT v. Sullivan, 1964*) is privileged over commercial speech, which has strict liability laws that prohibit falsity by misrepresentation or omission. Supreme Court rulings make it clear that commercial speech has only limited constitutional protection (*Bigelow v. Virginia, 1975*) and that "false, deceptive, or misleading" communication has no First Amendment protection (FTC Policy Statement on Deception, 1985). Within the continuum of speech, between the poles of political speech and commercial speech, lies the expression of ideas that could loosely be described as general. Contribution of these to the marketplace in a meaningful way requires an important element: access to the marketplace.

Access: The Right to Speak and Hear Information

Following decades of judicial rulings on the breadth and depth of what constitutes the freedom of expression and its location within the First Amendment, *access*, broadly defined, is the right of individuals to freely express themselves and to receive information necessary for informed decision-making. A speaker's access to the marketplace is fundamental to the free flow of information and ideally the contribution of all available knowledge on a subject. Social media provide access for the average citizen to the contribution and consumption of information as never before, and media practitioners have a responsibility to provide the most comprehensive information necessary for authentic understanding of a subject by an individual.

Unfortunately, there remains a disparity among social media users regarding access. Some have more access than others. This is abundantly clear when one considers the technological divide, but it is perhaps less clear when considering the ability to contribute information via social networks. Social media are hailed as the great information equalizer. Anyone with access to the Internet can post information, regardless of whether the information comes from the *New York Times* or a cell phone in Libya. While that may be true on the surface, the resources available to the creator of the information can significantly affect the quality of the information and its value to the marketplace. For example, though the Lotso television commercial may have been exposed as a fraud by some on the Internet, many more will have viewed it and taken from it the idea that Lotso was a real toy from the 1980s. Media practitioners may wonder why a video about a stuffed bear is important; it's just about a toy in a movie. But it is really more than that. It is an example of how the many talented employees at Disney Pixar, with their range of high tech equipment and deep-pocket funding, can create videos that exploit advertising's social norms to intentionally mislead consumers. By failing to disclose the ad as a promotional piece for an upcoming movie, Disney Pixar can use it to mislead viewers about the video's true purpose, thereby preventing them from critically consuming the video. It's an example of failing to provide access *to the most available* information on a subject and an example of the different levels of access between wealthy corporations and individual citizens.

Process: The Creation and Distribution of Information

Legal rulings have made clear that political speech is privileged over commercial speech and that the value of speech is determined by the meaningful contribution it makes to the marketplace. This conclusion favors news from media outlets over persuasive information presented by advertising and public relations practitioners and plays an important role in the ethical use of social media. There remains the philosophical understanding that news outlets will use social media to present truthful information that is objective and factual unless the viewer (perhaps user is a more appropriate word when discussing social media) is informed otherwise. Persuasive communication is expected by the Federal Trade Commission to avoid false representations and deceptive omissions so that users may recognize persuasive information when exposed to it. Therefore, it is the *process* by which communication channels are accessed and information created and distributed that separates ethical media industry practitioners from unethical ones. Sending a Facebook friend request to a story subject or source to gain access to personal information without the reporter identifying him or herself as such is a clear violation of the socially responsible, and thereby ethical, use of social media. Using public information found on the subject's Facebook page, or any other social media site, is an ethical use because the person voluntarily contributed to the marketplace of ideas about him or herself.

ABC's *Nightline* co-anchor Terry Moran's tweet about President Obama's "jackass" comment to his more than 1 million followers is another example of the unethical use of social media for information dissemination (Obama calls Kanye West a "Jackass," 2009). During the 2009 Video Music Awards show, hip-hop singer Kanye West interrupted country singer Taylor Swift's acceptance speech by taking the microphone from her and proclaiming singer Beyoncé Knowles had the better music video. In an off-the-record conversation during an interview for CNBC, Obama was asked about West's stunt and replied West's behavior was that of a jackass. Moran sent the following tweet: "Pres. Obama just called Kanye West a 'jackass' for his outburst at VMAs when Taylor Swift won. Now THAT's presidential." Because the tweet was from an off-the-record conversation, ABC quickly deleted the tweet and issued an apology for it:

> In the process of reporting on remarks by President Obama that were made during a CNBC interview, ABC news employees prematurely tweeted a portion of those remarks that turned out to be from an off-the-record portion of the interview. That was wrong. We apologize to the White House and CNBC and are taking steps to ensure that it will not happen again.
>
> *(Obama calls Kanye West a "Jackass," 2009)*

Still, the damage was done. One post less than 140 characters in length resulted in instant, widespread discourse across the Internet and the apology of a national television network.

An example of the gray area surrounding the press' ethical use of social media for news purposes occurred during the attack on Fort Hood. When U.S. Army major Nidal Malik Hasan opened fire on his comrades at Fort Hood military base in November 2009, base commanders followed protocol by placing the base on lock down. There was limited movement on and off the base of both people and information. When supposed eyewitness accounts from inside Fort Hood began emerging via Twitter, traditional news outlets integrated the content into their own online and social media content. Complicating the matter was that the day before the shooting occurred microblogging site Twitter had launched a new feature called Twitter Lists, which allows users to sort the people they follow into lists (Heussner, 2009). A number of major news outlets like *The New York Times*, *The Washington Post*, and *The Dallas Morning News*, compiled lists of breaking news from Fort Hood. One of the most prolific tweeters from inside Fort Hood was Tearah Moore. Unfortunately, a number of her tweets provided inaccurate information. For example, at one point she tweeted: "Some guys just shot 19–25 people." Some of her tweets were criticized as insensitive, such as "[T]hey just brought a CART full of boxes w/transplant parts in them. Not good not good. #fthood." Considered most insensitive was the picture she tweeted of a soldier being brought into the hospital on a gurney with the caption, "The poor guy that got shot in the balls."

Moore was not a trained journalist. She was a person in a crisis situation sharing information the only way she could. Under those circumstances one can allow that Moore may not have used her best judgment when deciding what information to share, and that Moore could have understandably tweeted inaccurate information, even while sharing her phone number via tweets from inside Fort Hood encouraging followers to relay her number to media outlets so she could provide updates. What's more important than her sudden role of citizen journalist is how the news media used Moore's and others' tweeted information. By incorporating these tweets into a list of tweets from other local news agencies like TV station KCEN and the *Fort Hood Sentinel*, Moore's tweets and the tweets by others claiming to originate from inside Fort Hood were given more credibility than they would have under usual circumstances. But that is the point in this case. The Fort Hood shooting was not normal circumstances, which asks the question: For the press, where is the line between providing truth—honest and factual as required by its responsibility to society—and providing ideas to the marketplace before the value of those ideas has been evaluated?

It is the *process* that affects the information. In the Fort Hood shooting, the need to provide information to the marketplace was fundamental, and when little to no information was available from trusted sources, the press chose to disseminate the tweets, even though the source and accuracy of those tweets were not identifiable at the time of the event. This is an example of the Self-Righting Principle, the corollary to the Marketplace of Ideas. The Self-Righting Principle predicts that in the marketplace of ideas, truth will always overturn falsity. Indeed, as time progressed and more information became available, traditional news outlets engaged in their primary function of verifying the truth and accuracy of information before sharing it and of correcting the errors in previously shared information. Shortly after the attack by journalists, bloggers, and other citizens about her inaccurate and insensitive tweets, Moore ended her work as citizen journalist and changed her Twitter profile from public to private.

Other process issues to consider include the role journalists should play in the social media landscape, for these days most major news outlets, and many smaller ones, require their employees to blog, tweet, and contribute to the outlet's Facebook page. NPR, *The New York Times, The Wall Street Journal*, and numerous other news outlets have embraced social media as new information and dissemination tools. Journalists tweet while covering meetings and events, they post status updates on the outlet's Facebook page, they write pieces for the outlet's legacy format and its online site, and they blog about their stories. In all these cases reporters are reminded they represent the news agencies for which they work and are held to the same code of conduct as when writing, reporting, and editing for their traditional workplace. They are also told their personal participation in social media reflects on their workplaces and should be guided by the same code of ethics they use at work. In 2009, *The Los Angeles Times* updated its code of ethics to address journalists' personal online activities.

> Assume that your professional life and your personal life merge online regardless of your care in separating them. Don't write or post anything that would embarrass the LAT or compromise your ability to do your job. Assume that everything you write or receive on a social media site is public and knowable to everyone with access to a computer.
>
> *(Mashable.com, 2009)*

Also stated is that journalists should not join politically or morally charged groups via Facebook or other networking sites. They should not blog, tweet, or otherwise post opinions about subjects or people they cover, a guideline violated in summer 2011 when several AP journalists tweeted their opinions about two very controversial subjects: the New York Senate vote on gay marriage and the Casey Anthony trial in Florida of a young mother charged with killing her 3-year-old daughter. As a result, AP Deputy Managing Editor for Standards and Production Tom Kent issued a memo to AP journalists regarding their use of social networks, "however we may configure our accounts or select our friends, [social networks] should be considered a public forum. AP staffers should not make postings there that amount to personal opinions on contentious public issues" (Romenesko, 2011). In a more serious case of a journalist tweeting about a news subject, CNN's senior Middle East editor Octavia Nasr was fired in 2010 following a tweet through her official CNN Twitter account in which she expressed sadness for the death of Grand Ayatollah Mohammed Hussein Fadlallah, Lebanon's top Shia cleric with ties to the militant group Hezbollah, which the U.S. views as a terrorist organization (Bauder, 2010). In her tweet Nasr wrote, "Sad to hear of the passing of Sayyed Mohammad Hussein Fadlallah. One of Hezbollah's giants I respect a lot." CNN fired Nasr, who had been with the company for 20 years and had interviewed Fadlallah in 1990, saying the tweet did not meet CNN's editorial standards and had compromised her credibility as a journalist. Nasr's tweet was quickly removed from her Twitter feed and the following day she blogged on the CNN website that her tweet was "simplistic" and an "error of judgment." She explained she was praising Fadlallah for his stance on women's rights, particularly his call to end honor killings. Also in her blog Nasr wrote, "Reaction to my tweet was immediate, overwhelming and provides a good lesson on why 140 characters should not be used to comment on controversial or sensitive issues, especially those dealing with the Middle East."

The Process of Using Social Media Deceptively

On the commercial side of social media use, users have more latitude in their actions, as long as their communication is not misleading due to misrepresentation or an omission of information important to a consumer's decision to purchase a product or service (Fitzpatrick, 2006). In 2007, Marié Digby was a 24-year-old aspiring musician, uploading to YouTube homemade videos of her covering popular songs, including an acoustic rendition of Rihanna's "Umbrella," hoping she would become a viral success and record executives would sign her to a recording contract (Smith & Lattman, 2007). Her videos quickly gained traction. Her version of "Umbrella" was included in an episode of MTV's *The Hills*, was played on radio stations in Oregon and California, including Los Angeles, and was even available for purchase on iTunes. In July, she was interviewed by Los Angeles DJ Valentine on adult contemporary radio station KYSR-FM where they discussed her nearly instantaneous rise to fame. Digby modestly explained that she was "usually the listener calling in, you know, just hoping that I'm going to be the one to get that last ticket to the Star Lounge with [pop star] John Mayer!" In August, she posted on her Myspace page, "I NEVER in a million years thought that doing my little video of Umbrella in my living room would lead to this . tv shows, itunes, etc !!!" After 2.3 million views of her version of "Umbrella," Digby's wish came true. Walt Disney Co.'s Hollywood Records label issued in a press release: "Breakthrough YouTube Phenomenon Marié Digby Signs With Hollywood Records." Unfortunately, Digby was not what she claimed to be. Eighteen months before her YouTube success, Hollywood Records had already signed her to their label. In an elaborate marketing plan that relied heavily on social media, Hollywood Records and Digby concocted the idea of depicting her as an average girl who dreamed of being famous. YouTube was the perfect outlet for their plan because on YouTube anyone can be famous, just ask pop singer Colbie Calliat, who also signed a record contract based on the songs she wrote and posted on her Myspace music page.

In Digby's case, the farce was complex and widespread. One month after her supposed contract signing, *Wall Street Journal* reporters exposed the charade and the extent of Digby's and Hollywood Record's deception was revealed. The Apple computer and software she used to record her videos were given to her by Hollywood Records. The LA DJ who interviewed her? In on the ruse, as were station programming executives. The high-quality sound of Digby's version of "Umbrella" available on iTunes? It was recorded by Hollywood Records, which also released it to radio stations for play. How did Digby and Hollywood Record producers respond when confronted about their deception? They said it was difficult for new artists to break in to the music scene and that online publicity was an opportunity too good to pass up. "I was coming out of nowhere," Ms. Digby said. "I wanted to find a way to get some exposure."

Digby's case in some ways parallels Lots-o'-Huggin' bear's in that both were viral video hits on YouTube and both used deception as a ploy to attract viewers. The companies behind the deceptions intended them to result in monetary gain, either through viewers seeing the movie or listeners buying songs. And in that gray area between omitting information, such as Lots-o'-Huggin' bear not being a real toy, and using misleading information, as in Digby's case, neither failed to provide information material, or necessary, to the decision of an individual to purchase a product or a service. However, the *process* of deciding to deceive the public via a social media outlet bears evidence that the outlet itself carries heavy ethical weight because neither campaign would have been directed to a traditional media outlet.

Truth is Crucial to Serving the Public Good

While access and process make important contributions to the Marketplace of Ideas, truth is the most important of the four foundations. Every credible media organization lists truth as key to its mission. The Society of Professional Journalists directs journalists to "seek truth and report it." The Public Relations Society of America's code of ethics states providing "truthful information is essential to serving the public interest." The Word of Mouth Marketing Association, a professional organization for the social media industry, encourages members to "create an environment of truth between consumers and marketers." However, as with traditional media, not all social media companies value truth to the same extent as their professional organizations. Until mid-2011, Twitter was used as a non-disclosed conduit for payment by celebrity tweeters. Mention a product and make a buck or two, or $10,000. Kim Kardashian reportedly earned as much as $10,000 per testimonial in 2010 when tweeting about a product or service, or approximately $71 per character based on Twitter's 140-character limit (Evangelista, 2010). By November 2012, Kim was listed as being one of the highest-earning celebrity tweeters on Sponsoredtweets.com, a software platform used by IZEA Holdings, Inc. to facilitate social media-sponsored (SMS) campaigns (Sponsored tweets.com, 2012). With 16.6 million followers Kim's endorsement was in such high demand that companies who wanted Kim to sponsor their product via Twitter had to call Sponsoredtweets.com for her price-per-tweet fee. IZEA defines itself as a company that facilitates social networking promotional campaigns by compensating "bloggers, tweeters and mobile promoters (our publishers) to share information about companies, products, websites and events within their social media streams. Advertisers benefit from buzz, traffic and awareness; publishers earn cash, points and product samples" (IZEA.com, 2011).

IZEA isn't the only company in the business. MyLikes and Ad.ly also broker deals between sponsors and Twitter users. Social media-sponsored promotional campaigns in general came under the scrutiny of the Federal Trade Commission (FTC) after the agency issued guidelines for paid-for celebrity testimonials on blogs and social media sites (FTC, 2009). The FTC's guidelines stipulate that "material connections" between advertisers and endorsers, including bloggers and word-of-mouth marketers, must be disclosed and that celebrities must reveal their paid status when promoting a product outside the context of traditional advertisements. Given Twitter's 140-character limit, sponsored tweets often carry the short hash tag #spon or #ad or #paid or #samp at the end to indicate the tweeter was compensated either by cash or free samples. Sponsoredtweets.com is taking the FTC's directions to heart, both legally and ethically. On its website the company explains it uses a software program to automatically check for disclosure of sponsorship before a tweet is posted and provides tweeters with example disclosure statements to include in their tweets. However, if a company still wanted a Kardashian to tweet about it but couldn't afford Kim, her younger sister Khloe was available for $13,000 per tweet to her 7.7 million followers, ethical sponsorship disclosure included.

IZEA also owns Socialspark.com (2011), a company that functions in the same way as Sponsoredtweets.com except it connects advertisers with bloggers. For many advertisers blogging extends the product or service mentions in Twitter's microblog into full-blown conversations in other forums, such as Deal Seeking Mom and tech blogger Chris Pirillo. The FTC's social media guidelines apply to blogs as well. People who are paid to blog about a product or service, whether in money or sample products, are expected to do so truthfully by disclosing their compensation. The same is true for product and service reviews. At this point in the chapter it becomes clear that *access*, *process*, and *truth* cannot be considered without discussing *disclosure*, which is the transparency of the information individuals use to inform their decisions and behaviors.

Disclosure: Key to Building Trust

One example of undisclosed sponsored blogging that resulted in a wave of negative publicity when exposed was the "Wal-Marting Across America" blog. In this case, two supposedly average Americans traveled across the United States in an RV, staying overnight in Wal-Mart parking lots and blogging about their encounters with Wal-Mart employees (Gogoi, 2006). Jim and Laura, who did not use their last names, began their blog in Las Vegas, the starting point of their journey, and ended it when they reached their destination in Georgia. The couple blogged about the Wal-Mart employees they met, all of whom provided excellent service to the travelers. In Amarillo, Texas, the pair blogged about an employee whose son had a potentially fatal heart disease requiring $300,000 worth of medical treatment. He told the two that if it weren't for his Wal-Mart health insurance, his son might not be alive today. A stop in Bentonville, Arkansas, the headquarters of Wal-Mart, introduced readers to a former Wal-Mart cashier, now project manager for corporate sustainability, who talked in detail about how proud she was of Wal-Mart's effort to go green. What Jim and Laura didn't disclose was that Wal-Mart was indirectly funding the trip by paying for their RV, gas, food, and other expenses through the organization Working Families for Wal-Mart, a company founded the year before by Wal-Mart's public relations firm Edelman. Working Families for Wal-Mart described itself as a grassroots organization dedicated to countering criticism by labor groups, but in no way did it disclose that Wal-Mart was its primary benefactor or that the organization's blogs were written by three Edelman employees.

In an interview with *Business Week* early in their travels Laura said she and her partner, who live together and have three children, came up with the idea of taking an RV trip to see their children and staying in Wal-Mart parking lots to save money. Laura said she contacted Working Families for Wal-Mart about their plan and the organization offered to fund their expenses. The organization flew the pair to Las Vegas where an RV with Working Families for Wal-Mart emblazoned across the sides was waiting for them. Working Families for Wal-Mart also set up a website for Laura and Jim to blog on, and paid Laura a freelance fee to chronicle their adventure. Although there was a Working Families for Wal-Mart banner on their blog site, nowhere was the mention that Wal-Mart was the biggest benefactor of Working Families for Wal-Mart and that the organization had been created less than a year earlier by Wal-Mart's public relations firm. Just days after the couple's road trip began, the press identified Laura as Laura St. Clair, a freelance writer, and Jim as Jim Thresher, a professional photographer who was in his 25th year as an employee for *The Washington Post*. Very quickly the newspaper's executive editor said Thresher had spoken with an editor about the trip but did not explain that it would be a sponsored venture and that Thresher's actions violated the newspaper's policy on doing freelance work for special interests. While *The Washington Post* was an unintended victim, Edelman's public relations plan from the beginning was to promote its client's image via social media, ignoring its professional organization's key principle of being "honest and accurate in all communications." Shortly after Edelman's elaborate social media PR stunt was exposed, president and CEO Richard Edelman addressed the situation on his own blog. "I want to acknowledge our error in failing to be transparent about the identity of our two bloggers from the outset." As a lesson to persuasive media outlets engaging in social media campaigns, transparency is the key to success. Honest communication in any social media outlet is crucial to success. Because of the openness of social media and the ability of the public to engage directly with the information provider and with others interested in the information provided, imperfect communication is ethically necessary and effective. "Packaged, filtered, controlled conversations" are not (Gunther, 2006).

Another situation that speaks to the need for identity disclosure when using social media is that of *The Los Angeles Times*' Pulitzer Prize-winning reporter and columnist Michael Hiltzik, who used pseudonyms to post comments on his own blog and the blogs of other people (Kurtz, 2006). Hiltzik had long-standing public feuds with conservative bloggers Hugh Hewitt, a radio talk show host, and Patrick Frey, an assistant Los Angeles district attorney. On his *Times* blog Hiltzik posed as "Mikekoshi," praising his own work and criticizing Frey's and Hewitt's. About Frey's blog Mikekoshi wrote Hewitt shouldn't be "running around loose in public without a muzzle" and on another site Mikekoshi criticized one of Frey's blogs as a "buffoonish post" and congratulated him for reaching "a new high-water mark in dopey criticism." Hiltzik was exposed when he used his Mikekoshi pseudonym to respond to criticism of him in Frey's column. Frey traced the IP address of Mikekoshi and discovered it was actually Hiltzik. *The Los Angeles Times* responded by suspending Hiltzik's blog after he admitted to using the pseudonym, saying he violated the paper's policy by using a false identity to post derogatory comments. Failing to disclose one's relationship with a media outlet, be it a news organization or a buzz marketing business like Sponsoredtweets.com, robs the marketplace of valuable information and creates an imbalance of power because one perspective appears to have more support than another.

Sony's PSP Marketing Campaign and the Four Foundations

While laws are in place that protect speech within the marketplace, media practitioners have an ethical responsibility to self-regulate their actions, thereby ensuring the most complete version of the truth is presented in the marketplace at all times. Lying by omission, as in undisclosed sponsored tweets by celebrities, is an example of unethical behavior that fails to provide the public with the most available information. Other cases, such as Marié Digby's meteoric rise to musical fame, are examples of outright deception, but neither fail to provide information "material" to a person's ability to make a reasoned decision to buy a product or service. In these cases and many others, the ethical responsibilities of social media use pick up where legal ones leave off. For example, Sony's PSP social media debacle "All I Want for Xmas is a PSP" violates all four marketplace principles (Nudd, 2006). In this campaign Sony, with the help of marketing firm, Zipatoni, created a fake video/blogging website about two target-demographic guys trying to drum up support in convincing their families to buy them a PSP for Christmas. By presenting information in a stealth format, Sony failed to provide the most available information to the marketplace, a tactic that backfired when gamers quickly identified the website as registered to Zipatoni. Internet users' *access* to more information than what Sony/Zipatoni provided quickly righted the imbalance in the marketplace.

Well-funded businesses can sometimes dominate the marketplace, thereby limiting other voices, and by deceiving the public about the source of certain information and the level of support their particular interest really has, the businesses can affect the *process* of communication. Such was the case with Sony/ Zipatoni when it attempted to embed its campaign within legitimate social media networks. The contribution of misleading or false information to the marketplace obstructs the public's ability to discern an objective *truth*, and failing to *disclose* the origin of communication limits the transparency necessary for informed decision-making. Unfortunately for Sony and its PSP, their attempt at blending in with other authentic social media users was quickly identified. Sony took down the website and issued an apology for its ploy.

> Busted. Nailed. Snagged. As many of you have figured out (maybe our speech was a little too funky fresh???), Peter isn't a real hip-hop maven and this site was actually developed by Sony. Guess we were trying to be just a little too clever. From this point forward, we will just stick to making cool products, and use this site to give you nothing but the facts on the PSP.
>
> *(Nudd, 2006)*

The Penny Arcade gaming site addressed Sony's campaign and the new communication model of social media as exemplified by viral marketing with this statement: "The reality is that no agency can create viral marketing, this is the sole domain of the consumer. Viral marketing is what happens when a campaign works—when we allow their message to travel via our own super-efficient conduits" (Graft, 2006).

The Ethical Use of Social Media

A common element among major professional media organizations is that all address the four foundations of the marketplace of ideas in their codes of ethics. All stress the need for the free flow of information in a democracy. All go into specific detail about the ethical processes for gathering and disseminating information, and each addresses the overriding need for truth, which should be accessed via full disclosure. Many have extended their codes of ethics to specifically address social media, reminding their employees that while the ways and means of reporting and writing may have changed, the ethics behind them haven't. As representative of the social media and word of mouth industry, the Word of Mouth Marketing Association's (WOMMA) code of ethics presents little difference between legacy media's and WOMMA's expectations: to use only ethical means in conducting business; to adhere to ethical standards that may exceed those required by law; and avoid deception.

Granted the Self-Righting Principle should eventually correct any false or misleading information that finds its way into the marketplace, and in all the cases presented in this chapter has done so, ethical use of social media by media professionals ensures the Self-Righting Principle need not be employed to assure a free flow of communication. As demonstrated in the Sony PSP example, the four foundations of the marketplace of ideas can provide a framework for assessing the ethical legitimacy of media communication practices (Fitzpatrick, 2006). While social media offer media practitioners the opportunity to ethically contribute information to the marketplace in ways radically different from the traditional push model of sending out information for the general public to find, a wide variety of publics can engage with modern information and persuasion professionals on an equal footing as part of a richer, more complex conversation, even if at times it's limited to 140 characters.

References

Abrams v. United States, 250 U.S. 616 (1919), 630.

Bauder, D. (2010, July 8). Octavia Nasr fired by CNN – the editor tweeted admiration for Grand Ayatollah Mohammed Hussein Fadlallah. *The Washington Post*. Retrieved Nov. 9, 2011, from: http://www.washingtonpost.com/wp-dyn/content/article/2010/07/07/AR2010070704948.html.

Bigelow v. Virginia, 421 U.S. 809 (1975), 818.

Evangelista, B. (2010, January 12). Startups cash in on Twitter with pay-per-tweet: Firms sponsor celebrities, users to promote products. *San Francisco Chronicle*. Retrieved Nov. 8, 2011, from: http://articles.sfgate.com/2010-01-12/business/17824144_1_twitter-users-san-francisco-s-twitter-advertisers.

Federal Trade Commission (2009, October 5). FTC publishes final guides governing endorsements, testimonials. Retrieved Nov. 1 2011 from: http://www.ftc.gov/opa/2009/10/endortest.shtm.

Federal Trade Commission Policy Statement on Deception, 103 F.T.C. 174 (1984).

Fitzpatrick, K. (2006). Baselines for ethical advocacy in the "Marketplace of Ideas." In Fitzpatrick, K., & Bronstein, C. (Eds). *Ethics in public relations: Ethical advocacy*. Thousand Oaks, CA: Sage.

Fitzpatrick, K., & Bronstein, C. (Eds). (2006). *Ethics in public relations: Ethical advocacy*. Thousand Oaks, CA: Sage.

Gogoi, P. (2006, October 8). Wal-Mart's Jim and Laura: The real story. *Business Week*. Retrieved Oct. 28 2011 from: http://www.businessweek.com/bwdaily/dnflash/content/oct2006/db20061009_579137.htm.

Graft, K. (2006, December 19). Sony screws up. Retrieved Oct. 28 2011 from: http://www.businessweek.com/innovate/content/dec2006/id20061219_590177.htm.

Gunther, M. (2006, October 18). Corporate blogging: Wal-Mart's fumbles. Retrieved Nov. 1 2011 from: http://money.cnn.com/2006/10/17/technology/pluggedin_gunther_blog.fortune/.

Heussner, K. (2009, November 11). Fort Hood soldier causes stir on Twitter. Retrieved Nov. 4 2011 from: http://abcnews.go.com/Technology/AheadoftheCurve/tweeting-uniform-ft-hood-soldier-stir-twitter/story?id=9042726.

Izea.com. Retrieved Nov. 10 2011, from: http://izea.com/.

Kietzmann, J. H., Hermkens, K., McCarthy, I. P., & Silvestre, B. S. (2011). Social media? Get serious! Understanding the functional building blocks of social media. *Business Horizons, 54*, 241–251.

Kobe Bryant jumps over an Aston Martin car [YouTube] Retrieved Nov. 3 2011 from: http://www.youtube.com/watch?v=7hWJkdUMiMw.

Kurtz, H. (2006, April 24). Columnist's blog: He hasn't been himself lately. *The Washington Post*. Retrieved Oct. 21 2011 from: http://money.cnn.com/2006/10/17/technology/pluggedin_gunther_blog.fortune/.

Lots-o'-Huggin' bear commercial. (2009, June 8) [YouTube] Retrieved Nov. 19 2012 from: http://www.youtube.com/watch?v=z6dZtNYGlLM&noredirect=1.

Mashable.com (2009, June 8). How social media is radically changing the newsroom. Retrieved Oct. 20 2011 from http://mashable.com/2009/06/08/social-media-newsroom/.

Meiklejohn, A. (1948). *Free speech and its relationship to government*. New York: Harper and Brothers.

New York Times v. Sullivan, 376 U.S. 254 (1964), 272-73.

Nudd, T. (2006, December 12). Sony gets ripped for a bogus PSP blog. Retrieved Nov. 3, 2011 from: http://www.adweek.com/adfreak/sony-gets-ripped-bogus-psp-blog-17996.

Obama calls Kanye West a "Jackass" (2009, September 15). Retrieved Nov. 2 2011 from: http://www.foxnews.com/politics/2009/09/15/obama-calls-kanye-west-jackass/.

Romenesko, J. (2011, July 8). AP warns staff about expressing opinions on social networks. Retrieved Nov. 3 2011 from: http://www.poynter.org/latest-news/mediawire/138288/ap-warns-staff-about-expressing-opinions-on-social-networks/.

Smith, E., & Lattman, P. (2007, September 7). Download this: YouTube phenom has a big secret. *The Wall Street Journal*. Retrieved Nov. 2 2011 from: http://online.wsj.com/article/SB118903788315518780.html.

SocialSpark.com. Retrieved Nov. 19 2012 from: http://socialspark.com/.

Sponsoredtweets.com. Retrieved Nov. 19 2012 from: https://app.sponsoredtweets.com/tweeters.

Toy Story 3 drops in at toy fair. [YouTube] Retrieved Nov. 2 2011 from: http://www.youtube.com/watch?v=G6bvTo3xh9A.

8

TRADITIONAL NEWS MEDIA'S USE OF SOCIAL MEDIA

Tracy Collins Standley

Social Media and the Citizen Journalist

One of the great hopes for social media at its inception was the creation of "citizen journalists." Blogs created for the purpose of allowing regular citizens the opportunity to share news during the London bombings and Hurricane Katrina, both in 2005, showed the possibility of a joint venture of news reporting between people near or on the scene and reporters and editors who were unable to get to the scene (Allan, 2006). This arrangement was particularly helpful for garnering photos and video from the scene. Likewise, citizens released information and photos about the bombings in Mumbai in 2008 and the US Airways crash in 2009 through Twitter (Murthy, 2011). The difficulty for the citizen journalist lies in access to sources to adequately cover a story (Reich, 2008). This is where a partnership between the citizen journalist and the professional journalist is necessary.

In addition to providing actual content for journalists, social media can also suggest areas of reporting. Journalists can learn which topics are important to the audience through the use of social media and can set their reporting agendas accordingly. While reporters embrace this idea, they haven't embraced the practice (Lariscy, Avery, Sweetser, & Howes, 2009). It seems that journalists have largely used the social media and the Web as a method for one-way communication with little reception of information from the audience (Gordon, 2009).

Social Media as a Delivery Method

According to Greer and Ferguson (2011), television stations are more frequently using social media, specifically Twitter, to deliver news content, rather than as a method of promoting their news product. One of the benefits of social media is the ability to hyperlink news stories to a deeper coverage of the story provided by the news organization. It is simple to click on a hyperlink to obtain more information. In comparison, a member of the audience who is told of a place to go for further information during a news broadcast must remember the website address and go to a computer to look it up.

One study examining young adults found that they demand immediacy in their information acquisition (Urista, Dong, & Day, 2008). In a world of instant access, social media can provide instant news. In an interesting example of both providing immediate coverage and providing coverage when more traditional methods are not available, many of the reporters of Wilmington, N.C.'s *Star-News* used social media during Hurricane Hanna in 2008 to connect with the audience and to provide information as to what was going on (Schulte, 2009).

Social Media as Method of Increasing Viewers/Readers

Facebook (2011) reports that it has "more than 800 million active users." According to Socialbakers (2012), Facebook has 155,699,640 users in the United States. By comparison, the U.S. population is approximately 312 million people (U.S. Census Bureau, 2011). When examining Nielsen (2011b) ratings for the week of November 7, 2011, the highest rated news program, *60 Minutes* on CBS, received an audience of 13.1 million people. Only approximately 4.2% of the population watched the highest rated news program; whereas approximately 50% of the population are Facebook users. Clearly, users enjoy utilizing social media.

But why is Facebook so popular? A survey of 172 college students found that users went to Facebook to fulfill certain needs (Sheldon, 2008). Users go to Facebook not only for entertainment, but also for the maintenance of relationships. By creating a relationship with the online community through social media rather than being a one-way vehicle of information, news organizations can take advantage of both the entertainment and relationship development that a college student desires.

It is commonly believed that young Americans are not interested in the news. Part of this has been attributed to the Internet and its ability to allow the individual to search out only what interests the individual to the exclusion of any other news or contradictory opinions (Mindich, 2005). However, Mindich (2005) found that in the case of New Orleans, a vastly diverse but interrelated community engages the public, both young and old, in learning about the news. The news media have the potential to create this same diverse but communicative community through the use of social media.

Social media have the potential to transform news coverage into a more attractive and meaningful experience for the audience. Through its interactivity, social media can be used to create a two-way dialogue between the news organization and the audience. It can also be used to bring news and visual images more quickly from a location to the masses. Considering the potential that social media have in two-way communication with the audience and the fact that traditional news media are using social media, the following research questions were investigated:

R1: What forms of social media are the traditional news media using?
R2: How are traditional news media using social media?

Method

A content analysis was conducted of the websites of 112 news sources. To get a clear picture of how the entire news industry is using social media, a sample was created of newspapers, network television, cable news channels, and local television.

The newspapers selected for the sample were those on the Pew Research Center's *The State of the News Media 2011* report. Newspapers listed in the "Top 25 Circulating Newspapers," "Top 25 Newspapers in Growth of Total Audience (Print and Online) in 2010," and "Top Newspapers Local Audience: Print and Online Combined" were combined to create a sample of 46 newspapers for analysis (Edmonds et al., 2011).

National television was represented in the sample by examining both networks with national news programs and cable news networks. Broadcast and cable news networks included those listed in the Pew Research Center's *The State of the News Media 2011* report. These were ABC, CBS, NBC, PBS, CNN, FoxNews, and MSNBC (Guskin et al., 2011; Holcomb et al., 2011).

Local television stations used in this sample were each local television station within the top 10 television markets in the United States that included a news component on its website (FCC, 2010; Nielsen Company, 2011a). This gave a sample of 59 local television stations.

The websites of a total sample of 112 news organizations were examined. Two methods of utilizing social media were studied. First, the social media sites that the news organization used as an additional method of distributing news product were recorded. Second, the social media sites that the news organization enabled for audience members to redistribute news product were recorded. In this content analysis, all coding was conducted by the author.

Twitter and Facebook were used ubiquitously across the news organizations. Of the 112 organizations sampled, 111 or 99.11% had a presence on Facebook and Twitter. Because of this, Facebook and Twitter were examined more closely. To begin with, the links to the Facebook and Twitter accounts from each website were inspected.

Each news organization's Twitter feed and Facebook posts were also examined for content. Specifically, the list of posts and tweets, ordered by the time they were posted from most recent to least recent, were analyzed as to whether they included breaking news messages, comments to the audience, non-news promotions or advertisements, news story promotions, audience comments or suggestions, requests for story research, or solicitation of user comments.

A breaking news message was considered a post or tweet that gave information without referring the audience to a place for further information. A comment to the audience was a personal comment directed to a member of the audience. A non-news promotion or advertisement was any content that promoted the news organization that was not news content. This also included advertisements. A news story promotion was information about a news story that referred the audience to the website, publication, or news broadcast for more information. An audience comment or suggestion was any comment from the audience that was directed at the news staff. A request for story research was a post or tweet from a reporter asking for information to include in an upcoming story. A solicitation of user comments was a post that included a statement asking the audience for a response (i.e. what do you think?).

The list of recent posts and tweets was also examined to discover who created posts. In some cases, the post was listed as having been created by the organization, while in other cases posts came from multiple sources. Posts and tweets that were listed as having been authored by the organization only (i.e. *New York Times*) were coded as being authored by the main organization. Posts and tweets that had multiple authors (i.e. specific audience members, specific reporters, and the actual organization) were coded as being authored by multiple submitters.

For Twitter, the number of tweets from November 7 to November 13, 2011 were counted. The statistics that Twitter provides for each account were also recorded. These are the total number of tweets, the number of accounts that the organization follows, the number of accounts that follow the news organization, and the number of accounts that have the organization as part of a list.

For Facebook, the statistics that Facebook provides for each account were recorded. These are the number of people that like this page and the number of people that are talking about this page.

Overall Usage of Social Media

Overall, Facebook and Twitter are the most frequently used social media tools; they are used almost universally (Table 8.1). Surprisingly, they are used more frequently than any of the older and more established forms of Internet communication such as email distribution, RSS feeds, or blogging. No other form of social media comes close to the usage of Facebook and Twitter.

Although media organizations for the most part do not use other forms of social media, they allow the audience to share information through many other forms. Of the 112 news organizations in the sample, only eight (7.14%) allowed the audience to share news stories solely through Facebook, Twitter, or email. All others had at least one other method of sharing (Table 8.2). In addition, 57 organizations (50.89%) in the sample utilized either Addthis or Sharethis in their full capacities. Addthis and Sharethis are both utilities that are added to a website that give sharing access to hundreds of social media outlets. (The remaining 14 websites that include Addthis or Sharethis have limited numbers of social media available through them.)

Since news organizations are spending the time creating and updating Twitter and Facebook accounts, these accounts should be publicized on the organizations' website. While this is predominantly true, 14 organizations (12.61%) did not have a direct link (Table 8.3).

TABLE 8.1 Social media used by news organizations

Social media	Number of organizations using	Percentage of organizations using
Facebook	111	99.11
Twitter	111	99.11
RSS Feeds	98	87.50
Mobile Delivery	88	78.57
Email Distribution	72	64.29
Blogs	55	49.11
MyYahoo!	14	12.50
YouTube	9	8.04
Podcasts	8	7.14
Foursquare	5	4.46
Google	4	3.57
Tumblr	2	1.79
Flickr	2	1.79
Myspace	1	0.89
Other social media	8	7.14

TABLE 8.2 Social media listed for audience sharing

Social media	Number of organizations listing	Percentage of organizations listing
Facebook	110	98.12
Twitter	108	96.43
Email	105	93.75
Google	93	83.04
Reddit	77	68.75
Digg	74	66.07
StumbleUpon	69	61.61
LinkedIn	52	46.43
Delicious	50	44.64
Addthis	37	33.04
Sharethis	34	30.36
Tumblr	34	30.36
Blogger	25	22.32
Messenger	20	17.86
Fark	19	16.96
Myspace	18	16.07
Yahoo!	12	10.71
Newsvine	7	6.25
Meebo	5	4.46
Other social media	20	17.86

TABLE 8.3 Links to Facebook and Twitter

Links	Number for Facebook	Percentage for Facebook	Number for Twitter	Percentage for Twitter
Links to account	97	87.39	97	87.39
Story feed show, but no link	3	2.70	0	0
Links to reporters but not main account	1	0.90	1	0.90
Allows login to individual's own account	1	0.90	2	1.80
Allows audience to recommend	2	1.80	0	0
No reference or link	7	6.31	11	9.91

Although similarities do exist, there is a significant difference in the way that news organizations use Twitter and Facebook ($\chi^2 = 55.55$, df = 36, $p < 0.05$) (Table 8.4). Although both Twitter and Facebook are frequently used to promote upcoming news content, Twitter is more frequently used to release breaking news with no reference to an upcoming story. For example, reporters were using Twitter to release weather warnings, traffic updates, and play-by-play updates from court trials. Twitter was frequently the place for a reporter to go to update the audience quickly on a story.

In contrast, Facebook was more frequently used for communication with the audience. More non-news promos, audience comments, and soliciting of comments occurred on Facebook than Twitter. When posting news promos, reporters were more likely to ask for the audience's opinion on Facebook. Facebook was also used by the audience. Audience members were more likely to propose news story ideas on Facebook. More non-news was posted on Facebook as well. This included promotions for the newspaper or television station that was not related to news. This also included posts that were advertisements for products or services that were posted either by the news organization or by the audience.

TABLE 8.4 Subjects that news organizations cover in Twitter and Facebook posts

Subject	Number tweeting	Percentage tweeting	Number Facebook posting	Percentage Facebook posting
News promos	107	97.27	109	98.20
Solicit comments	27	24.55	80	72.07
Non-news promos	34	30.91	57	51.35
Audience comments	13	11.82	28	25.23
Breaking news	70	63.64	27	24.32
Comments to audience	19	17.27	10	9.01
Story research	8	7.27	8	7.21

The difference in who posted the messages on Twitter and Facebook for each news organization was statistically significant ($\chi^2 = 31.17$, df = 1, $p < 0.05$) (Table 8.5). Most news organizations restricted Facebook wall posts to only the news organization. In contrast, the majority of news organizations allowed tweets from multiple sources. These generally included tweets from multiple reporters and re-tweets from other sources.

Across all news organizations, the average number of tweets in one week was 177.11 (Table 8.6). The number of tweets in one week ranged from a minimum of 1 to a maximum of 719. The total number of tweets by a news organization ranged from 162 to 149,463 with an average across all organizations of 20,747.83. The number of followers of news organizations on Twitter ranged from 529 to 3,985,020, while the number of "Likes" on Facebook ranged from 420 to 3,075,942. The average number of Twitter followers was 181,382.32, and the average number of Facebook "Likes" was 107,338.95.

Comparing Newspapers and Television

For the most part, there is not much difference in how newspapers and television utilize social media (Table 8.7). With Twitter, most newspapers and television organizations promote news stories in their tweets. Almost three quarters of television organizations tweet about breaking news, whereas only about half of the newspapers tweet this. Not many newspapers or television organizations are using Twitter for much beyond this.

TABLE 8.5 Who posts for the news organization on Twitter and Facebook?

Who posts?	Number tweeting	Percentage tweeting	Number Facebook posting	Percentage Facebook posting
Main organization	36	32.73	78	70.27
Multiple submitters	74	67.27	33	29.73

TABLE 8.6 Twitter and Facebook statistics

Statistics	Average	Maximum	Minimum
Number of tweets in one week	177.11	719	1
Total number of tweets	20,747.83	149,463	162
Number following on Twitter	4,986.92	173,837	3
Number of followers on Twitter	181,382.32	3,985,020	529
Number listed on Twitter	4,276.11	89,270	24
Number of Facebook "Likes"	107,338.95	3,075,942	420
Number of Facebook talking about	4,315.57	55,698	3

TABLE 8.7 Comparing newspapers and television tweets

Subject	Number of newspapers tweeting	Percentage of newspapers tweeting	Number of television tweeting	Percentage of television tweeting
Breaking news	23	51.11	47	72.31
Comments to audience	6	13.33	13	20.00
Non-news promos	11	24.44	23	35.38
News promos	43	95.56	64	98.46
Audience comments	8	17.78	5	7.69
Story research	4	8.89	4	6.15
Solicit comments	7	15.56	20	30.77

Similar to Twitter, most newspaper and television organizations are using Facebook to promote news stories (Table 8.8). A large percentage of both newspapers and television organizations are also using Facebook as a method of soliciting audience comments. This is contrary to how news organizations are using Twitter. A larger percentage of television organizations than newspapers are also using Facebook to report breaking news, to respond to the audience, and to receive audience comments.

When examining the origination of tweets between newspapers and television organizations, a larger percentage of newspapers have multiple submitters of news content than do television organization (Table 8.9). Many of these multiple submitters are different reporters from the newspaper that are tweeting under their own names rather than under the name of the organization.

Interestingly, the opposite is true for Facebook. More newspapers only allow posts from the main organization on Facebook, although there is not much difference between the percentages of newspapers and television organizations in this case (Table 8.10).

TABLE 8.8 Comparing newspapers and television Facebook postings

Subject	Number of newspapers posting	Percentage of newspapers posting	Number of television posting	Percentage of television posting
Breaking news	3	6.52	24	36.92
Comments to audience	0	0.00	10	15.38
Non-news promos	23	50.00	34	52.31
News promos	46	100.00	63	96.92
Audience comments	8	17.39	20	30.77
Story research	6	13.04	2	3.08
Solicit comments	32	69.57	48	73.85

TABLE 8.9 Comparing tweet authors in newspapers and television

Who tweets?	Number newspapers tweeting	Percentage newspapers tweeting	Number television tweeting	Percentage television tweeting
Main organization	12	26.67	24	36.92
Multiple submitters	33	73.33	41	63.08

TABLE 8.10 Comparing post authors in Facebook between newspapers and television

Who posts?	Number newspapers posting	Percentage newspapers posting	Number television posting	Percentage television posting
Main organization	34	73.91	44	67.69
Multiple submitters	12	26.09	21	32.31

Newspapers tweet slightly more on average than television organizations in a week and also have a larger average for total number of tweets (Table 8.11). The average number of newspaper tweets for the sample week was 180.56, while the average for television was 174.69. The average total number of tweets for newspapers was 22,556.38. For television, this average was 19,476.20. This is interesting since the average number of followers on Twitter and the average number of "Likes" on Facebook are greater for television than for newspapers. The average number of followers for television organizations is 199,432.97, but for newspapers, the average is only 155,710.29. The difference is even more noticeable on Facebook, where the average number of "Likes" for television organizations is 134,381.51, whereas the average number for newspapers is 69,126.63.

TABLE 8.11 Comparing averages of newspapers and television

Statistics	Newspaper average	Television average
Number of tweets in one week	180.56	174.69
Total number of tweets	22,556.38	19,476.20
Number following on Twitter	3,779.31	5,836.02
Number of followers on Twitter	155,710.29	199,432.97
Number listed on Twitter	4,962.40	3,793.56
Number of Facebook "Likes"	69,126.63	134,381.51
Number of Facebook talking about	4,315.57	33,302.84

Comparing Local and National Organizations

Local news organizations seem to be using social media more fully than national news organizations (Table 8.12). Although both local and national news organizations are primarily using Twitter to promote their news coverage, national news organizations are not using social media much beyond that. No national news organization used Twitter to comment to the audience, to receive audience comments, or to conduct story research. Only one national news organization solicited any sort of audience response through Twitter.

Much the same could be said of the media's usage of Facebook (Table 8.13). Again, both local and national news organizations are using Facebook primarily to promote the news. And once again, there is more variety in how the local news media are using Facebook as opposed to the national news media. Again, no

TABLE 8.12 Comparing subjects of local and national news organization tweets

Subject	Number of local news tweeting	Percentage of local news tweeting	Number of national news tweeting	Percentage of national news tweeting
Breaking news	64	64.65	6	54.55
Comments to audience	19	19.19	0	0.00
Non-news promos	31	31.31	3	27.27
News promos	97	97.98	10	90.91
Audience comments	13	13.13	0	0.00
Story research	8	8.08	0	0.00
Solicit comments	26	26.26	1	9.09

TABLE 8.13 Comparing subjects of local and national news organization Facebook postings

Subject	Number of local news posting	Percentage of local news posting	Number of national news posting	Percentage of national news posting
Breaking news	23	23.00	4	36.36
Comments to audience	10	10.00	0	0.00
Non-news promos	54	54.00	3	27.27
News promos	98	98.00	11	100.00
Audience comments	28	28.00	0	0.00
Story research	8	8.00	0	0.00
Solicit comments	73	73.00	7	63.64

national news provider used Facebook to comment to the audience, to receive unsolicited comments from the audience, or to conduct story research.

The national news media is much less likely to allow any tweets from someone other than the main organization (Table 8.14). Primarily, their tweets come from within the news organization. They do not retweet any information.

All of the national news media prevent anyone from posting on their Facebook wall as well. In contrast, only 67% of local media prevent wall posts on Facebook (Table 8.15).

Considering the larger size of the national news media's audience as compared to the local news media, it is not surprising that the national news media has a far larger average number of followers on Twitter and "Likes" on Facebook. The national news media average number of followers on Twitter is 1,639,892.18, whereas the local news media average is only 17,672.03. Likewise, the national news media average number of "Likes" on Facebook is 891,664.82, and the average for local news media is only 21,063.10. It is interesting to note that the national news media have more followers on Twitter than "Likes" on Facebook, while the opposite is true of local news media.

National news media on average had more tweets in the sample week than did the local news media (Table 8.16). The average number of tweets for national media was 236, and the average number of tweets for local media for the week was 170.5. The average total number of tweets for the national news media was also over twice that of local media. This average for the national news media was 43,959.09, but for local media it was 18,142.49.

TABLE 8.14   Comparing authors of tweets in local and national news

Who tweets?	Number local news tweeting	Percentage local news tweeting	Number national news tweeting	Percentage national news tweeting
Main organization	26	26.26	10	90.91
Multiple submitters	73	73.74	1	9.09

TABLE 8.15   Comparing authors' Facebook posts in local and national news

Who posts?	Number local news posting	Percentage local news posting	Number national news posting	Percentage national news posting
Main organization	67	67.00	11	100.00
Multiple submitters	33	33.00	0	0.00

TABLE 8.16 Comparing local and national news organizations' averages

Statistics	Local news average	National news average
Number of tweets in one week	170.50	236.00
Total number of tweets	18,142.49	43,959.09
Number following on Twitter	3,718.28	16,289.36
Number of followers on Twitter	17,672.03	1,639,892.18
Number listed on Twitter	964.61	33,778.55
Number of Facebook "Likes"	21,063.10	891,664.82
Number of Facebook talking about	2,241.36	23,172.00

Conclusion

In examining how traditional news media are utilizing social media, it appears that traditional news media are still primarily using social media as a delivery system for news and are not fully embracing the social aspect of social media. Part of the attraction of social media is their ability to create and maintain two-way relationships between groups and people. For the most part, the traditional news media are not taking advantage of this. Rather than using social media to create a dialogue with the audience, the news media are delivering news content to the audience. This is particularly true of the national news media. National news media are almost exclusively using social media to deliver information to the audience rather than communicating with that audience. Local media, although still predominantly using social media in one-way communication, are more varied in their usage.

A far better way to utilize social media would be to play to its strengths. Since the audience is interested in using social media to create a dialogue, the news media should provide that dialogue. Very few organizations used social media as a way to research stories or to determine which stories the audience was interested in. This is a potential research tool that is being neglected. By examining exactly which stories are garnering the greatest response, the news media can determine exactly what the audience wants to know.

Much of the time, the news media are using social media, particularly Twitter, to deliver news rather than to promote their traditional delivery method. The problem that faces traditional media when they use social media as a delivery method is that they are effectively competing with themselves. If the audience can get the same news through Facebook and Twitter, why should they then go to the traditional delivery method, be it newspaper or television? Ideally, social media should increase the audience for the traditional delivery method.

Likewise, news organizations are limited in how they allow the audience to share information. Most organizations allow the audience to share stories with friends through Facebook, Twitter, and email. Every time a story is shared from a news source, it brings new potential audience members with a click of the link.

Allowing the audience to share stories through many venues maximizes that increase in audience.

If news organizations are going to use social media, the social media links should ideally be prominently displayed on the organization's website so that the audience knows where to look for them. Although most news organizations have links to their Facebook and Twitter accounts on their website, not all did. And for many of the organizations that did have the links displayed, the links were difficult to find. If the audience is not aware of the news organization's presence in social media, that presence is not benefitting the news organization.

Limitations and Future Research

This study largely examined the breadth of social media usage by news organizations. As such, a major limitation for this study was the lack of depth. Future research should more deeply analyze the individual messages that are being posted or tweeted. Which news story topics receive the most attention? What messages are the audience members posting in response?

Although a content analysis can show what content is available on the given websites, it cannot reveal anything about the decision-making process of the media professionals providing that content. Therefore, an area for future research would be to examine the various media outlets' philosophies on utilizing social media. Is there an overarching social media policy for the media outlet, or does the information being posted depend on each individual reporter? It would be beneficial to survey the various media organizations to determine what strategy they are using, if any, for their social media connections.

In addition to the media professionals' thoughts on how social media should be used, the audience opinions of what is most beneficial to them should be analyzed. A survey of the audience will provide information as to what specifically the audience wants from social media communication from media news outlets. With this information, the most effective usage of social media can be created.

References

Allan, S. (2006). *Online news*. New York: Open University Press.

Edmonds, R., Guskin, E., & Rosenstiel, T. (2011). Newspapers: By the numbers. In *The State of the News Media 2011*. Retrieved November 11, 2011, from: http://stateofthe media.org/2011/newspapers-essay/data-page-6/.

Facebook. (2011). *Facebook statistics*. Retrieved November 21, 2011, from: http://www. facebook.com/press/info.php?statistics.

FCC. (2010). *Updated maps of all full-service digital television stations authorized by the FCC*. Retrieved November 13, 2011, from: http://transition.fcc.gov/dtv/markets/.

Gordon, R. (2009). *Social media: The ground shifts*. Nieman Reports, 63(3), 7–9.

Grabe, M.E., Kamhawi, R., & Yegiyan, N. (2009). Informing citizens: How people with different levels of education process television, newspaper, and web news. *Journal of Broadcasting & Electronic Media, 53*(1), 90–111.

Greer, C.F. & Ferguson, D.A. (2011). Using Twitter for promotion and branding: A content analysis of local television Twitter sites. *Journal of Broadcasting & Electronic Media, 55*(2), 198–214.

Guskin, E., Rosenstiel, T., & Moore, P. (2011). Network: By the numbers. In *The State of the News Media 2011*. Retrieved November 11, 2011, from: http://stateofthemedia. org/2011/network-essay/data-page-5/.

Holcomb, J., Mitchell, A., & Rosenstiel, T. (2011). Cable: By the numbers. In *The State of the News Media 2011*. Retrieved November 11, 2011, from: http://stateofthemedia. org/2011/cable-essay/data-page-2/.

Lariscy, R.W., Avery, E.J., Sweetser, K.D., & Howes, P. (2009). An examination of the role of online social media in journalists' source mix. *Public Relations Review, 35*, 314–316.

Mindich, D.T.Z. (2005). *Tuned out: Why Americans under 40 don't follow the news*. New York: Oxford University Press.

Murthy, D. (2011). Twitter: Microphone for the masses? *Media, Culture & Society, 33*(5), 779–789.

Nielsen Company. (2011a). *Local television market universe estimates comparisons of 2010–11 and 2011–12 market ranks*. Retrieved November 13, 2011, from: http://www.nielsen. com/content/dam/corporate/us/en/public%20factsheets/tv/nielsen-2012-local-DMA-TV-penetration.pdf.

Nielsen Company. (2011b). *Nielsen: Top 10 TV ratings, top 10 TV shows*. Retrieved November 21, 2011, from: http://www.nielsen.com/us/en/insights/top10s/television. html.

Reich, Z. (2008). How citizens create news stories: The "news access" problem reversed. *Journalism Studies, 9*(5), 739–758.

Schulte, B. (2009). The distribution: How news organizations are intensifying their use of social networking venues like Twitter and Facebook to circulate their stories and connect with their communities. *American Journalism Review, Winter*, 22–25.

Sheldon, P. (2008). Student favorite: Facebook and motives for its use. *Southwestern Mass Communication Journal, 23*(2), 39–53.

Socialbakers. (2012). *United States Facebook statistics*. Retrieved February 2, 2012, from: http://www.socialbakers.com/facebook-statistics/united-states.

Urista, M.A., Dong, Q., & Day, K.D. (2008). Explaining why young adults use MySpace and Facebook through uses and gratifications theory. *Human Communication, 12*(2), 215–229.

U.S. Census Bureau. (2011). *U.S. & world population clocks*. Retrieved November 21, 2011, from: http://www.census.gov/main/www/popclock.html.

Wonneberger, A., Schoenbach, K., & van Meurs, L. (2011). Interest in news and politics – or situational determinants? Why people watch the news. *Journal of Broadcasting & Electronic Media, 55*(3), 325–343.

9

PRIVACY AND SOCIAL MEDIA

Laurie Thomas Lee

Introduction

Privacy issues are at the center of a polarized debate because of social media (Sullivan, 2011; Madden, 2012). On one side, privacy advocates and scholars argue that the public is more concerned than ever about their online privacy and is demanding and deserving greater protections. Internet users value privacy and deeply care about personal information being accessed, tracked, used, and shared (Madden, 2012). Indeed, polls show that at least two-thirds of social media users and non-users alike are concerned they are losing control over their privacy (Sullivan, 2011). Of Facebook users alone, nearly seven out of ten say they are "somewhat" or "very concerned" about their privacy (Acohido, 2011b).

On the other side are those who contend that the age of privacy is over because people are now willingly sharing personal details on social networking sites (Kirkpatrick, 2010). They argue that social media use has made privacy just an illusion and privacy protection is an oxymoron (Debatin, 2011; Schneier, 2010). Facebook founder Mark Zuckerberg and others in social media are leading the "privacy-is-dead" argument, justifying their reasons for making personal data more publicly available on their sites (Madden, 2012; Schneier, 2010).

This battle over privacy has some worried that while social media companies and others are racing to amass vast amounts of personal data on users, users are giving up their privacy rights, willingly or otherwise (Acohido, 2011a). This imbalance over privacy is likely to only increase as social media use increases. Is privacy dead in the age of social media? Is social networking privacy a contradiction? If privacy is still an important value, how might it be preserved while social networking and its many advantages continue to flourish?

Risks to Social Media Privacy

Social media sites provide an incredible opportunity for millions of users to intentionally share personal information about themselves and others with friends, acquaintances, strangers, businesses, and government agencies. Consumers know they have to provide certain identifying information in order to take advantage of software applications that provide a host of benefits such as location-based advertising coupons or social gaming competitions. They appreciate heightened police protection and journalistic coverage that rely on social networks as well as the economic growth of new businesses that thrive on targeted data. Most of all, users value the ability to search personal profiles and find and connect with friends and loved ones (Smith, 2011).

Yet engaging in social networking can put privacy at risk. Information on social media sites may not only be searched without permission or knowledge but may be permanently stored, meaning some material intended to be private may never enjoy a cloak of privacy. Photos, rants, relationship statuses, and people's whereabouts, for example, may always be "out there" for future employers, dates, neighbors, police investigators, and commercial businesses to mine, share, and utilize.

The ramifications of privacy loss are real. Making personal information publicly available can cause harm to users, including threats to their health and safety as well as repercussions when affiliations are revealed. Pages and Friends lists can reveal potentially controversial political views or other sensitive information such as business relationships to prospective employers, business competitors, and government agencies. People want to interact yet need to be guaranteed privacy in their personal information if they are escaping an abusive relationship, fear they will lose or not obtain a job, worry they will be refused a loan, health insurance, child custody or adoption, or fear they will be marginalized or harassed for their religious or sexual preferences. In addition, people are concerned about government intrusions and monitoring, companies tracking their purchases and interests, hackers and phishers stealing their identity, and GPS tracking of their physical movements. They fear, for example, unwelcome contacts from cyberstalkers or zealous advertisers who can infer their location from social sites such as FourSquare and Gowalla.

Evidence shows that privacy protections over social media sites are easy to circumvent. It takes some people just a few minutes to search social media sites to learn plenty about another person. For example, someone's age can be determined by searching tagged Facebook photos and scrutinizing the posted birthday photos (Bilton, 2011). A search for a person based on only a photo might start with searching the relationships of others known in the photo and checking those people's Facebook Friend lists. Facial recognition software now expedites searches. In one case, a link to a running app was able to reveal the path of another person's morning jog (Bilton, 2011). Identities are also more vulnerable today as social media companies are linking social identities and users are staying logged on as they move from one social network to another. The ability to search and track individuals over social media sites has even prompted the Department of Homeland Security and FBI to announce monitoring plans (Marks, 2012).

Social media companies are also motivated to aggregate and make users' personal data available. As they strive to monetize their operations, they realize the value of their user information, not only to their own operations, but to marketers and third-party software applications who will pay to mine the data, target individual users, and develop personalized services. Privacy trade-offs occur as the social media weigh divulging or providing access to user data to losing the trust of users and potentially their business. At the same time, users also engage in a privacy negotiation as they weigh the benefits of engaging in social media to the loss of their personal information. Users essentially contribute private information in the form of profile content, communications with others, and behavioral tracking, in exchange for receiving useful services such as access to the network, communication tools, photo sharing, data storage, and a host of other applications (Rodrigues, 2010). Users engage in non-price bargaining as they typically pay nothing to register with a social medium, essentially paying with information about their personal habits, whereabouts, and interests. Every player in the equation is at least somewhat aware of the balance, techniques used, legal implications, and consequences, although consumers are generally the least aware of when and how their privacy may be compromised.

The Nature of Privacy and Social Networking

What is privacy in the context of social media? What does it mean? We know that privacy in general has various meanings and functions in different contexts and disciplines, such as psychology, biology, philosophy, and communications. In terms of a definition, it is oftentimes considered the "right to be let alone," as coined over a century ago. Dictionary definitions point to the Latin term "privatus," meaning "withdrawn from public life" (*Oxford Dictionaries*, 2012). It was Westin (1967) who provided the first systematic analysis of the multi-dimensional nature of privacy, proposing four fundamental states as solitude, reserve, intimacy, and anonymity. Since then, privacy has come to also mean such things as seclusion, dignity, involvement with neighbors, secrecy, and autonomy or control over information about oneself.

Yet social media presents an interesting contradiction when it comes to privacy. The very nature of social networking actually suggests anything but privacy. After all, if one is engaged in networking and social interactions, then one is hardly preserving anything private and is not "withdrawn from public life." In this sense, social media privacy is not about solitude or seclusion. Other reasons for seeking privacy include a feeling of crowdedness and a need to escape identification and social pressures or obligations (Marshall, 1974; Pastalan, 1970), but those reasons would not apply when engaged in social networking. Likewise, social media use would also seem somewhat removed from any interest in preserving anonymity or refraining from intimacy because people go on to social networks precisely to expose their thoughts, beliefs, activities, and photos. It might seem that privacy would only come into question as a right not to engage in social media in the first place. Thus, an argument may be made that unless social networking is compelled or done without knowledge or consent, it may not infringe on privacy.

Of course this simplistic view does not account for the range of social inter-actions that include elements intended and desired to be private. For example, people may choose to share intimate thoughts with close friends but not with the rest of their networks. Moving about in a social network anonymously can also be important to some, such as job seekers, potential buyers, and people seeking help without embarrassment. Even solitude can come into play when users resist getting bombarded with advertisements and requests. One can choose to go into seclusion and essentially go off the grid and refrain from engaging in social media, but this is hardly a practical solution to privacy concerns when social networking is an integral part of communications today. And privacy concerns associated with social media most certainly focus on autonomy or the ability or inability to control one's information over a social network. Indeed, one reason for seeking privacy is out of fear of losing control (Katz, 1987) and associated consequences (Laufer & Wolfe, 1977). Being fully informed about changes in privacy practices and given the clear option to opt in and out is a key privacy concern with social media. Thus, when it comes to social networking, privacy may be thought of in different ways.

The primary concern with social media privacy, however, seems to center on this latter need and interest in control. Indeed, Westin referred to privacy as the "claim of individuals, groups, or institutions to determine for themselves when, how, and to what extent information about them is communicated to others" (1967, p. 7). Smith expressed this further as a "right to control information about yourself, as in the right to prevent disclosure of private facts or the right to know which information is kept on you and how it is used" (1979, p. 323). This type of privacy interest in autonomy in an information age is often referred to as "information privacy." Social media concerns certainly focus on the ability to manage one's networks and determine who can see one's profile and other information. What information is collected by Facebook, Google, and others, and how it is compiled and divulged to advertisers, government, and other users are of particular concern. DeCew (1997) further defines privacy as control over making decisions about one's lifestyle and family. Indeed, social media users are especially concerned about having control over who sees their relationship statuses, Friends lists, "Likes," and postings, as well as the ability to permanently delete such information and control photo tags.

Privacy Perceptions

There are individual differences in how people perceive privacy that pertain to social media use. Studies show that women tend to disclose more (Derlega & Chaikin, 1977), yet also tend to be more concerned about privacy (O'Neil, 2001) and more likely to use blocking strategies (Burgoon, 1989). A recent study of Facebook profile disclosures, however, found that most people, regardless of gender, will enter full name, facial pictures, hometown, and e-mail addresses in their profiles (Taraszow, Aristodemou, Shitta, Laouris, & Arsoy, 2010). In fact, males were found to be more likely than females to disclose their mobile phone number, home address and instant messaging (IM) screen names. Other studies indicate that younger people are less likely to prefer reserve, but more likely to prefer solitude (Marshall, 1974). Trust and the type of relationship involved can also affect perceptions of privacy, with established and close relationships prompting less concern (Culnan, 1993). In this sense, social networking provides a fertile ground for encouraging private, less-reserved exchanges among friends, particularly teens and young adults, in the privacy of their home.

For the same matter, perceptions of privacy vary with perceptions of control. If people believe they can control their privacy, there is less concern (Culnan, 1993). Oddly enough, some argue that young people view the online world as more private and controllable compared to their home (Johnson, 2010). People also find a disclosure to be less invasive if they gave permission. The purpose and judged benefit of an exchange can also mitigate privacy concerns (Culnan, 1993). Thus, social media participants may not be worried about privacy invasions if they perceive they are in control, have the opportunity to agree to stated privacy policies, and consider the purpose of the exchange to be more beneficial than any potential privacy loss.

Changes in Social Media Privacy Attitudes and Behaviors

Expectations for privacy have been changing over the years (Katz, 1987) along with corresponding social norms, and this transformation is especially pronounced with the rise of social media. In just a few short years, attitudes and behaviors have radically changed, from an initial reluctance to public posts, to a new norm of openness with social networking (Johnson, 2010). While people seem to be more aware of and value privacy, many at the same time are freely giving up some of their privacy to strangers, as they willingly friend strangers and post information and images they would never have shared so publicly before. Indeed, when Facebook began in 2004, people questioned why they would want to put any information on the Internet (Kirkpatrick, 2010). The service took off by allowing people to communicate privately or with a small group of friends. Then the service quickly evolved, with Facebook and its users putting more information in public view.

The lines between public and private have arguably eroded, and Facebook founder Mark Zuckerberg says privacy is no longer a "social norm" (Johnson, 2010). Zuckerberg argues that people have gotten comfortable not only sharing more information and different kinds, but more openly and with more people. Evidence of this new openness include Twitter, Myspace, posted website comments, blogs, and the rise of Reality TV (Kirkpatrick, 2010). Zuckerberg contends that people simply no longer have an expectation of privacy (Johnson, 2010), a standard used to determine a legal right to privacy.

These changing attitudes about privacy reflect a new polarized view of privacy. While just a few years ago, an increasing number of Internet users feared they were losing their privacy, now the concerns are mixed. The Ponemon Institute did a study that asked people if they cared more or less about privacy today compared to five years ago, and about one-third said it was more important and one-third said less (Sullivan, 2011). The difference in views depended on the use of social media. By overwhelming numbers, non-users care more about privacy while avid users of social media care less about privacy today. A *USA TODAY*/Gallup Poll further found that the more people use Facebook, the less likely they are to be concerned about privacy invasion (Acohido, 2011a). Only one-fourth of daily Facebook users said they were "very concerned" about privacy, compared to nearly two-fifths of infrequent users.

How has this willingness to part with privacy evolved? In the first place, there is social pressure to engage in online social networking, which relies on active participation. Users face peer pressure to "friend" people (Irvine, 2012), stay connected and never go off the grid, indicate their whereabouts and latest activities, post family photos, and respond to queries 24/7. They are also simply more likely to expose personal information if their peers are doing it (Schneier, 2010).

This tendency toward social media exposure may be driven by some renewed sense of individualism and drive for recognition and self-promotion. Teenagers in particular are considered to have many friends, little sense of privacy, and a narcissistic fascination with self-display (Livingstone, 2008). A study of younger teenagers on social networking sites found them to "relish the opportunities to recreate continuously a highly-decorated, stylistically-elaborate identity" (Livingstone, 2008). History has shown various revolutions in personal sharing and exposure, from an era of urban anonymity and individualism that began in the late 1800s (Henderson, 1999; Westin, 1970), to the confessional culture and sexual revolution of the 1960s (Horn, 1998). Private exposures via social networking online today largely represent a switch to less privacy in the larger community and more in the home, made possible by the technological networking capabilities of the 21st Century. People today are more likely alone with their electronic devices and willing to reach out and interact with outside online communities.

Lack of awareness is also a factor in explaining social media exposure and lax privacy concerns. Studies show that many people are not aware of the extent to which their personal data is captured, tracked, retained, and disclosed. They do not have time to investigate online practices and may not understand the technological capabilities involved (Acohido, 2011b). Youth in particular, have been unaware of the potential dangers they face when entering real personal and contact information in their profiles while accepting friendship requests from strangers (Taraszow, et al., 2010). People are also distracted from thinking about the privacy implications when they use social media. Social networking sites constantly remind users of how much fun it is to share photos, comments, and conversations while downplaying and sometimes deliberately hiding information about the privacy risks (Schneier, 2010). Users are encouraged to forget that they are being directly monitored (Sloop & Gunn, 2010). Most users also skip or barely skim the posted privacy policies before agreeing to give up their personal information.

Users may also be lulled into a false sense of security when it comes to social media privacy. Culnan (1993) found less of a privacy concern when individuals (1) perceive that they have the ability to control future use of their information, and (2) believe that the information will be used to draw reliable and valid information about them. Some may simply believe they have the upper hand in control as they use social media to create and manage their persona. They delete unflattering photos, post content and "like" things that effectively bolster their image, and use social media like Twitter for self-promotion (Irvine, 2012). This perception of control may justify or negate any perceived loss of privacy.

Trust in others may also encourage social media exposure. Social network services in particular focus on building online communities of people with shared interests and activities that form and rely on a foundation of trust. Trust is especially important to social networking because it influences the acceptance and use of social networks (Shin, 2010). People use social networking sites to deepen bonds with friends and family members (Smith, 2011) and believe they are sharing information with trusted friends. Trust is known to be a precondition for self-disclosure because it reduces perceived risks involved in revealing private information (Metzger, 2004). Essentially, people are more likely to share more with those they trust, and they may presumably trust those they friend online.

An inability to assess and weigh online privacy risks can be another factor. The need to balance and even negotiate one's privacy has become increasingly important in an online world, and in the case of social media, these decisions are made almost constantly. Social exchange theory posits that individuals weigh the costs and rewards in deciding whether to engage in social transactions. Unfortunately, as users weigh the tradeoffs of potential privacy loss to the value and need for social networking, they are not operating on a level playing field. The power relationship in a transaction is rarely equal between consumer and service provider (Schneier, 2010). Studies also show that people, especially teens, can be poor judges of risk. Teens are more willing to disclose information online when they perceive more benefits from online disclosure (Youn, 2005). Another study found that people lacking in sufficient risk information are complacent about what happens to their personal data, judging the benefits they feel they gain through online transactions and believing they can adopt coping strategies to minimize dangers (Viseu, Clement, & Aspinall, 2004). Even people with negative attitudes toward personal information disclosures will paradoxically disclose their information for no apparent benefit (Norberg & Horne, 2007).

Finally, there is speculation that social media users have simply grown complacent when it comes to their privacy because they have not personally experienced any negative privacy event (Sullivan, 2011). A 2010 Pew study found only 4% of online adults experienced embarrassing or inaccurate information about themselves posted online, a number that has not increased since 2006 (Madden & Smith, 2010). When users are among millions who are actively engaged in social networks on a daily basis and they do not personally witness a privacy infringement, they may easily conclude that their private information is secure or otherwise uninteresting. Others will conclude that bad things only happen to others, or will rationalize that they have nothing to hide. Some may also feel that they, like millions of others, can realistically do little to protect their privacy.

Privacy Protection Resurrected

Proponents of the "privacy-is-dead" stance are facing a backlash, however, from new evidence that shows privacy is still very much on the minds of social media users. A new wave of privacy protective behaviors may be emerging and possibly reversing a trend in social media privacy loss and attitudes that privacy concerns are no longer salient.

A Pew Research report finds people are getting more privacy-savvy on social networks and becoming more active in protecting their privacy by pruning "Friends" lists, removing unwanted comments, and restricting access to their profiles (Madden, 2012). Nearly two-thirds have deleted people from their "Friends" lists, with women and young adults the most likely to "unfriend" others. More than two-fifths have deleted comments made by others on their profile, and more than one-third have removed their names from photos that were tagged to identify them. These actions are up considerably from the previous year. Likewise, a majority of social network site users say their main profile is set to private so that only friends can see it, while about one-fifth set their profile to partially private so that friends of friends can view it. Women are significantly more likely to set the highest restrictions.

Other studies show teens and young adults, in particular, are becoming more highly engaged in protecting their privacy. Compared with older users, young adults are actually the most attentive to customizing their privacy settings and limiting the visibility of their profiles (Madden & Smith, 2010), and they will take steps to complain when they feel their privacy is violated (Schneier, 2010). Now the vast majority of teens say they have private profiles set visible only to select friends (Lenhart, et al., 2011). More teens are also now migrating to Twitter for purposes of privacy (Irvine, 2012). Since parents have joined the Facebook craze, teens are turning to Twitter where they can have a smaller circle of friends and multiple accounts. They can also interact anonymously or pseudonymously because they do not have to use their real names.

Why a resurgence in privacy interest and protection? Like the push to engage in social networking, privacy protection behavior may also be subject to social influences. One study found that students are more likely to make their profile private if their friends and roommates have private profiles (Lewis, Kaufman, & Christakis, 2008). More than half of online teens also choose not to post something because they are concerned it will reflect badly on them in the future (Lenhart, et al., 2011).

Trust may also play a greater role in determining privacy protection behaviors than social media disclosures. A study of trust and privacy in Facebook and Myspace actually found trust to be a less significant factor in the willingness to share information and form new relationships online (Dwyer, Hiltz, & Passerini, 2007). A survey in the UK shows a decline in the trust of the security of social networks with very few naming it as the platform they trust most, despite the continued increase in the use of social networks ("The decline of trust in social networking platforms," 2012). Young adults are also generally less trusting of the sites that host their content than older users (Madden & Smith, 2010). When asked how much of the time they think they can trust social networking sites like Facebook, Myspace, and LinkedIn, more than one quarter said "never." This decline in trust may be prompting users to exercise more caution in their social media use.

Some argue that privacy norms have not changed and that social media like Facebook are the major agents of social change, not the other way around (Kirkpatrick, 2010). Privacy advocates and scholars contend that the public still cares about their privacy, but those sensitivities have been ill-served by technology companies that stand to profit from the sharing and availability of personal information (Madden, 2012; Schneier, 2010). If anything, social networking companies like Facebook are complicit in changing the way people think about their online privacy (Johnson, 2010). The very companies whose CEOs eulogize privacy make their money by controlling vast amounts of their users' information (Schneier, 2010). Whether through targeted advertising, cross-selling or simply convincing their users to spend more time on their site and sign up their friends, more publicly means more profits. This means these companies are motivated to continually ratchet down the privacy of their services and give users the illusion of control, while at the same time pronouncing privacy erosions as inevitable (Schneier, 2010). Just because people are more comfortable posting information publicly does not mean they wish to quietly surrender all control over their personal information they choose to share over social media. People are learning from the privacy debacle and some are not giving privacy up for dead (Bilton, 2011).

Evolution of Social Media Privacy Infringements

The Case of Facebook

Users have certainly been witness to an increasing loss of their privacy over social media, and their reactions have not gone unnoticed. When Facebook started, for example, it was limited to college students who essentially communicated privately. The company kept user data siloed inside its site alone, saying that a high degree of user privacy would make users comfortable enough to share more information with a small number of trusted people (Kirkpatrick, 2010). By 2006, however, Facebook began to alter the level of user privacy control when it introduced its News Feed feature, which gathered information on the actions of all of a user's contacts and compiled it into a chronological list on the user's home page. The News Feed changed the way people viewed information about their friends. While privacy was not truly breached because users could not see more information than before, the change to an illusion of control created a large uproar (Schneier, 2010). Thousands of users complained that the News Feed violated their privacy because they had no notice or warning and did not give consent. Facebook apologized, but the News Feed remains central to Facebook's service (Electronic Privacy Information Center [EPIC], 2012).

A year later, Facebook launched Beacon, a contentious advertising system that allowed advertisers to track user activities online. Beacon notified Facebook friends about a user's online purchases and transactions. Users were unaware they were being tracked and could not opt out at first from the unwelcome publicity (EPIC, 2012). Facebook shut down Beacon in 2009 and settled a lawsuit for $9.5 million (Johnson, 2010).

That privacy fiasco did not stop Facebook from introducing a host of new privacy changes in 2009, which resulted in an even larger outcry and ultimately government intervention. At first it changed its Terms of Service to allow Facebook to use anything a user uploaded to the site for any purpose (EPIC, 2012). Facebook then returned to its previous Terms of Service. Then later in the year, it essentially mandated the disclosure of previously protected profile information to the public and third-party developers without the ability to opt out. One group called the changes "plain ugly" (Johnson, 2010).

The December 2009 policy changes became one of the biggest privacy blunders for Facebook and prompted the Federal Trade Commission to file an eight-count complaint against Facebook in late 2011. The FTC cited Facebook for unfair and deceptive trade practices in changing its users' privacy settings, which Facebook told users would give them "more control" (*In the Matter of Facebook, Inc*, 2011).

The FTC complained that Facebook failed to adequately disclose that its 2009 privacy changes overrode existing user privacy settings that restricted access to a user's Name, Profile Picture, Gender, Friends List, Pages, or Networks. Users' Friends Lists were now accessible to other users, and although Facebook reinstated the settings shortly thereafter, they were not restored to the Profile Privacy Settings and were effectively hidden (*In the Matter of Facebook, Inc.*, 2011).

Other complaints dealt with control over who can see the user's profile and personal information. In the first place, Facebook provided apps with unrestricted access to user profile information that they did not need to operate, despite suggesting that access would only be to information the app needed to function. For example, an app for a quiz about a television show could also access unrelated information about a user's Relationship Status as well as the URL for every photo and video that the user uploaded to Facebook (*In the Matter of Facebook, Inc*, 2011). In addition, the control of apps was limited to only the user's apps, meaning an app authorized by a friend could access the user's profile information without authorization. For example, if a Friend authorized an app that provided reminders about other Friends' birthdays, that app could access, among other things, the birthday information of those Friends, even if those Friends never authorized the app (*In the Matter of Facebook, Inc*, 2011). While the language changed over time, the privacy information provided was not always clear. Facebook also did not specially verify the security of its so-called "Verified Apps," which users were told had passed Facebook review and displayed a badge.

Another complaint focused on user control over deleting and deactivating accounts. Facebook had promised in its privacy policy that when a user deleted or deactivated an account, no user would be able to see it or even search for it. Instead, the FTC found that Facebook continued to display photos and videos uploaded by users of deleted or deactivated accounts (*In the Matter of Facebook, Inc*, 2011).

Finally, various privacy policies stated that Facebook does not "share information with advertisers without your consent" (*Facebook Privacy Policy*, November 19, 2009). Even their 2009 Statement of Rights and Responsibilities stated "We do not give your content to advertisers" (*Facebook Statement of Rights and Responsibilities*, May 1, 2009). The FTC determined that Facebook did indeed share information about users with Platform Advertisers by identifying to them the users who clicked on their ads and to whom those ads were targeted. Advertisers could access a user's profile page to obtain information such as a name, and then could combine that name with targeted traits, such as interests and likes, as well as information about the user's visit to the advertiser's website (*In the Matter of Facebook, Inc*, 2011).

The complaints against Facebook resulted in a settlement that barred Facebook from making future changes without giving users clear and prominent notice and getting affirmative consent. It also required the company to implement a comprehensive privacy protection program, submitting to independent privacy audits for 20 years (EPIC, 2012). Mark Zuckerberg responded to the FTC settlement by announcing a commitment to "making Facebook the leader in transparency and control around privacy" (Zuckerberg, 2011). New tools and resources were announced, such as an easier way to select one's audience when posting, a tool to view one's profile as others would see it, a new apps dashboard to control what apps can access, the ability to review tags made by others, and the ability to share with smaller sets of people (Zuckerberg, 2011).

Privacy advocates argue that the settlement does not go far enough. They contend that Facebook should restore privacy settings to what users had in 2009, give users access to all of the data that Facebook keeps on them, stop making facial recognition profiles without users' consent, make audit results public, and stop secretly tracking users across the web (EPIC, 2012). They argue Facebook may still post archived user information, making old posts now available under downgraded privacy settings. Users were also told they would have just a week to clean up their history before the "Timeline" feature would go live (EPIC, 2012), which would further detail private information about a user in chronological form.

Other Social Media Cases

Privacy conflicts have also escalated with other social media companies, ultimately resulting in similar FTC settlements. Google experienced a strong backlash from users when it introduced Buzz, a social networking service that linked to Google's email service Gmail. On February 9, 2010, Gmail users were suddenly confronted with a list of followers and "people who you follow" (EPIC, 2012). Google Buzz launched as an opt-out service that compiled a Gmail user's social networking list based on address book and Gchat list contacts. The lists of address book contacts were publicly viewable and Google profiles were searchable. Users were shocked and unhappy that the names and addresses of personal contacts and their relationships were now publicly known (Schneier, 2010). While opt-out options were available at every turn, users were upset that opt-in was the default. Many simply checked out Buzz without realizing that their information was now publicly available (Schneier, 2010). Google responded by making changes to allow users to pre-screen people it suggested to follow, but it placed the burden on users to block any unwanted followers. The FTC filed a complaint about Buzz, and a settlement was reached in early 2011 that required Google to obtain users' consent, draft a "Comprehensive Privacy Plan," and run audits to assess privacy and data protection for the next 20 years (EPIC, 2012).

The Google Buzz case illustrates the scope of privacy protections needed, because Google utilized one kind of Internet service, email, and transformed it into a social networking service without user consent (EPIC, 2012). Buzz was eventually dropped but effectively replaced with the social networking service Google+ in 2011. A consumer watchdog group filed suit to prevent Google from making sweeping changes in 2012 to its privacy policies which would enable Google to bundle the personal information gathered by its Internet search engine and other services, such as Gmail, YouTube, and Plus (Watchdog group sues FTC in attempt to prevent Google from changing privacy policies, 2012).

Twitter has also faced FTC scrutiny for having serious lapses in its data security that allowed hackers to gain control and for making nonpublic tweets accessible. The FTC took significant enforcement action in 2010, resulting in a similar settlement, barring Twitter from misrepresenting its privacy and security (*In the Matter of Twitter, Inc.*, 2010). Yet in early 2012, Twitter joined a list of companies in confessing to uploading user smart phone address books and storing the data on its servers for 18 months without clearly disclosing this practice to its users (Copeland, 2012).

Other Social Media Privacy Issues

Many other social media privacy issues have arisen that are gaining the attention of social media users as well as lawmakers. Tracking and monitoring users is one issue that is prompting legislative interest and lawsuits. Aside from the use of cookies to track social media users, therefore applications such as "Open Graph," which automatically share notices about websites visited and content accessed (Acohido, 2011a).

Location-based services also threaten social media privacy. Location-based services track where a user's mobile device is physically. Location-based services such as FourSquare, Gowalla, Google Latitude, Facebook Places, and Shopkick are a part of social media that rely on GPS, Wi-Fi, and other location tracking techniques for purposes of games, advertisements, information, and social sharing. Location privacy complaints include people being tagged as being at a location even when they did not allow it, and Facebook Places having no easy opt-out feature. Location apps may also have posts linked to Facebook, Twitter, and other social media, ensuring wide coverage and a permanent record of one's where-abouts. Consumers are starting to demand location privacy, meaning the ability to move in public space with the expectation that under normal circumstances, one's location will not be systematically and secretly recorded for later use (Blumberg & Eckersley, 2009), at least not without explicit consent. Several bills in Congress currently seek to make opting-out a required consumer choice and to make it illegal to intercept, use, or disclose geolocation information without permission (*Do Not Track Me Online*, 2011; *Geolocational Privacy and Surveillance Act*, 2011).

Social gaming sites are also presenting privacy concerns. Another FTC settlement recently involved a social game site RockYou, which the FTC said had failed "to protect the privacy of its users, allowing hackers to access the personal information of 32 million users," particularly children without parental consent (Federal Trade Commission, 2012). The settlement bars the company from making future deceptive claims about its privacy and security (Federal Trade Commission, 2012). Unfortunately, when it comes to the third-party applications themselves, they remain largely unregulated (McCullagh, 2011). Much here rests on the strength of the privacy policies that users agree to when they subscribe. This presumes, of course, that an app presents a privacy policy and that users read the policy. One federal bill currently being proposed requires entities to at least establish a privacy policy and provide consumers notice of any use unrelated to a transaction (*Consumer Privacy Protection Act of* 2011).

Who has access to personal data on social networking sites has also become a privacy issue. What happens to one's privacy on a site when they die, for example, leaving the accounts in limbo? This is important if the deceased recorded personal thoughts and posted photos and uploaded other digital mementos that family members would like to control as digital assets of an estate. Facebook's policy has been to put a deceased person's account in a memorialized state, removing certain information and restricting the privacy to friends only. The profile and wall are left so friends can make posts in remembrance. But without the password, prior consent from the deceased, or a legal mandate, family members cannot take control of the account and download its data because of privacy. Lawmakers in at least two states are considering proposals that would require Facebook and other social networks to grant access to loved ones when a family member dies, basically making the contents of the site part of a person's digital estate.

The right of government to access personal social networking data is a serious legal matter. Government surveillance programs have turned their attention to social media, and the Department of Homeland Security (DHS) has stated that it will routinely monitor the public postings of Twitter and Facebook, creating fictitious accounts and scanning posts of users for key terms (EPIC, 2012). Although the agency would not actively seek personally identifiable information, post it, or interact on social media sites, it would monitor activities on social media for information that it can use "to provide situational awareness and establish a common operating picture" ("Publicly Available Social Media Monitoring and Situational Awareness Initiative System of Records," 2011). Such data may be stored for several years and shared with other government agencies. Privacy advocates question the legal authority of the program. Twitter was required to give up personal information to the Justice Department after a federal district judge in Virginia ordered Twitter to make available such information as IP addresses, session times, and relationships of people who may have supported Wikileaks. It was argued, in part, that transmitting IP address information to Twitter did not constitute surveillance of private spaces, and that voluntarily revealing information to a third party eliminated an expectation of privacy and a Fourth Amendment claim (*In Re Application of the United States of America for an Order Pursuant to 18 U.S.C. Section 2703(d), Memorandum Opinion*, 2011).

Yet another access issue that has taken the spotlight is access to people's social networks by employers and potential employers. Some employers are scouring social networking sites of job applicants and even asking job seekers to share their social networking login information (Valdes & McFarland, 2012). It has become common for managers to review publicly available Facebook profiles, Twitter accounts, and other sites to learn more about job candidates and check for inappropriate relationships and activities. But because many users are setting their profiles to private, some managers have resorted to asking applicants to "friend" them or simply provide their password. Some companies will use third-party applications such as BeKnown to comb through Facebook profiles. Other companies such as Sears will allow applicants to log into their job site through Facebook, allowing a third-party app to draw profile information, such as Friend lists, and monitor the applicant's work history. For example, the city of Bozeman, Montana, had a policy of asking job applicants for online passwords (Valdes & McFarland, 2012). Facebook tells employers not to seek passwords, saying it is an invasion of privacy and opens companies to legal liabilities. At least two states have proposed legislation forbidding public agencies from asking for access to social networks (Valdes & McFarland, 2012).

Conclusion

As the battle lines are drawn between privacy advocates and "privacy-is-dead" proponents, it seems clear that privacy control is tipped in favor of the social media industry and will slip away from protection unless efforts are made to preserve privacy. Solutions to an apparent decline in social networking privacy will have to come from regulatory and judicial action, marketplace/economic pressures, and changes in behavior and attitude. Enhanced oversight and enforcement of social media privacy practices as well as marketplace-driven options for privacy protection will be needed to change the course of privacy. User expectations, demands, and efforts to seek and employ privacy protections will ultimately be needed to help spur marketplace and legal protections as well as improve self-protection. Otherwise, the "privacy is dead" declaration in this new era of social networking will be realized.

Regulation needs to keep up with the rapid changes in technology, otherwise expectations of privacy and the standards by which regulatory oversight is allowed will continue to change as the privacy balance moves in favor of the social media companies and their partners. The Federal Trade Commission needs to continue monitoring social media firms and require them to engage in fair information practices and submit to monitoring. This must include third parties, such as software apps and advertisers. Privacy policies must be clear and concise, not overly long and buried. Users must also have the opportunity to give informed consent and have the clear ability to opt in and opt out. Chances are good that as the FTC holds a company like Facebook to certain standards, other social media sites will voluntarily toe the same line as well, for fear of similarly being subjected to government scrutiny (Wassom, 2012).

Competition in the market for social networking privacy protection can also be an effective means of protecting user privacy. In this sense, marketplace forces must work to encourage social media to provide users with privacy protection. One area where social networking sites engage in non-price competition is privacy (Rodrigues, 2010). This can involve competition in privacy policies, whereby principles or statements of rights and responsibilities can be promoted, along with privacy practices that are true to those policies. The provision of privacy control features and enhanced and guaranteed data security may also be competitive. Just as there is a market for social networking, there is a market for social networking privacy protection. This may be met by social media sites themselves or third-party sites.

Perhaps the most effective efforts should be devoted to helping users become properly educated about social media privacy procedures, their choices and their rights, gaining an enlightened understanding of the technology and unintended consequences. In this sense, more attention is needed in "privacy literacy" that can enable users to make educated choices in their use and protection (Debatin, 2011). Negotiations for privacy protection fail, for example, if consumers are lacking perfect information. This would include not only raising awareness but also diminishing indifference. Consumers need to understand the range, likelihood, and potential severity of privacy encroachments and not dismiss that information as hype without properly assessing that information. Users would need to be equipped with the skills to grasp and investigate privacy infringements as well as execute the available privacy protections. The social media would need to assist in these efforts and would do so if properly incentivized via marketplace and legal remedies.

Finally, users need to adjust their privacy attitudes and behaviors to ensure continued protection. While the latest evidence shows more people are "unfriending," restricting their networks, and limiting access to profiles, more effort is needed in exercising discretion in terms of the scope and availability of personal information. Essentially, reducing the flow of personal information and exercising self-restraint would lessen risk. This would mean that user attitudes would need to reflect greater expectations of privacy, while behaviors would need to embrace a mode of self-protection.

Privacy needs will likely continue to be the focus of debate, thanks to social media. Social media privacy concerns may only escalate as more services link to social media sites and more personal information is collected and shared. For the same matter, users may proceed to unknowingly, complacently, and even willingly share personal details in exchange for the benefits these services and communications provide. Social networking adoption and use will likely continue to soar, despite serious threats to privacy.

Yet privacy may not be "dead." Social networking may seem to be the antithesis of individual privacy, but users still appear to have an expectation of privacy as evidenced by an increase in privacy protection strategies. The notion of privacy may simply be evolving as opportunities for disclosure as well as protection grow. With more people moving online and engaging in social networking, privacy expectations may adjust. But marketplace, regulatory, and behavioral responses to any shift in privacy should also occur and evolve. Finding that proper balance in this new age of social networking is the challenge.

References

Acohido, B. (2011a, October 17). Facebook's new features remain unpopular. *USA Today*. Retrieved October 18, 2011, from http://www.usatoday.com/tech/news/story/2011-10-14/gallup-facebook-poll/50806620/1.

Acohido, B. (2011b, February 9). Most Google, Facebook users fret over privacy. *USA Today*. Retrieved March 31, 2012 from: http://www.usatoday.com/tech/news/2011-02-09-privacypoll09_ST_N.htm.

Bilton, N. (2011, December 12). BITS; Privacy fades in Facebook era. *The New York Times*. Retrieved March 25, 2012 from: http://query.nytimes.com/gst/fullpage.html?res=9D02E2D9163BF931A25751C1A9679D8B63&ref=privacy.

Blumberg, A. & Eckersley, P. (2009). *On locational privacy, and how to avoid losing it forever.* White Paper. Electronic Frontier Foundation. Retrieved March 27, 2011 from: http://www.eff.org/wp/locational-privacy.

Burgoon, J. K., Parrott, R., LePoire, B. A., Kelley, D. L., Walther, J. B., & Perry, D. (1989). Maintaining and restoring privacy through communication in different types of relationships. *Journal of Social and Personal Relationships, 6,* 131–158.

Consumer Privacy Protection Act of 2011. (2011). H.R. 1528, 112th Congress.

Copeland, D. (2012, February 15). Twitter is the latest company to admit it uploads your address book. *ReadWriteWeb.* Retrieved March 25, 2012 from: http://www.readwriteweb.com/archives/twitter_is_the_latest_company_to_admit_it_uploads.php.

Culnan, M. J. (1993). How did they get my name?: An exploratory investigation of consumer attitudes toward secondary information use, *MIS Quarterly, 17*(3), 341–361.

Debatin, B. (2011). Ethics, privacy, and self-restraint in social networking. In S. Trepte, & L. Reinecke (Eds.), *Privacy online: Perspectives on privacy and self-disclosure in the social web.* New York: Springer.

DeCew, J. W. (1997). *In pursuit of privacy: Law, ethics, and the rise of technology.* Ithaca, NY: Cornell University Press.

Derlega, V. J., & Chaikin, A.L. (1977). Privacy and self-disclosure in social relationships. *Journal of Social Issues, 33*(3), 102–115.

Do Not Track Me Online Act. (2011). H.R. 654, 112th Congress.

Dwyer, C., Hiltz, S., & Passerini, K. (2007). Trust and privacy concern within social networking sites: A comparison of Facebook and MySpace, *Proceedings of the thirteenth Americas conference on information systems.* Retrieved March 24, 2012 from: http://csis.pace.edu/~dwyer/research/DwyerAMCIS2007.pdf.

Electronic Privacy Information Center (EPIC). (2012). Social networking privacy, Retrieved February 6, 2012 from: http://epic.org/privacy/socialnet/.

Federal Trade Commission. (2012, March 27). FTC charges that security flaws in RockYou game site exposed 32 million email addresses and passwords. Retrieved March 28, 2012 from: http://www.ftc.gov/opa/2012/03/rockyou.shtm.

Geolocational Privacy and Surveillance Act. (2011). H.R. 2168, 112th Congress.

Henderson, H, (1999). *Privacy in the information age.* New York: Facts on File, Inc.

Horn, M. (1998, October 26). Shifting lines of privacy. *U.S. News & World Report, 125* (16), 57.

In Re Application of the United States of America for an Order Pursuant to 18 U.S.C. Section 2703(d), Memorandum Opinion. U.S. District Court, Eastern District of Virginia, case number 1: 11-dm-00003-TCB-LO, filed Nov. 10, 2011. Retrieved February 6, 2012 from: http://www.wired.com/images_blogs/threatlevel/2011/11/twitter_wikileaks_ruling.pdf.

In the Matter of Facebook, Inc. (2011). Complaint. Federal Trade Commission, No. 092314. Retrieved March 22, 2012 from: http://ftc.gov/os/caselist/0923184/111129facebook cmpt.pdf.

In the Matter of Twitter, Inc. (2010). Agreement Containing Consent Order, File No. 0923093, Federal Trade Commission. Retrieved March 22, 2012 from: http://ftc.gov/os/caselist/0923093/100624twitteragree.pdf.

Irvine, M. (2012, March 31). Teens migrating to Twitter—for privacy? *Associated Press.* Retrieved March 31, 2012 from: http://today.msnbc.msn.com/id/46182268/ns/today-today_tech/t/teens-migrating-twitter-sometimes-privacy/#.T3e-6yOXQzG.

Johnson, B. (2010, January 10). Privacy no longer a social norm, says Facebook founder. *The Guardian.* Retrieved January 15, 2012 from: http://www.guardian.co.uk/technology/2010/jan/11/facebook-privacy/print.

Katz, J. E. (1987). Telecommunications and computers: Whither privacy policy? *Society, 25*(1), 81–86.

Kirkpatrick, M. (2010, January 9). Facebook's Zuckerberg says the age of privacy is over. *ReadWriteWeb,* Retrieved January 15, 2012 from: http://www.readwriteweb.com/archives/facebooks_zuckerberg_says_the_age_of_privacy_is_ov.php.

Laufer, R. S., & Wolfe, M. (1977). Privacy as a concept and a social issue: A multidimensional development theory. *Journal of Social Issues, 33*(3), 22–42.

Lenhart, A., Madden, M., Smith, A., Purcell, K., Zickuhr, K., & Rainie, L. (2011, November 9). Teens, kindness and cruelty on social network sites, *Pew Internet & American Life Project.* Retrieved February 8, 2012 from: http://pewinternet.org/Reports/2011/Teens-and-social-media.aspx.

Lewis, K., Kaufman, J., & Christakis, N. (2008). The taste for privacy: An analysis of college student privacy settings in an online social network. *Journal of Computer-Mediated Communication, 14,* 79–100.

Livingstone, S. (2008). Taking risky opportunities in youthful content creation: Teenagers' use of social networking sites for intimacy, privacy and self-expression. *New Media & Society, 10*(3), 393–411.

Madden, M. (2012, February 24). Privacy management on social media sites. *Pew Internet & American Life Project.* Retrieved March 24, 2012 from: http://pewinternet.org/Reports/2012/Privacy-management-on-social-media/Summary-of-findings.aspx.

Madden, M., & Smith, A. (2010, May 26). Reputation management and social media. *Pew Internet & American Life Project.* Retrieved March 24, 2012 from: http://www.pewinternet.org/Reports/2010/Reputation-Management/Summary-of-Findings/Findings.aspx.

Marks, J. (2012, February 16). DHS defends social media monitoring program. Nextgov. Retrieved February 22, 2012 from: http://www.nextgov.com/nextgov/ng_2012 0216_6216.php.

Marshall, N. J. (1974). Dimensions of privacy preferences, *Multivariate Behavioral Research, 9,* 255–272.

McCullagh, D. (2011, May 19). Senators press Apple, Google on location privacy. CNET. Retrieved May 30, 2011, from http://news.cnet.com/8301-31921_3-20064395-281.html#ixzz1NsiBeXhf.

Metzger, M. (2004). Privacy, trust, and disclosure: Exploring barriers to electronic commerce. *Journal of Computer-Mediated Communication, 9*(4). Retrieved May 30, 2011 from http://jcmc.indiana.edu/vol9/issue4/metzger.html.

Norberg, P., & Horne, D. (2007). Privacy attitudes and privacy-related behavior. *Psychology & Marketing, 24*(10), 829–847.

O'Neil, D. (2001). Analysis of Internet users' level of online privacy concern. *Social Science Computer Review, 19*(1), 17–31.

Oxford Dictionaries (2012). Private. Retrieved April 20, 2012 from: http://oxford dictionaries.com/definition/private.

Pastalan, L. A. (1970). Privacy as a behavioral concept. *Social Science, 45*(2), 93–97.

Publicly Available Social Media Monitoring and Situational Awareness Initiative System of Records (2011, February 1). *Federal Register*, Vol. 76 (21), 5603–5606, FR Doc No: 2011–2198.

Rodrigues, R. (2010). Privacy on social networks: Norms, markets, and natural monopoly. In S. Levmore, & M. Nussbaum (Eds.), *The offensive Internet: Speech, privacy, and reputation* (pp. 237–258). Cambridge, MA: Harvard University Press.

Schneier, B. (2010, April 6). Google and Facebook's privacy illusion. *Forbes*. Retrieved March 22, 2012 from: http://www.forbes.com/2010/04/05/google-facebook-twitter-technology-security-10-privacy.html?boxes=Homepagechannels.

Shin, D. (2010). The effects of trust, security and privacy in social networking: A security-based approach to understand the pattern of adoption. *Interacting with Computers, 22*(4), 428–438. Retrieved May 30, 2011, from http://www.sciencedirect.com/science/article/pii/S0953543810000494.

Sloop, J., & Gunn, J. (2010). Status control: An admonition concerning the publicized privacy of social networking. *The Communications Review, 13*, 289–308.

Smith, A. (2011, November 15). Why Americans use social media. *Pew Internet & American Life Project*. Retrieved March 24, 2012 from: http://pewinternet.org/Reports/2011/Why-Americans-Use-Social-Media.aspx.

Smith, R. E. (1979). *Privacy: How to protect what's left of it*. Garden City, NY: Anchor Press.

Sullivan, B. (2011, March 10). Study: Social media polarizes our privacy concerns. *MSNBC*. Retrieved March 24, 2012 from: http://www.msnbc.msn.com/id/41995992/ns/technology_and_science/t/study-social-media-polarizes-our-privacy-concerns/#.T294 OiOXQzH.

Taraszow, T., Aristodemou, E., Shitta, G., Laouris, Y., & Arsoy, A. (2010). Disclosure of personal and contact information by young people in social networking sites: An analysis using FacebookTM profiles as an example. *International Journal of Media and Cultural Politics, 6*(1), 81–102.

The decline of trust in social networking platforms (2012, March 6). *Help Net Security*. Retrieved March 8, 2012 from: http://www.net-security.org/secworld.php?id=12542.

Valdes, M., & McFarland, S. (2012, March 20). Employers ask job seekers for Facebook passwords. *MSNBC*. Retrieved March 24, 2012 from: http://www.msnbc.msn.com/id/46792017/ns/local_news-clarksburg_wv/t/employers-ask-job-seekers-facebook-passwords/#.

Viseu, A., Clement, A., & Aspinall, J. (2004). Situating privacy online. *Information, Communication & Society, 7*(1), 92–114.

Wassom, B. (2012, January 5). 5 predictions for social media law in 2012. *Mashable Social Media*. Retrieved January 15, 2012 from: http://mashable.com/2012/01/05/social-media-legal-predictions/.

Watchdog group sues FTC in attempt to prevent Google from changing privacy policies (2012, February 8). *Associated Press*. Retrieved February 8, 2012 from: http://www.therepublic.com/view/story/abd25acb8c074e0b92932e28c84c074a/US—Google-Privacy-Lawsuit/.

Westin, A. F. (1967). *Privacy and Freedom*. New York: Atheneum.

Westin, A. F. (1970). *Privacy and Freedom*. New York: Atheneum.

Youn, S. (2005). Teenagers' perceptions of online privacy and coping behaviors: A risk–benefit appraisal approach. *Journal of Broadcasting & Electronic Media*, *49*(1), 86–110.

Zuckerberg, M. (2011, November 29). Our commitment to the Facebook community. *Facebook Blog*. Retrieved January 8, 2012 from: http://blog.facebook.com/blog.php.

10

USES AND GRATIFICATIONS OF FACEBOOK MEMBERS 35 YEARS AND OLDER

Aimee Valentine

Introduction

The Internet provides a vast range of new ways to communicate that continue to evolve. Communication tools on the Internet have become an essential part of our lives (Subrahmanyam, Reich, Waechter, & Espinoza, 2008). One of the Internet's major benefits is helping people connect through social networks. Online social networking sites continue to grow in popularity as they provide a selective and convenient way to communicate, allowing constant and immediate interaction (Sheldon, 2008; Urista, Dong, & Day, 2009). According to Nielsen, activity on social media sites accounted for 23% of all time on the Internet in the U.S. as of May 2011, up from 17% in August 2009 (Lacy, 2009; Nielsen, 2011). According to Nielsen's *State of the Media: The Social Media Report Q3 2011*, Facebook is the most popular online social network in the U.S., with 70% of active Internet users having Facebook accounts as of May 2011 (Nielsen, 2011). Due to its popularity, the study discussed in this chapter focuses on Facebook over other available online social networking sites.

According to Facebook.com, the site had more than 750 million registered users worldwide as of July 2011, with roughly 20% (150 million) of those users living in the United States. This is an increase of 46.2 million U.S. members since August 2009, according to Nielsen (Facebook.com, 2010; Lacy, 2009; Shields, 2010). In addition to the number of Facebook users, time spent on the site is also increasing. During May 2011, Americans spent almost 53.5 billion minutes on facebook.com from computers at home and work, up 6% from May 2010 (Lacy, 2009; Nielsen, 2011). In August 2009, the average person spent 5 hours and 46 minutes per month on the site, up from 1 hour and 40 minutes in August 2008 (Lacy, 2009). The people spending so much time on Facebook are not just the tech-savvy young people that the site originally aimed to serve. The members behind Facebook's accelerating growth rate are older audiences. Facebook's U.S. audience growth is primarily fueled by the expansion of users 35 and older (Hempel, 2009). Facebook.com states, "the fastest growing demographic worldwide is among people 35 years and older" (Facebook.com, 2010).

The biggest growth in terms of new members in the U.S. came from users aged 35–44 from September 2008 to February 2009, with the addition of over 4 million women and nearly 3 million men in this age group. Facebook has also grown rapidly among people over 45 in the U.S. with a 165% increase in adults aged 45–54 from October 2008 to January 2009 (Smith, 2009). In January 2010, there were 10.6 million users aged 13–17 (10.4%), 26 million aged 18–24 (25.3%), 25.5 million aged 25–34 (24.8%), 29.9 million aged 35–54 (29.4%), and 9.7 million over 55 (9.5%). As shown in Figure 10.1, about 38.9% of all current Facebook users are over 35 years old, which is quite a change from Facebook's roots as a social networking tool for college students just a few years ago (Corbett, 2010).

Earlier studies argue that communication preferences differ for people of various generations (Fox & Madden, 2005; Westlake, 2008). According to Strauss and Howe (1991), commonly referenced generations for the U.S. are shown in Table 10.1. The Millennial generation was dubbed Generation Y by marketers after the media tendency to refer to the "Thirteenth" generation as Generation X.

Westlake (2008) suggests that people in the Silent, Baby Boomer and Thirteenth generations do not have the same perspective on the Internet as a means for social networking as the Millennial generation. Members of the Millennial generation are likely to have a different perspective on the Internet as they are the first generation to have grown up with the Internet; they are often referred to as "Digital Natives" (Sheldon, 2008). One claim is that the crucial generational difference stems from older Internet users lacking the need to engage with more

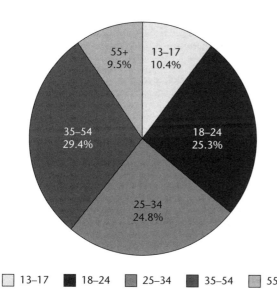

FIGURE 10.1 U.S. Facebook users by age group

Source: Corbett (2010)

TABLE 10.1 Commonly referenced generations of the U.S.

Generation	Years born
Silent	1925 to 1944
Baby Boomer	1945 to 1960
Thirteenth (Dubbed Generation X)	1961 to 1981
Generation Y	1982 or later

Source: Strauss and Howe (1991).

active forms of communication, such as messaging and "feeds." The argument is that older Internet users prefer communication via email or telephone and are not as comfortable with online chatting and text-messaging (Westlake, 2008).

The perceptions of this claim are present in an exploratory study of how college students are influenced by Internet technology. Participants reported perceived differences in the way their generation used technologies compared to the generations of their parents and grandparents. Respondents felt older generations did not understand the potential of interactive technologies (McMillan & Morrison, 2006). In addition, the Pew Internet and American Life Project reports that Generation Y is significantly more likely than older Internet users to engage in instant messaging, play online games, create blogs or download music (Jones & Fox, 2009).

However, Dye (2007) proposes that the Internet and growth of social networking sites have created a new sub-generation, which is not defined by age, but of individuals whose identities are defined by their connections and the content they produce online. This generation is called Generation C—for content. Although the majority of this group is made up of the Millennial generation, it encompasses all ages.

As is evident from Facebook's current audience statistics, older Internet users have begun to engage and become active on Facebook and are responsible for the majority of current growth. There are numerous studies that investigate the use of Facebook by college students; however, there is a lack of studies that have investigated the use of Facebook by older audiences.

Uses and Gratifications Theory

Uses and gratifications theory is a communication theory that focuses on how people use media and other forms of communication to fulfill their interpersonal needs and wants (Rubin, 2002). The basis of this theory is that selection and usage of media are a purposive and motivated action (Rosengren, 1974). In general, uses and gratifications theory is used to determine motives of media use, factors that influence those motives, and outcomes from media usage. It is often used to investigate "how and why" questions about media usage from a user perspective (Sheldon, 2008; Stafford, Stafford, & Schkade, 2004).

The uses and gratifications theory is a widely used approach for establishing initial audience research for a specific medium, type of media content or demographic group. Numerous studies have applied the uses and gratifications theory to investigate motivations for selection and gratifications obtained from usage of mass media. In the past, communication needs were met through a combination of face-to-face human interaction and traditional mass media such as television and radio. However, the Internet and social networking sites allow individuals to play an active role in media consumption, changing the traditional effects of media. Internet communication offers new ways for people to relate to each other and has blurred the lines between interpersonal communication and mass media (Parks & Floyd, 1996; Ruggiero, 2000; Urista, et al., 2009; Valenzuela, Park, & Kee, 2009a).

Uses and Gratifications of the Internet

As scholars began to apply uses and gratifications theory to the Internet, they quickly began to consider that some gratifications for online media may be different from those of traditional mass media. Ruggiero (2000) identified three differentiating attributes of the Internet compared with traditional media: interactivity, demassification (lack of control), and asynchronicity (staggered in time). Several studies identified unique social gratifications in measuring motivations for the Internet (Eighmey & McCord, 1998; Flanagin & Metzger, 2001; Papacharissi & Rubin, 2000; Stafford, et al., 2004).

An early study of college students' Internet usage introduced several Internet motive categories: entertainment, social interaction, passing time, information, and website preference (Kaye, 1998). Papacharissi and Rubin (2000) used a combination of interpersonal, media, and new technology gratifications to measure Internet usage. Gratifications established in their study were interpersonal utility, pass time, information seeking, convenience, and entertainment; with the strongest motivations indicated as entertainment and information seeking. Charney and Greenberg (2001) identified similar gratifications, in addition to a few new factors for the Internet: to keep informed, diversion and entertainment, peer identity, good feelings, communication, sights and sounds, career, and coolness. Another study, using a sample of AOL users, established similar Internet-specific gratifications that motivate users, including searching, gathering information, communication, and socialization (Stafford & Gonier, 2004; Stafford, et al., 2004).

Previous studies have established that some Internet gratifications differ from those found for traditional mass media, such as television and radio. Many studies have identified similar motives for Internet-based applications as entertainment, interpersonal communication, social interaction, information seeking, diversion/passing time, and convenience (Charney & Greenberg, 2001; Eighmey & McCord, 1998; Flanagin & Metzger, 2001; Kaye, 1998; Papacharissi & Rubin, 2000; Stafford & Gonier, 2004; Stafford, et al., 2004).

Uses and Gratifications of Social Networking Sites

Social networking sites satisfy an array of needs from one location. Ray (2007) explored the use of social networking sites for simultaneously fulfilling entertainment, information, surveillance, diversion, and social utility gratifications. Respondents in the study illustrated that one of the major benefits of social networking sites is the ability to meet multiple needs on multiple levels. Results of the study indicated that the sum of these gratifications motivated users to continue to use the sites.

Sheldon (2008) conducted a survey of students at a large southern university to investigate how motives and demographics predict attitudes and behaviors on Facebook. While passing time was found to be the predominant motivation for Facebook use, relationship maintenance and entertainment were also strong gratifications sought. Coolness, companionship, and meeting new people were found to be less likely motivations.

Lampe, Ellison, and Steinfield (2007) explored the use of social networking sites among college students and found that students used social networking sites most often for social reasons. The study also found that students used Facebook primarily to maintain or strengthen existing offline connections rather than to form new relationships. Urista, Dong, and Day (2009) conducted focus groups at a university in central California to investigate how young adults use Myspace and Facebook to fulfill their needs. The study identified five motivational themes: efficient communication, convenient communication, curiosity about others, popularity, and relationship formation and reinforcement. The most predominant theme to emerge was that social networking sites are an "efficient way to communicate with friends" (2009, p. 221). Participants viewed these sites as an easy way to spread news and information to many of their friends at once.

The predominant motivation found for using social networking sites is associated with connecting users with people, including keeping in touch with friends, those they see often and those they are not able to see often, locating old friends, learning about events, and making plans with friends. Other strong motivations found are sharing photos, entertainment, passing time, and information gathering (Lampe, et al., 2007; Pempek, Yermolayeva, & Calvert, 2009; Raacke & Bonds-Raacke, 2008; Subrahmanyam, et al., 2008).

Interpersonal Communication

Facebook facilitates interpersonal communication by providing channels for public and private communication, feedback, and peer acceptance (Valenzuela, et al., 2009b). To understand the role of online communication, some have used the theoretical proposal that users of interactive online forums, including blogs and social networking sites, are co-constructing their online environments. The co-construction model implies that a user's online and offline worlds are psychologically connected. With this model, it is expected that users bring people and issues from their offline worlds into their online worlds (Subrahmanyam, et al., 2008).

Previous research on social networking sites has indicated that these sites may be used to bridge online and offline social networks (Boyd & Ellison, 2007; Haythornthwaite, 2005; Lampe, et al., 2007). One study included a qualitative analysis of autobiographical essays written by college students (McMillan & Morrison, 2006) in which participants used the Internet to solidify their offline identities. The study stated that participants used their virtual online communities to sustain their "real-life" communities that existed offline, such as using online tools to plan social events with their offline friends. Lampe, Ellison, and Steinfield (2006) found students were using Facebook more for "social searching," investigating information about someone they already knew offline, rather than "social browsing," or finding people or groups they would like to connect with offline.

Subrahmanyam, Reich, Waechter, and Espinoza (2008) measured the overlap between face-to-face friends and online social network friends. Results showed that 49% of respondents' top face-to-face friends were also their top online social networking site friends and 16% of the sample reported 100% overlap between their top 10 face-to-face friends and top 10 online social networking friends. In addition, the majority of respondents in the study indicated that they only added people as friends in their online social networking account if they had met them at least once in person. This is consistent with findings by Pempek, Yermolayeva, and Calvert (2009), where the majority of respondents (77%) said that none of their Facebook friendships originated online and 68% reported accepting only people they know offline as friends to their Facebook network.

Socialization and Community

While socialization is very similar to interpersonal communication, the difference is in the reason for seeking the communication channel (Stafford & Gonier, 2004). The socialization motive encompasses several reasons including identifying with others and gaining a sense of belonging; finding a basis for conversation and social interaction; connecting with family, friends, and society; and gaining insight into the circumstances of others. Social interaction allows people to develop trust and reciprocity with others, which encourages participation in cooperative activities. Facebook allows users to feel connected to the community and increases their knowledge of other members (Putnam, 2002; Urista, et al., 2009; Valenzuela, et al., 2009a).

Facebook provides a surveillance tool allowing users to monitor behaviors, beliefs, and interests of their network. This function allows users to gain social cues for establishing group norms (Lampe, et al., 2007; Shoemaker, 1996). Donath and Boyd (2004) argue that analysis of a person's connections helps other people to gain information, form trust, and make decisions about them. Each time a user logs into Facebook, they get the latest updates about people within their network and can reciprocate by posting their own updates. News feeds can also be used as a way to facilitate or collect opinions and advice from within a users' network. In addition, Facebook allows users to create or join groups based on common interests and activities via the "Facebook Groups" application (Valenzuela, et al., 2009a).

Facebook Activities and Time Spent

In addition to investigating why college students use online social networking sites, uses and gratification studies generally examine how college students use these sites. Lampe, Ellison, and Steinfield (2007) investigated the amount of time spent on social networking sites by college students and found that 91% of respondents used Facebook an average of 10–30 minutes per day. Pempek, Yermolayeva, and Calvert (2009) reported respondents using Facebook an average of 28 minutes per day, with the total time being dispersed throughout the day and not taking place in one session. The authors also found that Facebook was integrated as a daily activity regardless of how busy the participants reported being during the time of the study. Raacke and Bonds-Raacke (2008) discovered participants spending 88 minutes on their accounts and 66 minutes on others' accounts per day. Users also reported logging into their account an average of 4.19 times per day.

Several studies have explored and reported consistent findings regarding frequent activities performed on social networking sites. Most frequent activities reported are reading and responding to messages, news feed posts or invitations; commenting and posting on the wall or homepage; browsing friends' profiles, walls, and pages; viewing and commenting on photos; updating the profile; and interacting with Facebook applications (Lampe, et al., 2007; Subrahmanyam, et al., 2008).

The Current Study

Several studies have employed the uses and gratifications theory to understand the motives and needs fulfilled through online social networking sites. The Internet and online social networking sites have begun to merge the concepts of interactive communication and mass media; therefore, presenting unique motivations and gratification factors. Online social networking sites have been linked with facilitating interpersonal relationships, socialization, and community involvement.

As online social networking sites continue to emerge as an essential communication tool in society, it is important to understand how they are utilized by all segments of the population. Previous studies have investigated the use of Facebook among college students and young adults. However, as illustrated by current Facebook audience data, older adults represent a substantial portion of the social networking site's members and account for the majority of growth. Older age demographics are a fairly new segment of the online social networking landscape that has not been investigated in previous studies. This study represents the first large-scale study to explore older audiences' use of social networking sites in the U.S. The findings of this study seek to provide a baseline of knowledge for this audience on Facebook.

This study explored motivations for this segment rapidly joining Facebook, as well as how this audience uses Facebook. A large-scale online survey was utilized in seeking quantitative data about usage and motivations of Facebook among members 35 years of age and older. Participants were provided an Internet link to a survey about Facebook. An online questionnaire was relevant for this study as all respondents were required to be Internet users. The survey included closed-ended questions, as well as two open-ended questions to investigate Facebook usage, frequent activities, and motives. The questionnaire was constructed using adaptations of measurements from earlier studies reviewed in the previous section. The following research questions were investigated:

RQ1: How much time do Facebook members 35 and older spend on the site?

RQ2: What are the most frequent activities conducted on Facebook by members who are 35 years or older?

RQ3: What gratifications are obtained from Facebook by members 35 and older?

Procedures and Sampling

To find respondents for this study, a convenience sample of adults 35 years of age or older was developed using a snowball effect from Facebook networks and groups. Individuals were contacted via a message to their Facebook inbox, wall or news feed, email inbox or other social networking site inbox or news feed. Additional social networking sites utilized in gathering respondents for the study were LinkedIn and Twitter.

Although the survey link was exposed to Internet users of all demographics, an accompanying message provided with the survey link outlined the qualifications for participation in the survey. Qualifications for the study were adults 35 years or older who had a Facebook account and were residents of the United States. After refining the study with feedback from a pretest, the final survey questionnaire was implemented December 8, 2010, and data was collected until January 24, 2011. A total sample of 350 qualified participants was collected.

The sample skewed female with 69.4% (n = 243) and 29.4% male (n = 103) subjects. In terms of age, the majority of the sample were 35–44 years old (43.4%, n = 152) followed by the 45–54 age group (29.4%, n = 103) and the 55–64 age group (22.3%, n = 78), with the 64 and older age group making up the smallest portion of the sample (3.7%, $n = 13$). There were four cases of missing values for both age and gender. In terms of ethnicity, the sample was heavily skewed toward Anglos (76.6%, $n = 268$), followed by Hispanics (8.9%, $n = 31$), African Americans (2.3%, $n = 8$), Asians (1.1%, $n = 4$), and other race (9.1%, $n = 32$). There were seven participants who chose not to indicate their ethnicity.

The majority of the sample had attended some college, with 50.6% ($n = 177$) completing some college and 32.6% completing some graduate school ($n = 114$). The remaining 15.1% of the sample had completed a high school education ($n = 53$), with the exception of one respondent who reported having less than a high school education. Overall, the bulk of respondents reported having household incomes over \$75,000 (59.7%, $n = 209$), followed by household incomes of \$25,000 to \$75,000 (34.6%, $n = 121$), and below \$25,000 (3.7%, $n = 13$). There were five cases of missing values for education level and seven respondents did not indicate household income level.

Findings of the Study

Time Spent, Access, and Membership Longevity

The survey sought to answer three research questions investigating uses and motivations of Facebook among members 35 years of age and older. The first research question explored the amount of time spent on Facebook by members 35 and older. In determining how much time this audience spends with Facebook, three different measurements were collected. First, the most straightforward answer was sought by asking respondents to indicate how much time in hours and minutes they spent on the site in an average day. Responses to this question on the survey proved problematic as the answers ranged from 5 minutes to 45 hours spent on Facebook in a given day. Due to the large number (18.8%, $n = 66$) of respondents who reported time spent with Facebook exceeding the possible number of hours in a day, this portion of the sample was eliminated from the results in an effort to report a more accurate average. Of the responses included (81.1%, $n = 284$) in the results, participants indicated spending an average of 4 hours and 53 minutes on Facebook each day ($\overline{\chi} = 293.6$, SD = 354.110).

When compared to previous studies that examined time spent on Facebook by younger adults and students, time spent reported in this study of older audiences is much higher. Prior findings reported for time spent on Facebook by younger adults and students has ranged from 10 minutes to 2.5 hours (Lampe, et al., 2007; Pempek, et al., 2009; Raacke & Bonds-Raacke, 2008; Sheldon, 2008). To some extent, this finding could be an indication of the overall increase in presence and consumption of social networking sites across all audiences, as well as a reflection of the difficulties experienced with this question on the survey instrument as discussed. However, these findings are a clear indication that this older audience is spending similar amounts of time, if not more, compared to younger audiences on Facebook.

Furthermore, a question was included to determine how often this audience tends to access Facebook. Participants were asked to select from options including never, 1–3 per week, 4–6 per week, 1–2 per day or 3+ times per day. The majority (63%) of participants in this study reported accessing the site daily, with 37% accessing the site 3 or more times a day. This is consistent with earlier findings among younger adults and students that indicated total time being dispersed throughout the day and not taking place in one session (Pempek, et al., 2009; Raacke & Bonds-Raacke, 2008; Sheldon, 2008). However, 36% of respondents in this study also reported accessing the site on a weekly basis, with 18.6% (n = 65) accessing the site 1–3 times per week and 16.9% (n = 59) accessing the site 4–6 times per week. Only a small number (1.7%, n = 6) of the sample reported that they never access Facebook. This suggests that frequency of access on the site is diverse among this older audience on Facebook.

This could be due to the fact that many Facebook members within this older demographic are new to the site, with over half (54%, n = 189) of the sample joining the site only 1–2 years ago and over a quarter (27.4%, n = 96) having an account for 3–4 years. Some respondents (14.3%, n = 50) were very new to Facebook, joining the site less than a year ago and only a small number (4.3%, n = 15) reported having an account for over 5 years.

Previous studies have found that longevity of Facebook membership may result in varied amounts of time spent on the site. Lampe, Ellison, and Steinfield (2007) conducted two identical surveys a semester apart and found that while the same number of users in the second survey reported spending less than 30 minutes per day on the site, a fewer number of users reported spending more than an hour a day on Facebook. Also, the age demographic of 35 years and older is much broader compared with a sample of college-age students and a much more diverse set of characteristics is represented.

Facebook Activities

The second research question examined the most frequent activities engaged on Facebook by this audience. Frequent activities were defined using 28 typical Facebook activities, some of which were adapted from Pempek, Yermolayeva, and Calvert (2009), and are listed in Table 10.2. Although the majority of Facebook activities were adapted from this previous study, there were additions and exclusions to the list executed for this study as updates to the site have changed the way users interact on the site, as well as the growing presence of company and organizational pages on Facebook. Participants were asked to indicate how often they engaged in each activity; selecting from the following options: never, occasionally, monthly, weekly or daily.

Many activities reported by participants of this study were very similar to earlier findings reported among younger audiences, including reading and responding to wall posts, news feeds, and invitations, updating the profile, looking at and reading

TABLE 10.2 Frequency of engagement with Facebook activities

Facebook Activities	(%) Daily	(%) Weekly	(%) Monthly	(%) Occasionally	(%) Never
Reading my own wall posts	47.1	20.0	5.4	21.1	6.3
Reading/responding to news feeds	45.1	14.9	2.9	25.1	12.0
Looking at photos	29.1	30.0	8.3	30.9	1.7
Reading private messages from others	20.6	32.0	9.1	29.1	9.1
Sending private messages	11.4	31.4	11.4	36.6	9.1
Updating or editing profile	1.4	7.7	14.3	65.7	10.9
Adding or removing friends	6.6	18.3	17.1	54.0	4.0
Resending to/reviewing events or invitations	4.3	15.1	10.3	48.0	22.3
Looking at/reading other people's profiles	23.1	19.1	7.1	46.6	4.0
Posting photos	2.6	14.3	24.3	45.4	13.4
Looking at video links	8.3	18.0	8.6	43.7	21.4
Looking at groups	2.9	8.6	12.3	43.7	32.6
Commenting on photos	10.3	24.3	12.6	43.1	9.7
Tagging or untagging photos	2.6	10.6	14.3	42.6	30.0
Getting information from others	11.7	13.4	11.1	40.3	23.4
Reading posts on others' walls	27.7	22.6	7.7	34.6	7.4
Posting on others' walls	23.4	27.1	8.9	33.7	6.9
Updating current status or news feeds	23.1	24.3	8.0	32.9	11.7
Interacting with the live chat function	5.1	12.3	7.4	36.3	38.9
Browsing company or organization pages	2.0	6.6	8.6	40.3	42.6
Adding or removing groups	0.9	3.4	7.1	41.1	47.4
Creating groups	0.6	0.9	1.4	17.4	79.7
Creating events and sending invitations	0.6	1.4	4.9	22.9	70.3
Interacting with applications, quizzes or games	11.7	2.0	3.4	23.7	59.1
Interacting with company or organization pages	0.9	3.4	7.7	34.6	53.4
Interacting with groups	0.9	6.6	6.0	36.0	50.6
Posting videos or links to videos	2.6	9.4	7.7	33.1	47.1
Posting links to other websites	4.0	11.7	9.7	28.3	46.3

Note: ($n = 350$).

other people's profiles, and looking at photos (Lampe, et al., 2007; Pempek, et al., 2009; Subrahmanyam, et al., 2008). In general, Facebook members 35 and older tend to use the site most often for communication with people in their network, which is also reflected in previous findings reported for younger audiences (Lampe, et al., 2007; Pempek, et al., 2009; Ray, 2007; Subrahmanyam, et al., 2008; Urista, et al., 2009).

There were only two activities for which the bulk of respondents reported performing on a daily basis: reading one's own wall posts ($\bar{\chi} = 3.81$, SD $= 1.38$)

and reading and responding to news feeds ($\overline{\chi}$ = 3.56, SD = 1.54). Among these activities, just over 40% of responses for reading one's own wall posts were also allocated to weekly or occasionally, and a quarter of respondents reported reading and responding to news feeds occasionally.

Overall, responses were fairly dispersed when reporting engagement frequency among Facebook activities. Most respondents reported engaging in a majority of activities occasionally, although within this category, diverse distribution among responses was present with a number of responses also ranging from daily to never. For instance, posting photos was among the activities with a majority of respondents indicating occasional activity although almost a fourth of participants also reported posting photos monthly. There were a few activities where responses spanned daily, weekly or occasional engagement: reading private messages ($\overline{\chi}$ = 3.26, SD = 1.32), sending private messages ($\overline{\chi}$ = 2.99, SD = 1.23), and looking at photos ($\overline{\chi}$ = 3.54, SD = 1.25). There were also three activities where frequency of engagement was almost evenly dispersed among occasionally and never: interacting with the live chat function ($\overline{\chi}$ = 2.09, SD = 1.19), browsing company or organization pages ($\overline{\chi}$ = 1.85, SD = .97), and adding or removing groups ($\overline{\chi}$ = 1.69, SD = .82).

There were also a number of activities where the majority of respondents reported never engaging. It is important to note that among all activities where the bulk of respondents reported never engaging, a large number of respondents also reported performing those tasks occasionally. The Facebook activity with the least amount of reported engagement was creating groups, with almost 80% of participants indicating they never create groups. A full disclosure of the Facebook activities measured and reported engagement is listed in Table 10.2.

One finding unique to this study is the more frequent reported use of private messages than indicated in earlier studies of younger audiences. Pempek, Yermolayeva, and Calvert (2009) found that respondents from their sample of undergraduate students preferred interacting with friends in a public wall space over private exchanges. This could be due to inexperience of this older audience on Facebook as this segment tends to be newer to the online social media environment and may be more familiar with email, as suggested by Westlake (2008) in discussing differences of generational perspectives on technology. Boyd (2010) also argues that teens are more equipped to navigate social networking sites since they have grown up with the Internet and are inherently familiar with the social rules that accompany online networks. This finding may also be linked to an increased awareness of privacy concerns on the Internet. A series of updated privacy settings have been released for Facebook over the last few years, as well as pending government regulations for Internet consumer data mining and advertising targeting (Valentino-Devries & Steel, 2011).

Lastly, in regards to frequent activities, Facebook members within this older audience reported more frequent engagement in activities of surveillance rather than participation. For example, a large percentage of respondents reported reading wall posts and looking at pictures on a daily or weekly basis, while only updating their own status or news feed or posting pictures themselves occasionally. Furthermore, many participants reported occasionally accepting event invitations or looking at, adding or removing groups, but the majority reported that they never create event invitations or interact with groups.

Older audiences have been found to demonstrate more passive media consumption online as is associated with traditional forms of media, such as broadcast television or radio. A collaborative research project conducted by PHD and MRI research firms highlighted some key generational differences in consumption of new media platforms. The research focused on three age categories, including Generation Y, representing ages 18–29, Generation X, as ages 30–44, and boomers, referring to ages 45–60. Authors of the study noted that adoption of new media platforms is different from embracing the technology.

PHD and MRI found that use of new media platforms among the boomer group was indicated as more of an extension of traditional media behaviors, while Generation X respondents were more likely to adopt new media behaviors. Members of both Generation X and boomer groups indicated a perception of media production as an area for "specialists," while Generation Y participants felt constrained by traditional media creators. In addition, although boomer groups reported consuming user-generated content, they were more likely to be passive users. Members of this group reported viewing, but not creating content (White, Vogel, Baim, Galin, & Murnane, 2007). Similar findings are reflected in a study commissioned by Motorola, which found that a vast majority of Millennials (71%) were interested in customizable applications for their televisions, compared to 56% of Generation X and 46% of boomers. These findings reinforce the idea that younger generations are more likely to engage with media, while older audience tend toward more passive consumption.

Media consumption habits begin formation early in life and the media with which an audience grows up can have an effect on the way they perceive media as they age. Older generations' familiarity with traditional, one-to-many media formats that foster more passive consumption may extend to their behaviors on social networking sites. While many participants of the PHD and MRI study said they had modified their media habits in some way, most participants admitted that their parents' media habits had an impact on their media consumption. Therefore, members of older generational groups had more traditional media habits passed down to them. Respondents of the boomer group reported parents reading more newspapers, while TV was indicated as a major medium among Generation X and Generation Y parents. Only members of Generation Y reported Internet usage as a media consumption habit passed on to them from their parents.

Gratifications Obtained from Facebook

The final research question explored gratifications obtained from Facebook by members 35 and older. Motives for Facebook use were evaluated using a series of scales adapted from previous studies (Kim & Haridakis, 2009; Lin, 2005; Papacharissi & Rubin, 2000; Schaedel & Clement, 2010; Sheldon, 2008). These motives scales were selected from multiple previous studies in order to maximize the number of gratifications measured in this study, due to the exploratory nature of investigating the older audience on Facebook. Ten motivation scales were measured in the survey: (1) relationship maintenance, which focuses on maintaining or strengthening existing offline relationships; (2) passing time; (3) virtual community, which is the opposite of the maintaining relationships' motive and emphasizes relationships developed on Facebook; (4) entertainment; (5) coolness; (6) companionship, which is related to loneliness and often considered an interpersonal need; (7) information seeking; (8) escape; (9) habit; and (10) self-expression.

Factor analysis of the motive scale responses was conducted, yielding five factors accounting for 60.31% of the total variance: interpersonal habitual entertainment, virtual companionship escape, information seeking, self-expression, and passing time. The interpersonal habitual entertainment factor consisted of the greatest number of variables (13) and accounted for 37.54% of variance. Gratification measurement scales from the survey represented in this factor were relationship maintenance (5 of 6 items), habit, entertainment (3 of 4 items), and coolness (2 of 3 items). Virtual companionship escape was the factor with the second highest number of variables (12) and accounted for 9.65% of variance. All items from the virtual community, companionship, and escape motive scales were represented in this factor, as well as one item from the coolness gratification measurement.

The remaining three factors were composed of items specific to the motive scales used in the survey. The information-seeking factor contained five variables, representing all items included in the motive scale, and accounted for 5.73% of the variance. The self-expression factor included all five variables used for the motive scale and accounted for 3.91% of variance. The last factor, passing time, consisted of all three items included in the motive scale and accounted for 3.45% of variance.

Of the five gratification factors identified as motives for using Facebook among participants, only three factors were determined as salient. The strongest gratification factor for Facebook use indicated in this study was interpersonal habitual entertainment ($\bar{\chi}$ = 4.14, SD = 0.71). This suggests that participants view the site as an entertaining way to communicate with people they know. Kim and Haridakis (2009) also identified a motive factor that combined entertainment and habit for uses and gratifications of the Internet, composed of items that reflected both habitual use and using the Internet to be entertained. The interpersonal habitual entertainment gratification factor consists of similar items found to be central motives for social networking sites among younger audiences in previous studies, including relationship formation and reinforcement, relationship maintenance, convenient communication, social utility, entertainment, and habit. Social gratifications, such as connecting with new and old friends, keeping up with friends and family, and a convenient way of interpersonal communication, are the dominant overarching gratifications found for Facebook use across all audiences. However, entertainment is also indicated as a strong motivation for using social networking sites (Lin, 2005; Raacke & Bonds-Raacke, 2008; Ray, 2007; Sheldon, 2008; Urista, et al., 2009).

The other two significant gratification factors identified in this study were passing time ($\overline{\chi}$ = 3.88, SD = 0.59) and self-expression ($\overline{\chi}$ = 3.52, SD = 0.62). Earlier studies of younger Facebook audiences also identified similar motives to passing time (Ray, 2007; Sheldon, 2008). Self-expression is an effective gratification factor established in this study that is not as consistent in prior studies. Raacke and Bonds-Raacke (2008) found that students reported items of self-expression as less common than other items, while the findings of Lampe, Ellison, and Steinfield (2007) suggested that students utilized Facebook profiles as an accurate representation of themselves online. Neither of these motives is as widely represented in previous studies of younger social networking site audiences. Further research could establish whether self-expression is more salient among older audiences and if passing time emerges as a substantial motive for using social networking sites. A list of the three significant factors and eigenvalues can be seen in Table 10.3.

Due to the explorative nature of this study in examining an older audience on Facebook, two open-ended questions were also included in the survey questionnaire to gather additional qualitative responses regarding possible motivations or influences for this audiences' use of Facebook. The two questions included in the questionnaire were: "Please indicate the number one reason you use Facebook" and "What was the most influential factor in your decision to join Facebook?" Responses to each question were categorized into general groups of similar answers for a comprehensive analysis.

The first open-ended question asked participants to indicate the number one reason they use Facebook. This question yielded 19 response groups. The largest number of responses indicated that members use Facebook to connect with people. The largest response group was to connect with friends, family, and coworkers; to see what people I know are up to; and to see what people post (46.2%, n = 147). A list of the response groups and frequencies for the first open-ended question can be found in Table 10.4.

The second open-ended question asked, "What was the most influential factor in your decision to join Facebook?" This question yielded 22 groups of responses. The largest number of responses indicated participants were influenced by other people who had become members of the site or the ability to stay in touch with friends and family. The three response groups with the greatest number of

TABLE 10.3 Factor loadings of Facebook motives

"Please indicate how much you agree with each statement"

Factor 1: Interpersonal Habitual Entertainment

Using Facebook is enjoyable	.893	−.001	.004	−.126	−.007
I just like to use Facebook	.891	.013	−.006	−.242	.157
It allows me to communicate with my friends	.816	−.099	−.031	.081	−.042
Visiting Facebook is a habit	.786	.155	−.171	.045	.104
It allows me to stay in touch with friends	.784	−.194	.043	.132	−.029
It is entertaining	.750	.033	.144	−.192	.152
Visiting Facebook is like second nature to me	.743	.186	−.166	.080	−.006
It is one of the routine things I do when I am online	.733	.067	−.150	−.009	.174
It helps me to get in touch with friends	.723	−.192	.151	.107	−.045
It allows me to have fun	.673	.064	.128	−.042	.090
I use it to send messages to friends	.647	−.079	.201	−.028	−.046
It is cool	.645	.173	.022	−.138	−.063
I post messages on my friends' walls	.644	−.066	.057	−.027	.140

Factor 4: Self-Expression

People can use Facebook to judge me	−.327	.163	.142	.723	.096
It portrays an image of me to others	−.096	.126	.117	.654	.121
Facebook gives me information about people	.328	−.214	.081	.538	.106
Facebook gives others information about me	.356	−.010	.113	.455	−.168
It is part of my self-image	.231	.395	−.103	.451	−.128

Factor 5: Passing Time

I visit Facebook when I have nothing better to do	.101	−.166	.109	.056	.761
I use it to pass time when I am bored	.292	.088	−.099	.013	.609
I use it to occupy my time	.276	.273	−.114	.026	.473
Cronbach's Alpha	0.94	0.91	0.84	0.70	0.80
Eigenvalue	9.73	7.79	3.22	2.82	1.84
% of total variance explained	37.54	9.65	5.73	3.91	3.48

responses were everyone was doing it or because so many people I know were on it (18.2%, n = 54), to stay in touch with friends and family or to read what others post (15.2%, n = 45), and I was encouraged or pressured by friends or family (14.9%, n = 44). A list of the response groups and frequencies for the second open-ended question can be found in Table 10.5.

Responses to the exploratory open-ended questions also revealed some additional unique possible motives to be considered in future research. When asked about the main reason for Facebook use or the most influential factor for joining the site, some participants indicated peer pressure, children, and business or job implications as being factors for their Facebook use. Further investigation into these elements might yield new information.

TABLE 10.4 Open-ended response groups: "Please indicate the number one reason you use Facebook"

	Frequency	(%) Total
It's a way to connect with friends, family and coworkers; See what people I know are up to; See what people post	147	46.2
To connect with people I don't see often or that live far away	47	14.8
To reconnect with old friends/classmates	35	11.0
To view/share pictures	15	4.7
To stay in touch with/keep an eye on my kids	13	4.1
I was encouraged by friends or family	13	4.1
It's entertaining; Just for fun	8	2.5
To gather information/Research	7	2.2
It seemed necessary; Because so many people I know are on it	6	1.9
For business/job purposes	6	1.9
Boredom; Just for something to do	5	1.6
To play games	5	1.6
Curiosity	4	1.3
I have a profile, but don't use Facebook	2	0.6
It is easy to use	1	0.3
Politics	1	0.3
To tell people about my blog	1	0.3
To keep up with the music scene	1	0.3
To show off my art	1	0.3
Total	318	100.0

Connecting with old friends or classmates was also a theme introduced through the open-ended questions included in the survey, and this is also a familiar trend introduced in prior studies of college students. Prior studies among undergraduate students have revealed that many participants used social networking sites to reconnect with old acquaintances, grade school, and high school classmates (Pempek, et al., 2009; Raacke & Bonds-Raacke, 2008).

Practical Implications

This study has several implications for consideration among marketing, advertising, and business industries. According to the U.S. Census Bureau as of 2009 projections, 52% of the population is 35 years of age or older. This represents a critical audience for marketers, not only by sheer size but for buying power as well. The baby boomer generation, born between 1946 and 1964, spent $3.8 trillion in 2007 and are projected to spend as much as $4.6 trillion by 2015 (Baby boomer buying power: A force to reckon with, 2008; Whitney, 2008). Older audiences represent the largest number of homeowners with families and make up the bulk of both household and high-end purchases. According to Nielsen, this audience

TABLE 10.5 Open-ended response groups: "What was the most influential factor in your decision to join Facebook?"

	Frequency	(%) Total
Everyone was doing it; Because so many people I know were on it	54	18.2
To stay in touch with friends and family; Read what others post	45	15.2
I was encouraged/pressured by friends or family	44	14.9
To reconnect with old friends/classmates	25	8.4
For business/job purposes	24	8.1
To stay in touch with/keep an eye on my kids	20	6.8
To connect with people I don't see often or that live far away	17	5.7
To view/share pictures	12	4.1
To keep up with a specific offline group or organization	11	3.7
Curiosity	8	2.7
Someone else created my profile	6	2.0
Don't remember	6	2.0
Easy to use	5	1.7
It is better than Myspace	5	1.7
Just thought it would be fun	3	1.0
Found it interesting	2	0.7
To exchange news and information	2	0.7
Politics	2	0.7
Privacy options	2	0.7
It is free	1	0.3
I have a profile, but don't use Facebook	1	0.3
To play games	1	0.3
Total	296	100.0

accounted for nearly $230 billion in sales of consumer packaged goods and represented 55% of total sales in the category in 2008. Nielsen tracked purchases of over 6500 brands and found that baby boomers were responsible for 50% of purchases for 72% of those brands (Nielsen, 2008).

As the influence of social media and those using social media continues to grow, it is crucial for traditional media, retailers, brands, and advertisers to understand how different consumer segments use and share content. As advertising budgets continue to shift from traditional media to the Internet, social networking sites are a platform that are increasingly included in marketing plans and strategies (eMarketer, 2007). Results of this study indicate that adults 35 and older are active consumers of Facebook content, spending an average of almost five hours per day on the site and the majority of the sample reporting access to the site on a daily basis. From these baseline findings regarding this audience, it is clear that this audience allocates a substantial amount of time to the site. Even with the increase of media multitasking and convergence, a shift in attention from other media to social networking sites is evident. Facebook represents a major opportunity for reaching this demographic segment as it is the social networking site with the greatest representation of this audience in the U.S.

As businesses and marketers seek to take advantage of Facebook as a valid strategy for reaching people who are 35 and older, creativity and strategic tactics are crucial. Nielsen reports that 60% of Americans who used at least three digital platforms for product research learned about a specific brand or retailer from a social networking site, while 48% of consumers responded to an offer posted on Facebook or Twitter. In addition, 53% of active social media users report following a brand (Nielsen, 2011). However, a majority of participants in this study reported never interacting with company or organization pages, while only 40% said they occasionally browse organization or company pages. Industry studies also show that click-through rates for display ads on Facebook are very low (Baker, 2009). According to these findings, hosting a company page or purchasing advertising space on Facebook is not a sufficient strategy for utilizing the site to make consumer connections. Businesses and marketers will need to consider audience insights, such as the findings offered in this study, to develop innovative solutions for engaging audiences on Facebook.

Findings presented in this study indicate that Facebook may be a more appropriate platform for building brand awareness and loyalty through applications or strategies that help facilitate communication with one's network or provide entertainment, as these were established as the strongest gratification factors among members who are 35 and older, as well as younger audiences. Strategies could also be implemented to drive traffic to a company or organization website. Opportunities may also exist for utilizing members' friend networks to garner social brand influence and reference. Consumers are much more receptive to brand information expressed by members of their social network over brand pages, as friends are perceived to have similar opinions and values (Hausman, 2010). Several digital technology companies, including Facebook, have begun to investigate how the friend networks on social networking sites might be exploited by marketers and advertisers (Baker, 2009).

Theoretical Implications

In addition to the business and marketing implications of this study, the growth of social networking sites among all audiences, including those who are 35 years and older, has an impact on the fundamental characteristics of interpersonal communication, development of community, collection of social norms, and formation of social identity. As discussed in regard to uses and gratifications theory, it suggests that people select media based on their needs which are influenced by social and psychological factors. Studying media outlets from this perspective provides insight not only about motivations and influences of the media, but also about which social and psychological functions they serve (Katz, Gurevitch, & Haas, 1973). boyd (2010) refers to social networking sites as "networked publics" and compares them to traditional publics, suggesting that as a result of their unique properties, networked publics will influence the roles people play in society and blur the boundaries between public and private.

In advancing interpersonal communication, social networking sites offer a new way of achieving a sense of belonging and community and, therefore, provide a new way of gathering social cues. Previous studies have explored perceptions of a sense of community in online environments and found that members often experience a virtual sense of community (Blanchard & Markus, 2004; Jones, 1997; Rotman, Golbeck, & Preece, 2009). Further studies have established that Facebook allows users to feel connected to the community by increasing their knowledge of other members (Putnam, 2002; Urista, et al., 2009; Valenzuela, et al., 2009a).

Individuals are often shaped by the communities they belong to, including the expected behaviors, morals, and ethics. Online social networks present similar characteristics to traditional communities and encourage the creation of community by facilitating more efficient means of communication between members (Donath & boyd, 2004; Hoffman, 2008).

One's attitudes, behaviors, and perceptions are significantly influenced by the social groups to which one belongs. Research presented in the area of group communication indicates that online social networks can function as groups that facilitate development of social norms and have a direct impact on people's behavior and judgment (Severin & Tankard, 2001). Sherif's (1936) experiments suggest that people depended on groups for guidance in uncertain situations, such as politics, religion or morality, whether the group is actually present or not. Sherif argues that even casual groups, or people who may not have actually interacted face-to-face, can have a strong influence on its members. This argument suggests that an individual's Facebook network can have a substantial influence on the beliefs and attitudes formed in these areas.

Limitations and Future Research

There were some limitations present in conducting this study. Although an adequate sample size was collected, a convenience sample beginning with the researcher's own network was used for the study. Random sampling of a larger number of participants would provide external validity. Additionally, the sample collected for this study skewed heavily toward females and Caucasians, with the largest percentage representing the 35–44 age group.

Measurements for this study relied heavily on descriptive statistics, which contributes to the low validity of the study. Descriptive statistics are useful in explaining characteristics of the sample collected, although utilizing only descriptive statistics for measurement increases the chance of different results from a replication of the study.

Although the motive measurement scales were replicated from several studies, these motives are not completely comprehensive. More authentic information may be discovered with the development of motive scales specific to older audiences. Some potential unique motives were identified through the open-ended questions explored in this study, such as peer pressure, children, and business or job implications.

Finally, when using a self-reported measurement there is usually a concern about response bias and inaccurate estimates. Self-reported measures are often criticized for the possibility of being influenced by social acceptability and researcher bias. Specific to uses and gratifications, there is often concern regarding the extent to which respondents are conscious of their motives for media usage (Palmgreen, 1984; Subrahmanyam, et al., 2008). Respondent anonymity was emphasized in recruitment of respondents for the study.

This study provides an inaugural investigation of Facebook members 35 years of age or older. Future research exploring relationships and differences among gender, usage groups or age brackets as related to Facebook gratifications and usage would benefit the literature. The age demographic of 35 and older was targeted specifically for this study since this group represents the fastest-growing audience on Facebook. However, a significant gap remains between the numerous studies that have investigated college students and young adults and the older adult audience examined in this study. Future research will need to assess Facebook usage among post-college members who are younger than 35 years old.

References

Baker, S. (2009, June 1). What's a friend worth? *BusinessWeek*, 32–36.

Becker, L. (1979). Measurement of gratifications. *Communication Research*, 6(1), 54–73.

Berelson, B. (1949). What "missing the newspaper" means. In P. F. Lazarsfeld, & F. N. Stanton (Eds.), *Communication research 1948–1949* (pp. 111–129). New York: Harper.

Blanchard, A.L., & Markus, M. L. (2004). The experienced "sense" of a virtual community: Characteristics and processes. *Data Base for Advances in Information Systems*, 35, 65–79.

Blood, R., Keir, G. J., & Namjun, K. (1983). Newspaper use and gratification in Hawaii. *Newspaper Research Journal*, 4(4), 43–52.

Blumler, J. G. (1979). The role of theory in uses and gratifications studies. *Communication Research*, 6(1), 9–28.

boyd, d. (2010). Social network sites as networked publics: Affordances, dynamics, and implications. In Z. Papacharissi (Ed.), *Networked self: Identity, community, and culture on social network sites* (pp. 39–58). New York: Routledge.

boyd, d. m., & Ellison, N. B. (2007). Social network sites: Definition, history, and scholarship. *Journal of Computer-Mediated Communication*, 13(1), 210–230.

Burgoon, J., & Burgoon, M. (1981). Functions of the daily newspaper. *Newspaper Research Journal*, 2, 29–39.

Charney, T., & Greenberg, B. (2001). Uses and gratifications of the Internet. In C. Lin, & D. Atkin (Eds.), *Communication, technology and society: New media adoption and uses and gratifications* (pp. 383–406). Hampton, NJ: Cresskill.

Corbett, P. (2010). Facebook demographics and statistics report 2010–145% growth in 1 year. Retrieved June 15, 2010 from: http://www.istrategylabs.com/2010/01/facebook-demographics-and-statistics-report-2010-145-growth-in-1-year/.

Dobos, J., & Dimmick, J. (1988). Factor analysis and gratification constructs. *Journal of Broadcasting & Electronic Media, 32*(3), 335–350.

Donath, J. & boyd, d. (2004). Public displays of connection. *BT Technology Journal, 22*(4), 71–82.

Dye, J. (2007). Meet generation C: Creatively connecting through content. *EContent, 30*(4), 38.

Eighmey, J., & McCord, L. (1998). Adding value in the information age: Uses and gratifications of sites on the World Wide Web. *Journal of Business Research, 41*(3), 187–194.

eMarketer. (2007). Online ad spending to reach $42B by 2011: Budget shift to accelerate. Retrieved March 16, 2011 from: http://www.marketingcharts.com/television/online-ad-spending-to-reach-42b-by-2011-budget-shift-to-accelerate-2292/emarketer-us-online-advertising-spending-2006-2011jpg/.

Facebook.com. (2010). Report. Retrieved July 6, 2010 from: http://www.facebook.com/adsmarketing/.

Flanagin, A., & Metzger, M. (2001). Internet use in the contemporary media environment. *Human Communication Research, 27*(1), 153–181.

Fox, S., & Madden, M. (2005, December). Memo: Generations online, Pew Internet & American Life Project. Retrieved June 15, 2010 from: http://www.pewinternet.org/PPF/r/170/report_display.asp.

Hausman, A. P. D. (2010). Marketing strategy: Using social media to create customer value. Retrieved March 22, 2011 from: http://hausmanmarketresearch.org/social-marketing/marketing-strategy-using-social-media-to-create-customer-value/.

Haythornthwaite, C. (2005). Social networks and Internet connectivity effects. *Information, Communication & Society, 8*(2), 125–147.

Hempel, J. (2009). How Facebook is taking over our lives. *Fortune, 159*(4), 48.

Hoffman, P. (2008). But are we really friends? Online social networking and community in undergraduate students. Unpublished dissertation. University of Akron, Ohio.

Jones, Q. (1997). Virtual communities, virtual settlements, and cyber-archaeology: A theoretical outline, *Journal of Computer-Mediated Communication, 3*(3). DOI: 10.1111/j.10 83-6101.1997.tb00075.x.

Jones, S., & Fox, S. (2009). Generations online in 2009. Pew Internet & American Life Project. Retrieved June 20, 2010 from: http://www.pewinternet.org/~/media//Files/Reports/2009/PIP_Generations_2009.pdf.

Kang, M., & Atkin, D. (1999). Exploring the role of media uses and gratifications in multimedia cable adoption. *Telematics and Informatics, 16*(1–2), 59–74.

Katz, E., Blumler, J. G., & Gurevitch, M. (1973). Uses and gratifications research. *Public Opinion Quarterly, 37*(4), 509–523.

Katz, E., Gurevitch, M., & Haas, H. (1973). On the use of the mass media for important things. *American Sociological Review, 38*, 164–181.

Kayahara, J., & Wellman, B. (2007). Searching for culture–high and low. *Journal of Computer-Mediated Communication, 12*(3), 824–845.

Kaye, B. K. (1998). Uses and gratifications of the World Wide Web: From couch potato to web potato. *New Jersey Journal of Communication, 6*(1), 21–40.

Kim, J., & Haridakis, P. M. (2009). The role of internet user characteristics and motives in explaining. *Journal of Computer-Mediated Communication, 14*(4), 988–1015.

Lacy, L. (2009). Nielsen: Social ad spending up sharply. Retrieved November 2, 2009 from: www.clickz.com/3635095.

Lampe, C., Ellison, N., & Steinfield, C. (2006). A Face(book) in the crowd: Social searching vs. social browsing. In *Proceedings of the 2006 20th Anniversary Conference on Computer Supported Cooperative Work* (pp. 167–170). New York: ACM Press.

Lampe, C., Ellison, N., & Steinfield, C. (2007). The benefits of Facebook "friends:" Social capital and college students' use of online social network sites. *Journal of Computer-Mediated Communication, 12*(4), 1143–1168.

Lenhart, A. (2008). The democratization of online social networks. Pew Internet Project. Retrieved June 20, 2010 from: http://fe01.pewinternet.org/Presentations/2009/41—The-Democratization-of-Online-Social-Networks.aspx.

Lichtenstein, A., & Rosenfeld, L. (1983). Uses and misuses of gratifications research: An explication of media functions. *Communication Research, 10*(1), 97–109.

Lin, C. A. (2005). Predicting online shopping via consumer motives, innovativeness, and off-line teleshopping activity. Paper presented at the annual meeting of the International Communication Association, New York City.

McMillan, D. W., & Chavis, D. M. (1986). Sense of community: A definition and theory. *Journal of Community Psychology, 14*, 6–23.

McMillan, S. J., & Morrison, M. (2006). Coming of age with the Internet. *New Media & Society, 8*(1), 73–95.

Mendelsohn, H. (1964). Listening to radio. In L. A. Dexter, & D. M. White (Eds.), *People, society and mass communications* (pp. 239–249). New York: The Free Press.

Motorola Home & Networks Mobility. (2009). Survey reveals shift in media consumption habits across generations. Retrieved April 27, 2011 from: http://www.mediazbiz.com/2009/12/05/shift-in-media-consumption-habits-across-generations.

Nielsen. (2008). Baby boomer buying power: A force to reckon with. Retrieved April 28, 2011 from: http://blog.nielsen.com/nielsenwire/consumer/baby-boomers-buying-power-a-force-to-reckon-with/.

Nielsen. (2011). *State of the media: The social media report Q3 2011.* Retrieved from: http://blog.nielsen.com/nielsenwire/social/. Retrieved from: http://www.nielsen.com.

Palmgreen, P. (1984). Uses and gratifications: A theoretical perspective. In R. N. Bostrom (Ed.), *Communication yearbook, 8* (pp. 20–55). Beverly Hills, CA: Sage.

Palmgreen, P., & Rayburn II, J. D. (1979). Uses and gratifications and exposure to public television: A discrepancy approach. *Communication Research, 6*(2), 155–180.

Palmgreen, P., & Rayburn II, J. D. (1982). Gratifications sought and media exposure: An expectancy value model. *Communication Research, 9*(4), 561–580.

Papacharissi, Z., & Rubin, A. M. (2000). Predictors of Internet use. *Journal of Broadcasting & Electronic Media, 44*(2), 175–196.

Parks, M. R., & Floyd, K. (1996). Making friends in cyberspace. *Journal of Communication, 46*, 80–97.

Pempek, T. A., Yermolayeva, Y. A., & Calvert, S. L. (2009). College students' social networking experiences on Facebook. *Journal of Applied Developmental Psychology, 30*(3), 227–238.

Price, V. (1988). On the public aspects of opinion: Linking levels of analysis in public opinion research. *Communication Research, 15*(6), 659–679.

Putnam, R. (2002). Bowling together. *American Prospect, 13*(3), 20–22.

Raacke, J., & Bonds-Raacke, J. (2008). MySpace and Facebook: Applying the uses and gratifications theory to exploring friend-networking sites. *CyberPsychology & Behavior, 11*(2), 169–174.

Ray, M. (2007). Needs, motives, and behaviors in computer-mediated communication: an inductive exploration of social networking websites. Paper presented at the annual meeting of the International Communication Association, San Francisco, CA. Retrieved June 20, 2010 from: http://www.allacademic.com/meta/p169242_index.html.

Rosengren, K. E. (1974). Uses and gratifications: A paradigm outlined. In J. G. Blumler, & E. Katz (Eds.), *The uses of mass communications: Current perspectives on gratifications research* (pp. 269–286). Beverly Hills, CA: Sage.

Rotman, D., Golbeck, J., & Preece, J. (2009). The community is where the rapport is–on sense and structure in the YouTube community. Paper presented at international conference on communities and technologies, ACM, University Park, PA.

Rubin, A. (2002). Media uses and effects: A uses-and-gratifications perspective. In J. Bryant, & D. Zillmann (Eds.), *Media effects: Advances in theory and research* (2nd ed.) (pp. 525–548). Hillsdale, NJ: Lawrence Erlbaum Associates, Inc.

Rubin, A. M. (1981). An examination of television viewing motivations. *Communication Research*, *8*(2), 141–165.

Ruggiero, T. (2000). Uses and gratifications theory in the 21st century. *Mass Communication and Society*, *3*(1), 3–37.

Sarason, S. B. (1974). *The psychological sense of community: Prospects for a community psychology.* San Francisco: Jossey-Bass.

Schaedel, U., & Clement, M. (2010). Managing the online crowd: Motivations for engagement in user-generated content. *Journal of Media Business Studies*, *7*(3), 17–36.

Severin, W., & Tankard, J. (2001). *Communication theories: Origins, methods, and uses in the mass media* (5th ed.). New York: Addison Wesley Longman Inc.

Sheldon, P. (2008). Student favorite: Facebook and motives for its use. *Southwestern Mass Communication Journal*, *23*(2), 39–53.

Sherif, M. (1936). *The psychology of social norms.* New York: Harper & Brothers Publishers.

Shields, M. (2010). Facebook hits 500 million mark. *Mediaweek.* Retrieved July 21, 2010 from: http://www.mediaweek.com/mw/content_display/news/digital-downloads/broadband/e3i588547861bb321c9a26df80eaf3fe9a8.

Shoemaker, P. J. (1996). Hardwired for news: Using biological and cultural evolution to explain the surveillance function. *Journal of Communication*, *46*(3), 32–47.

Smith, J. (2009). Number of US Facebook users over 35 nearly doubles in last 60 days. Retrieved November 2, 2009 from: http://www.insidefacebook.com/2009/03/25/number-of-us-facebook-users-over-35-nearly-doubles-in-last-60-days/.

Stafford, T. F., & Gonier, D. (2004). What Americans like about being online. *Communications of the ACM*, *47*(11), 107–112.

Stafford, T. F., Stafford, M. R., & Schkade, L. L. (2004). Determining uses and gratifications for the Internet. *Decision Sciences*, *35*(2), 259–288.

Strauss, W., & Howe, N. (1991). *Generations: The history of America's future, 1584 to 2069.* New York: William Morrow and Company, Inc.

Subrahmanyam, K., Reich, S. M., Waechter, N., & Espinoza, G. (2008). Online and offline social networks: Use of social networking sites by emerging adults. *Journal of Applied Developmental Psychology*, *29*(6), 420–433.

Towers, W. M. (1985). Weekday and Sunday readership seen through uses and gratifications. *Newspaper Research Journal*, *6*(3), 20–32.

Towers, W. M. (1987). Radio listenership and uses and gratifications: A replication. *Communication Research Reports*, *4*(1), 57–64.

Turner, J. C. (1982). Towards a cognitive redefinition of the social group. In H. Tajfel (Ed.), *Social identity and intergroup relations.* Cambridge: Cambridge University Press.

Urista, M. A., Dong, Q., & Day, K. D. (2009). Explaining why young adults use MySpace and Facebook through uses and gratifications theory. *Human Communication*, *12*(2), 215–229.

Valentino-Devries, J., & Steel, E. (2011, March 16). White House to push privacy bill. *The Wall Street Journal*. Retrieved March 16, 2011 from: http://online.wsj.com/article/SB10001424052748704662604576202971768984598.html?mod=ITP_marketplace_0.

Valenzuela, S., Park, N., & Kee, K. F. (2009a). Is there social capital in a social network?: Facebook use and college students' life satisfaction, trust, and participation. *Journal of Computer-Mediated Communication, 14*, 875–901.

Valenzuela, S., Park, N., & Kee, K. F. (2009b). Being immersed in social networking environment: Facebook groups, uses and gratifications, and social outcomes. *CyberPsychology & Behavior, 12*(6), 729–733.

Westlake, E. J. (2008). Friend me if you Facebook. *TDR: The Drama Review, 52*(4), 21–40.

White, A., Vogel, J., Baim, J., Galin, M., & Murnane, B. (2007). Media consumption pathways in an evolving world. Retrieved April 27, 2011 from: http://www.gfkmri.com/PDF/WP%20Media%20consumption%20pathways%20in%20an%20evolving%20world.pdf.

Whitney, D. (2008). Booming buying power. Retrieved April 28, 2011 from: http://www.tvweek.com/news/2008/02/booming_buying_power.php.

11

SOCIAL MEDIA AND YOUNG LATINOS

Alan B. Albarran

Introduction

Young demographics are among the heaviest users of social networks. According to Swartz (2009), young people are heading towards universal adoption of social networking usage while more than four in five adults in the United States are using social media at least once a month. Because of the vast numbers of users, social networking has been of huge interest to businesses. BIGresearch (2009) conducted a study to learn more about the habits and demographics of social media users, and determined they are more likely to use more than one platform. Social media users tend to skew towards females, younger than the general population and statistically have a slightly higher income. In terms of demographics, social media usage indexes high across different ethnic groups on most social media sites. Of interest to this project, the BIG study found that Latinos most often used Myspace, followed by Twitter, Facebook, and LinkedIn (Facebook, n.d.).

Baker (2009) reports friendships have changed as a result of the rise in social networking sites. Sites such as Facebook have yet to take off as an advertising platform because visitors tend to pay more attention to friends and socializing than the ads on the page. However, ad companies are attempting to analyze these linkages among friends because they recognize that friends are more likely to be influenced by other friends and use the same types of goods and services.

The popularity of Facebook has taken a direct toll on Myspace. Steel (2009) explains Myspace was forced to re-invent their brand because users were rapidly abandoning their site. The goal was to refocus Myspace in order to make it more entertainment based, as a place for users to connect with their friends over content like music and TV. Moving to a strategic position as an entertainment site puts Myspace in direct competition with other popular video sites such as Hulu, Netflix, and YouTube.

Twitter debuted in 2006, and brought in a new era of social media as users were limited to posting "tweets" that consist of no more than 140 characters. While many users and businesses were unsure how to utilize Twitter, others quickly gravitated to the new site and realized its potential as a medium for "broadcasting" to followers who wanted the latest updated information. Soon news organizations and all types of business and industry recognized the value of using Twitter as both a tool to send information and a way to expand marketing efforts.

Forrester Research is predicting that by 2013, an estimated 2.2 billion people worldwide will be online (Tweeting all the way to the bank, 2009). Social networking sites are hesitant to charge fees for their users, instead focusing on making as much money as possible via advertising on the sites. Facebook continues experimenting with different ad formats in order to gain better control over their advertising on the sites.

As the previous discussion illustrates, business and industry see immense value and economic potential in social media not only for the massive numbers that use the platforms, but for advertising and marketing purposes as well. Social media has also been embraced for its many possible research opportunities by the academic community, with a number of books already in print along with scholarly investigations in scholarly journals, edited volumes, and at conference venues. The academic literature on social media is limited. Many of the studies have limited their samples to college-age students found on one campus, and most studies lack much sample diversity in terms of ethnicity.

The study reported in this chapter seeks to contribute to the literature by examining young adult Latino social media users in the United States and five Latin American countries: Argentina, Chile, Colombia, Mexico, and Uruguay. We define "young adults" as between the ages of 18 and 25. This is a key demographic group with a large presence on social network sites that has largely been underrepresented in previous studies.

In the United States alone, the Latino population is now estimated by the government at approximately 51 million people, and these estimates do not include the undocumented population. Adding the undocumented population (conservatively estimated to be at least 10 million) makes the U.S. the second largest Spanish-language-speaking nation in the world. Spanish is a primary language for many U.S. Latinos. Globally, the Spanish-speaking population is much larger and even more diverse, estimated at somewhere around 452 million and growing (Worldwide Spanish speaking population statistics, n.d.).

Review of the Literature on Social Media

The scholarly literature regarding social media is limited in both size and scope due to the relatively short time that these sites have existed. The majority of academic studies have focused on the uses and gratifications of social networking, but some other studies exist that look at the uses of social media as part of a broader investigation of Internet usage.

A long-established theoretical domain, uses and gratifications theory focuses on how individuals use media and other forms of communication to fulfill social and psychological needs. This framework proposes that people select and use media based on specific motivations (Rosengren, 1974). Uses and gratifications theory also suggests people use the same media for different purposes. In general, the uses and gratifications theory is used to determine motives of media use, factors that influence those motives, and outcomes from media-related behavior (Sheldon, 2008). In the past, gratifications were often delayed due to the lack of interactivity with traditional media. However, social networking sites allow individuals to play an active role, changing the traditional effects of mass media (Valenzuela, Park, & Kee, 2009).

In one of the first studies involving uses and gratifications and social media, Lampe, Ellison, and Steinfield (2006) surveyed first-year students at Michigan State University and found the students were using Facebook as a means to "social search" and investigate people with whom they shared an offline connection. Students were less likely to engage in "social browsing" to meet new people online to then create an offline relationship. In a series of related studies, the same researchers examined Facebook users among college students to identify relationships between social media and the formation and maintenance of individual social capital (Ellison, Steinfield, & Lampe, 2007). The authors found that people were mainly using Facebook as means to keep in touch with individuals with whom they already shared an offline connection. Other findings indicated that the relationship between Facebook use and bridging social capital varied based upon the degree of self-esteem and satisfaction with their life.

Steinfield, Ellison, and Lampe (2008) conducted two more surveys one year apart to determine how Facebook use changes over time among a college-aged population. Between the years of 2006 and 2007, users reported time spent per day on Facebook was significantly higher, increasing by over one hour per day, while the average number of "friends" also increased by 50%. Findings also indicated that students with lower self-esteem had a higher relationship in regards to Facebook use and bridging social capital, while those with high self-esteem the effect was reversed.

Hargittai (2007) conducted a study with a diverse sample of students at the University of Illinois-Chicago regarding patterns of social networking use. Overall 88% of the sample used social networking sites. Facebook was the most popular social network, with about four in five respondents having an account. Myspace was ranked second in popularity. In regard to ethnicity, students of Hispanic descent were more likely to be Myspace users than the rest of the sample. There was also a correlation between the level of the parents' education and what site that student might be most likely to use. Those whose parents had a high school education or less were most commonly Myspace users, while those whose parents held college or graduate degrees were most likely on Facebook. Other findings suggest students who lived at home were less likely to spend as much time on social networking sites as those who lived away from home and Facebook use was more common among younger students (18–19).

Coyle and Vaughn (2008) used a survey and focus groups to gauge the habits college students use to communicate, including social networking. Just over half (53%) of the sample reported use of two social networking sites and slightly over one-third used only one account. Students reported logging in as many as three times a day, and used the time spent on these sites to keep in touch with friends and for entertainment. The authors concluded that social networking sites enable users to be both creative and expressive. Raacke and Bond-Raacke (2008) conducted a study with 116 students from a public East Coast university regarding Internet usage. Of those surveyed, 87.1% reported having either a Myspace or Facebook account. Most people used their account to keep in touch with old and current friends, and to post and look at pictures. Findings showed that students were typically spending around 3 hours per day on one or more social networking sites to keep in touch with friends, to learn about events and social functions, and to feel connected.

Subrahmanyam, Reich, Waechter, and Espinoza (2008) conducted a study at a university in Los Angeles regarding use of social networking sites as well as typical activities on the sites. Of the sample of 131 students, 78% reported having a profile on a social networking site. The most common activities reported while using social networking sites were reading and responding to notes and messages, reading comments and posts written on their profile page and wall, and browsing friends' profiles and walls. Other motives for using social networking sites were to keep in contact with people from their offline lives, and using the online connection to strengthen their relationships with offline friends.

Pempek, Yermolayeva, and Calvert (2009) examined social networking usage by using 92 undergraduate students to complete a diary-like measure for each day of the week to report daily time use and respond to an activities checklist to assess their use of Facebook. Time spent on Facebook averaged 27.9 minutes on week-days and 28.4 minutes per weekend day. Findings indicated students use Facebook as a medium to communicate with friends, as well as to establish their own personal identity. The authors also found students used Facebook to share content as content creators, and also post messages on the walls of others to be seen publicly.

In terms of research, these studies offer a baseline of material on how to examine social networking from a uses and gratifications perspective, especially among younger audiences. One shortcoming is the lack of data on how young Latinos use social networks. This chapter presents data from a large-scale study on social media uses and gratifications among young Hispanics/Latinos, collected by an international research team in six different countries: Argentina, Chile, Colombia, Mexico, the United States, and Uruguay. To be eligible to participate in the study, three criteria were used: subjects had to (1) be of Hispanic or Latino descent; (2) be between the ages of 18–25; and (3) use at least one social media site on a weekly basis. The study was designed to answer the following research questions:

RQ1: What social media sites do young Latinos use?

RQ2: How do the gratifications associated with social media sites compare among young Latinos?

RQ3: How do attitudes about social media sites differ among young Latinos?

Methodology

Following the recruitment of members of the research team in the individual countries, the investigators decided to use a two-stage research design involving both qualitative and quantitative approaches to answer the questions guiding this project. The first stage involved a series of focus groups conducted in each nation and then sharing the findings as a team. The second stage involved preparing, pre-testing, and administering a quantitative study using a survey methodology, based on the data obtained in the focus groups. These procedures are detailed below.

Focus Groups

Focus groups were organized and conducted during September–October 2009 in each country. In order to participate in a focus group subjects had to meet the criteria listed earlier (be of Latino descent, between ages of 18–25, and use one social media site on a weekly basis). Each research team also sought to maintain gender balance among focus groups by recruiting equal numbers of males and females. Two focus groups were conducted in each nation for a total of 12 groups. In each country focus groups were conducted by a trained researcher and adhered to all local human subjects requirements. A total of 106 subjects participated in the focus groups across the six nations.

Among the key findings gleaned from the focus groups were that social media had become a regular part of the subject's lives, and was used to maintain contact with friends and family members. Social media was identified as a good way to pass time, share photos, share links to music and videos, and to find out what other people were doing. While usage of sites varied from country to country, subjects reported the heaviest use among three sites: Facebook, Myspace, and Twitter. These three sites became the focus of the second stage of the study.

Questionnaire Preparation and Survey Administration

The qualitative data from the focus groups in each country were individually content analyzed and combined to provide a master set of findings. These data were used to prepare the questionnaire to be used in the main quantitative survey. Following the actual construction and pre-testing of the survey instrument, the data collection for the second stage of the project began in November 2009, and concluded in February 2010.

The research team set a goal to complete 250 surveys in each country. Sampling for the survey was done with a purposive sample, as researchers had to find subjects that met the three-fold criteria involving participation. Some nations recruited via college classrooms, while others recruited their samples in public venues outside of campus. Every effort was made to maintain gender balance in the study. A total of 1507 usable surveys were collected and coded for analysis. The most surveys were completed in Mexico (n = 270), with Uruguay, Colombia, and Chile each completing 250, followed by Argentina (n = 249) and the United States (n = 238).

The questionnaire first asked respondents to identify which social media sites they used on a regular basis, which sites they used most often, how much time they spent on the sites, how they accessed the sites, and how often they updated their status, or for Twitter users, how often they sent "tweets." Respondents were also asked how their time spent with social media impacted their use of television, radio, and newspapers.

The majority of the survey was concerned with the gratifications associated with using social media. Based on the focus groups, we asked the gratification items for three social media sites: Facebook, Myspace, and Twitter. The gratification items were adapted or modified from earlier studies discussed in the literature review. A total of 13 separate items were used, with the statement (e.g., "To provide entertainment, how helpful is . . .?") followed by a choice of responses (1 = very helpful; 4 = not at all helpful). Respondents answered separately for each of the social media sites they used. The survey concluded with a forced choice item (If you could only keep one social media site, which one would it be?), followed by a small set of demographic items (age, gender, educational level, and household income level).

Results

In terms of results, the findings are broken down into demographic characteristics, social media usage and access, an overview of the gratification items, and attitudinal items towards social media.

Demographic Characteristics

Regarding the total sample, 51.9% (n = 779) of the respondents were female, and 48.1% (n = 721) were males, achieving good gender balance. The mean age of the sample was 20.8 years, and in terms of education the majority of the sample was attending school (74.4%), while 14.5% had completed high school. Income levels were widely distributed with about half the sample split between lower income (less than $50,000 household income) and higher income (greater than $50,000). In many Latin American nations, younger people tend to live at home longer than they do in the United States, offering one explanation as to the split among household income levels.

Social Media Use and Access

In terms of the overall sample, Facebook was the most popular social media site, with 94.8% of the sample (n = 1419) having a profile on the site. Myspace ranked second with 25.6% (n = 385), followed by Twitter at 17.9% (n = 269). A total of

55 respondents (3.7%) reported using LinkedIn. The average amount of time spent per day on social media was 86 minutes as reported by the sample. Regarding access, 979 reported using a desktop computer, 929 respondents indicated they usually use a laptop, and 241 access their social media sites via a mobile phone.

Respondents were asked to identify how often they updated their "status" on their social networking profiles. A total of 112 (7.5%) reported several times a day; 139 (9.1%) indicated once a day; 173 (11.6%) reported updating their site 2–3 times a week; approximately 241 (16.2%) reported they only update their status once a week, while 118 (7.9%) reported they only update once a month. Interestingly, 707 (47.5%) participants indicated they rarely update their profile. Twitter users responded similarly in that only 10.8% of the users "tweeted" from several times to just once a day; 16.2% tweet 2–3 times a week; 3.9% tweet once a week; and 10.4% tweet just once a month, with approximately 58% indicating they "rarely" post a tweet.

Social Media Impact on Traditional Media

Respondents were asked if their use of social media resulted in "a lot less, a little less, no difference, a little more or a lot more" use of three traditional mediums: television, radio, and newspapers. Significant differences were observed across the sample for all three mediums. While the majority of the respondents reported "no difference," a larger number of the sample indicated they were spending less time with traditional media, and fewer reported spending more time with traditional media. For television, 636 respondents indicated they watched less TV (χ^2 = 68.15, $p < .001$); for radio, 352 reported less time spent with radio (χ^2 = 132.43, $p < .001$); for newspapers, 384 reported less time spent with newspapers (χ^2 = 180.53, $p < .001$).

Gratification Items

The means for the 13 gratification items for the total sample are reported in Table 11.1. As can be seen in Table 11.1, overall Facebook was rated the highest by the respondents on nine of the items. Sharing photos ($\overline{\chi}$ = 1.33) reconnecting with old friends ($\overline{\chi}$ = 1.39), and keeping in touch with others ($\overline{\chi}$ = 1.61) were the three highest ranked items for Facebook. Myspace users rated the site the highest on three items: to share music ($\overline{\chi}$ = 2.46), to give you control over privacy ($\overline{\chi}$ = 2.46) and to provide a feeling of social acceptance ($\overline{\chi}$ = 2.94). Twitter was the highest ranking on only one item, to access news and information ($\overline{\chi}$ = 2.33).

In breaking down the data a bit further to focus on the entertainment aspects of social media, significant differences were noted across countries in regards to using Facebook to share videos (χ^2 = 41.04, $p < .001$), to share music (χ^2 = 79.70, $p < .001$), and to provide entertainment (χ^2 = 65.15, $p < .001$). Myspace respondents across nations also differed significantly in terms of sharing videos (χ^2= 37.52,

TABLE 11.1 Mean scores for gratification items ($n = 1507$)

Item	Facebook users	Myspace users	Twitter users
To keep in touch with family/friends	1.61	2.50	2.96
To help pass time	1.66	2.35	2.67
To share photos	1.33	2.15	3.13
To share videos	1.95	2.51	3.16
To share music	2.95	2.16	3.29
To chat with others	2.04	2.52	2.86
To check messages received	1.69	2.13	2.45
Control over privacy settings	2.82	2.46	2.87
To provide entertainment	1.79	2.23	2.61
To reconnect with old friends	1.39	2.27	2.98
Provide feeling of social acceptance	2.97	2.94	3.28
Access news/information	2.57	2.74	2.33
Use different applications	2.15	2.63	3.02

Notes: Coding of variables: 1 = "very helpful"; 2 = "somewhat helpful"; 3 = "a little helpful"; 4 = "not at all helpful"

$p < .001$) and providing entertainment ($\chi^2 = 28.06$, $p < .001$). Regarding social media providing access to news and information, significant differences were also observed across countries for all three social media sites. Facebook users rated the site highly for news and information ($\chi^2 = 97.16$, $p < .001$), as did Twitter users ($\chi^2 = 68.18$, $p < .001$). Myspace users tended to rate the site less helpful in regards to news and information ($\chi^2 = 39.31$, $p < .001$).

Attitudes Toward Social Media

Three attitudinal questions followed the gratification items on the questionnaire. These items were "There is too much advertising on social media websites," "Social media has become a part of my daily routine," and "I feel out of touch if I don't/can't log in." Respondents were asked to indicate if they "strongly agree" (coded as 1) "agree," "disagree," or "strongly disagree" (coded as 4) with these statements. The mean scores of these three items for the users are listed in Table 11.2.

TABLE 11.2 Attitudes toward social media (n = 1507)

Item	Facebook users	Myspace users	Twitter users
There is too much advertising	1.94	1.84	2.61
Social media is part of daily life	1.93	2.61	2.61
Feel out of touch if can't log in	2.65	3.07	3.03

Notes: Coding of variables: 1 = "strongly agree"; 2 = "agree"; 3 = "disagree"; 4 = "strongly disagree"

As seen in Table 11.2, Myspace users feel there is more advertising on the website than either Facebook or Twitter users. In terms of the statement about social media becoming part of their daily life, Facebook outdistanced Myspace and Twitter, which were tied. Facebook users were also more likely to feel out of touch if they were not able to log in, followed by Twitter users and then Myspace users.

The final item prior to the demographic questions asked respondents to identify which social media site they would keep if they could use only one social media site. In this forced-choice item, Facebook (n = 1,251) was the overwhelming choice among respondents, followed by Myspace (n = 69) and Twitter (n = 41).

Discussion

This study represents one of the largest single research efforts to understand how young adult Latinos are using social media websites, and the gratifications obtained from their use. While a few of the U.S.-based studies in the literature have had Latinos as part of their sample (e.g., Hargittai, 2007; Raacke & Bond-Raacke, 2008), this study represents the largest investigation of this demographic group, and adds a rich dimension by its simultaneous investigation across five other countries in Latin America.

In terms of the key findings, young Latinos use Facebook more than other social networking sites, with Myspace a very distant second option. Twitter users are fewer in number, but no doubt this group will grow as Twitter is the newest site to debut among the three and is limited to its unique presentation of no more than 140 characters per tweet.

Facebook also satisfies most of their gratifications as well, especially in the ease with which users can share photos and other content, chat, and reconnect with friends. Myspace is the best in its ability to share music, which is critical as the social networking site emphasizes music and entertainment for its users. Myspace also scored highly on providing a feeling of social acceptance, a finding also seen in other studies involving examinations of social capital (Ellison, Steinfield, & Lampe, 2007). Twitter emerged as the leader in one important variable, that of accessing news and information, a trait ideally suited to the site especially for news organizations and other sites who want to keep followers updated with breaking news and other information.

Social media users are also concerned about the sites containing too much advertising, but that has not stopped users from feeling that social media is a part of their lives. Facebook users feel the strongest connection and are most likely to feel out of touch if they cannot log in or obtain access. Facebook was the clear leader in terms of the one social media site the user would keep, if given only one option.

In terms of the industry-based implications from the data, we first consider what this study means for advertisers and marketers. In an evolving and rapidly changing media environment, advertisers have been shifting more and more resources from legacy media to new media platforms. If companies are not including social media as a part of their marketing strategy, they are potentially missing a huge growing segment of the market.

The Hispanic audience is considered under-measured in a number of ways. This study offers a baseline perspective on how young Hispanics/Latinos use social media. A survey of senior marketing and advertising executives found that half of respondents do not target Hispanics in their marketing efforts. However, most respondents agreed that Hispanics/Latinos will impact product and service offerings in the U.S. over the next five years (Loechner, 2010; O'Leary, 2009). Social media must be part of the marketing mix, especially for targeting young adult Spanish-speaking consumers.

From an economic standpoint, it is hard to imagine that social media sites will not benefit from significant growth in advertising revenues over the next decade. In this sample, the average amount of time spent with social media on a daily basis was just below 90 minutes. While we can anticipate that some of this time was used in a multi-tasking environment, it demonstrates at the least that Hispanic/ Latino respondents in this sample are allocating a great deal of their time to social media—time that previously may have been used for other media activities. We also can anticipate that social media access will be facilitated as more and more of the world's population replaces their mobile phones with smart phones, enabling easier access through applications devoted to social media.

From an audience research perspective, Baker (2009) points out a number of research companies are starting to analyze networks of "friends" and "followers" on social media sites. As these research efforts come to fruition, marketers and advertisers will identify more efficient and targeted ways to reach their audiences through social media sites than through other forms of advertising. The relationship among friends and peers has long been established in the mass communication literature as influential in forming opinions, referrals, and recommendations. Social media cannot help but benefit in the potential explosion of marketing resources this new medium offers for targeting the Hispanic/Latino demographic and the general market.

From the standpoint of businesses and media companies, this study offers some additional considerations for engaging social media. Firms will need to recognize that their social media presence needs to consist of more than just creating "fan" pages. While these pages can be part of a strategy, much more must be considered. Social media sites must be updated regularly with relevant information, and can become a great tool to capture opinions and attitudes towards specific programs, services, and products. Social media can be leveraged as a working research tool to constantly receive feedback from potential audiences.

Firms also need to actively recruit followers for all of their social media sites, especially with services like Twitter. While a lot of Twitter users may not be sending "tweets" as this study illustrates, many more are using the medium to follow individuals and companies. Followers can receive the latest information on content, promotions, advertising incentives (such as sending coupons directly to customers at the point of sale), and other tools to engage audiences in this highly fragmented competitive environment. Once again, if reaching Latinos is part of the strategy, whether as Spanish-speaking or bilingual, a coherent and multifaceted strategy is warranted.

This sample also illustrates the higher usage and gratifications associated with sharing music and video content. Companies involved in content creation and distribution should be aware of this key aspect of the data. While many companies are debating the merits of offering content for free versus a paid basis, it is clear that social media sites can be a driver of different types of media content to share with friends. This makes social media a critical platform moving forward for sharing content, not necessarily as complete programs, but through trailers and snippets to attract users and their friends. Sharing links on Facebook accounts for 33% of all services offered by Gigya, a leading social optimization platform that offers social sharing widgets for over 5000 content providers (Schonfeld, 2010). The study also points out that social media is yet another way to disseminate news and information, and that Facebook and Twitter are perceived as more useful in this area than Myspace.

This study was limited in terms of its reliance on self-report data, and the typical issues encountered in any survey research project. The sample was not randomly generated, but the fact that the project involves data collected from six different countries may mitigate some of these concerns. This examination as to how young Latino adults are using social media can perhaps provide a baseline of research for other scholars and practitioners seeking to gain a better understanding of the global Latino audience.

Acknowledgments

This chapter is part of a larger study involving an international research team of scholars. My thanks to German Arango (Columbia), Maria Elena Gutierrez (Mexico), Eileen Hudson (Uruguay), Laura Vaillard (Argentina), and Aldo van Weezel (Chile) for their help in collecting data in their respective country.

References

Baker, S. (2009, June 1). What's a friend worth? *BusinessWeek*, 32–36.

BIGresearch. (13, August 2009). BIGresearch profiles social media users. Retrieved from http://www.rbr.com/media-news/research/16395.html.

Coyle, C. L., & Vaughn, H. (2008). Social networking: Communication revolution or evolution? *Bell Labs Technical Journal, 13*(2), 13–17.

Ellison, N. B., Steinfield, C., & Lampe, C. (2007). The benefits of Facebook "friends": Social capital and college students' use of online social network sites. *Journal of Computer-Mediated Communication, 12*(4), 1143–1168.

Facebook (n.d.) *Statistics.* Retrieved February 7, 2010 from http://www.facebook.com/press/info.php?statistics.

Hargittai, E. (2007). Whose space? Differences among users and non-users of social network sites. *Journal of Computer-Mediated Communication, 13*(1), article 14. Retrieved October 18, 2009 from: http://jcmc.indiana.edu/vol13/issue1/hargittai.html.

Lampe, C., Ellison, N. B., & Steinfield, C., (2006). A Face(book) in the crowd: Social searching vs. social browsing. In *Proceedings of the 2006 20th Anniversary Conference on Computer Supported Cooperative Work* (pp. 167–170). New York: ACM Press.

Li, C., & Bernoff, J. (2008). *Groundswell: Winning in a world transformed by social technologies.* Boston: Harvard Business Press.

Loechner, J. (2010). Half of U.S. advertisers missing trillion dollar Hispanic market. Retrieved March 23, 2010 from http://www.mediapost.com/publications/?fa=Articles. showArticle&art_aid=124694.

O'Leary, N. (2009, November 2). The Hispanic market is set to soar. *Adweek.* Retrieved from http://www.adweek.com/aw/content_display/news/agency/e3i26911e62ce1ee0 f7f41748d31d4e42a0?pn=1.

Pempek, T. A., Yermolayeva, Y. A., & Calvert, S. L. (2009). College students' social networking experiences on Facebook. *Journal of Applied Developmental Psychology, 30*(3), 227–238.

Raacke, J., & Bonds-Raacke, J. (2008). MySpace and Facebook: Applying the uses and gratifications theory to exploring friend-networking sites. *CyberPsychology & Behavior, 11*(2), 169–174.

Rosengren, K. E. (1974). Uses and gratifications: A paradigm outlined. In J. G. Blumler, & E. Katz (Eds.), *The uses of mass communications: Current perspectives on gratifications research* (pp. 269–286). Beverly Hills, CA: Sage.

Schonfeld, E. (2010, February 16). Facebook drives 44 percent of social sharing on the web. Retrieved from http://techcrunch.com/2010/02/16/facebook-44-percent-social-sharing/.

Sheldon, P. (2008). Student favorite: Facebook and motives for its use. *Southwestern Mass Communication Journal, 23*(2), 39–53.

Silverthorne, S. (2009, September 14). Understanding users of social networks. *Harvard Business Week.* Retrieved from http://hbswk.hbs.edu/item/6156.htm.

Steel, E. (2009, October 15). MySpace tries to recover its cool. *The Wall Street Journal.* Retrieved from: http://online.wsj.com/article/SB10001424052748703790404544473 523398458990.html.

Steinfield, C., Ellison, N. B., & Lampe, C. (2008). Social capital, self-esteem, and use of online social network sites: A longitudinal analysis. *Journal of Applied Developmental Psychology, 29*(6), 434–445.

Subrahmanyam, K., Reich, S. M., Waechter, N., & Espinoza, G. (2008). Online and offline social networks: Use of social networking sites by emerging adults. *Journal of Applied Developmental Psychology, 29*(6), 420–433.

Swartz, J. (2009, September 22). Real-time web keeps social networkers connected. *USA Today.* Retrieved September 28, 2009, from http://www.usatoday.com/tech/news/ 2009-09-22-social-networking-real-time-web_N.htm.

Tweeting all the way to the bank. (2009, July 25). *The Economist,* 61–62.

Valenzuela, S., Park, N., & Kee, K. F. (2009). Is there social capital in a social network?: Facebook use and college students' life satisfaction, trust, and participation. *Journal of Computer-Mediated Communication, 14,* 875–901.

Worldwide Spanish-speaking population statistics (n.d.). Retrieved March 31, 2010, from: http://www.spanishseo.org/resources/worldwide-spanish-speaking-population.

12

BRIDGING THE GREAT DIVIDE

African American and Asian American Use of Social Media

Maria Williams-Hawkins

The Digital Divide

The digital divide is the division of the world between those who have access to new information and communications technology (ICT) and those who do not. This issue has global impact because it affects economic growth for all countries. This issue is not new. Opinion leaders and researchers have talked about the possibility that access to information leads to greater success for decades. In 1999, the United Nations Development Programme commented that the network society was creating parallel community systems: one for those with income, education and literacy connections; the other for those without connections, blocked by high barriers of time, cost and uncertainty and dependent upon outdated information. However, not all futurists agreed. Some believed poor and developing countries would skip the technology of the day and move directly to the latest technology. It is suggested that information and communications technology has a leapfrogging characteristic that will enable the poor to catch up. Indeed, we are currently in a stage when many developing countries have skipped the traditional development phases and advanced to the latest technology. Additionally, the poor or digitally underserved have followed suit.

Associated with the issue of access to information is access to the technology that makes this possible. While technological access may have been a big issue at the end of the last century, that is no longer the case. In the late 20th Century, gaining access to a home computer was an expense that people in developing countries had to plan for; in the United States and many others, one could purchase a computer for less than $400.

While the divide still exists, it is much less of a problem for Asian Americans, African Americans and Latinos. It's more of a problem for the poor, those living in rural settings and immigrants. Additionally, the divide has taken on a new image. The new digital divide will be discussed at the end of the chapter.

African American Use of Technology

Analysis of African American use of technology has been based on a comparison of the general American population versus the African American community. This normally placed African Americans in the *have nots* category. To no one's surprise, lower-income African Americans' use of Internet-based activity correlates them with *have nots* while African Americans in the $50,000 or higher income groups mirror the rest of the general population (Graham & Smith, 2010).

Since the proliferation of handheld devices such as cell phones, iPads, iPods and smaller tablets, researchers have focused on rates of technology ownership. Rice and Katz (2003) focused on mobile phone access and the *haves* and *have-nots*. In this study African Americans were clearly in the *have not* category. By 2006, African Americans were clearly moving out of the *have not* category along with the Hispanic community (Castells, et al., 2006). Currently, research shows that due to the adoption of mobile technology, people of color are leading in the adoption rates of mobile technology (Barber, 2011; Pew Project for Excellence in Journalism, 2011) and African Americans talk more on mobile devices than any other ethnic group (Nielsen, 2010).

After 2000, research began to focus less on *who* had technology and more on *how* they use that technology (Chakroborty & Bosman, 2005; DiMaggio, et al., 2001; Hargittai, 2002; Mossberger, et al., 2006, Ono & Zavodny, 2008; Servon & Nelson, 2001; Warschauer, 2003). This research has focused on how access to mobile technology has helped people gather information, complete daily tasks, communicate and entertain themselves.

Gathering information (Cothey, 2002; Hargittai, 2006; Rieh, 2004) is the activity normally exhibited by nonusers. The amount of information sought is normally related to the users' facility with search engine functions (Hargittai, 2004). Completing daily tasks is usually related to information gathering (Page & Uncles, 2004). Madden (2003) focused on entertainment. Many researchers have examined the third factor, communication (Brunsting & Postmes, 2002; Diani, 2000; Rheingold, 1993; Warschauer, 2003). Communication online is a factor related to relationship development. Using the Internet to form "virtual cliques" has often led to face-to-face interactions (Adams & Roscgino, 2005; Brunsting & Postmes, 2002; Castells, 2001; Diani, 2000; Garafalo, et al., 2007; Morahan-Martin & Schumacher, 2003).

Computer Ownership

By 2003, most American households owned computers. Indeed, 62% of those households owned two or three computers. About 88% of those households had Internet service. In similar time periods, while 67% of the Caucasian households had computers in the home, only 45% of the African American households had the same. In 2007, the African American population indicated that 45.3% had computers for the home compared to 64% of Caucasian families.

Earlier research focused on technology ownership including home computer, Internet access, PDAs or other handheld devices. Researchers used income and education as the primary predictors of whether families were likely to have technology (Attewell & Battle, 1999; Madigan & Goodfellow, 2005). Race was a subordinate factor in the likelihood that technology would be available to a family (Chakroborty & Bosman, 2005; Gates, 2000; Lenhart, et al., 2003; Mossberger, et al., 2006; Warschauer, 2003). While African American ownership of desktop computers has increased significantly, only 51% of African Americans owned desktops compared to 65% of Caucasians. African Americans also own fewer laptops. According to Smith (2010), in 2009, only 34% of African Americans owned laptops. By 2010, the figure had increased to 51% ownership of laptops.

Cell Phone and Mobile Technologies

An analysis of the cell phone bills of 60,000 U.S. mobile subscribers indicates that African Americans out-talk and out-text all cell phone subscribers (Nielsen, 2010). The lower cost of mobile technology has increased the use of cell phones to accomplish many of the same tasks achieved by using desktop and laptop computers. African Americans and other minority groups use their cell phones to access social sites that others might use their desktop or laptop computers to access. Mobile technologies have enabled African Americans to do more than just be equal in technology use with Caucasians. African Americans are more likely to own cell phones than Caucasians (Smith, 2010).

African Americans are more likely to use a wider range of cell phone options than Caucasians. More than 70% of African American cell phone users text one another compared to only 50% of Caucasian users. Nielsen (2010) found that African Americans send and receive 780 SMS (short message service) messages every month. This figure is slightly higher than Hispanic/Latino users at 767 SMS messages each month and Caucasians with 566 SMS messages each month. African American cell phone users more frequently visit social networking sites, use the Internet, record and watch videos, donate money through text messages, use email, play games, listen to music, instant message and search for new music.

Use of Game Consoles

A slightly higher percentage of African Americans and other minority groups than Caucasians buy game consoles. While only 40% of Caucasians buy game consoles, about half of the minority groups buy gaming consoles. This relates to social networking in that across racial/ethnic groups around one in three game console users use their consoles to go online.

African Americans have the technology and the determination to stay abreast of the most recent technological developments. The next section examines how they use that technology.

The Social Media Fix: African American Use of Social Media

> Black Americans have an oral tradition which is a historical and social phenomenon. The oral tradition of the African societies and the necessity for oral traditions as a result of the slave system have helped the Black culture survive.
>
> *(Staggers, 1984)*

African American use of social media is believed to be the latest offshoot of the oral tradition. In advertising terms, we have returned to (if we ever left) word-of-mouth (WOM) communication. Popular today in media promotion, WOM tells us that if we hear the information from people we trust, we can believe what we heard. The Pew Research Center and Nielsen Social Media Reports have provided statistics on Internet and broadband adoption rates throughout this century. What neither has fully provided is what draws African Americans and other ethnic groups to social media. We will answer that question in various ways in this section when we hear from African Americans who let us know why they use social media and point out how and why they see it as relevant.

Smith (2010) noted the Internet population over the past ten years has come to mirror the racial composition of the U.S. population. In the first decade of the 21st Century, African American and Latino use of the Internet almost doubled from 11% to 21%. In this same period, African Americans made significant improvements in home broadband adoption rates. All of this was driven by increased levels of ownership of desktop and laptop computers, but African Americans still fell short compared to Caucasians. This disparity stopped some researchers from looking into how people of color were actually moving forward to embrace new technology. Those researchers were still stuck at the *have not* perception of people of color. Latha Sarathy, Vice President for insights and analytics at Interactive One, revealed that "compared to other ethnic groups, this [African American] audience segment does not have the same volume of consumer research" (WARC, March 26, 2012).

Like people from developing countries, African Americans, Latinos and Asians might have been left out when trying to follow traditional paths of technology adoption. Rather than try to catch up with the Caucasian American population, they followed the technological developments to gain access to the latest communication options. Mobile technology has led African Americans and Latinos to the next level of communication access.

African American adults gravitated to cell phones and utilize more of the phones' capabilities than their Caucasian counterparts. According to a Pew survey (Zickuhr & Smith, 2011) of 2277 cell phone users, within the cell phone population, 39% of the Black, non-Hispanic Americans and 35% of Hispanic Americans access social networking sites. Younger African Americans grew up texting and instant messaging. Social media seems like a direct derivative. New York-based social media strategist, Michael Street suggests that this generation communicates by sharing photos and information as closely as possible to real-time transactions (Eversley, 2012c). Lenhart et al. (2010) note that African American adults are the most active users of the mobile web, and their use is growing at a faster pace than that of Hispanic adults. About 70% of all African Americans use text messaging. Various studies indicate African Americans frequently visit social networking sites, use the Internet on their cell phones, record and watch videos, make charitable donations via text messages, use emails, play games, listen to music, use instant messaging and post multimedia content online (Smith, 2010).

According to the Pew Research (Madden & Zickuhr, 2011), African Americans use social media at higher rates than Caucasian Americans. Seven in ten African Americans use social networking sites on a daily basis. One quarter of the online African Americans use Twitter daily (Madden & Zickuhr, 2011; Townsend, 2011). Some researchers suggest that Twitter is the social technology of choice of African Americans. The 2008 presidential campaign provided numerous opportunities for minorities in general and African Americans in particular to use social media to let their opinions be known and to be able to hear from candidates and their supporters. African Americans and other minority groups felt that social media made governmental outreach more accessible and made them feel more informed than did Caucasian voters (Smith, 2010).

The next section presents specific ways that African Americans gather information, complete daily tasks, communicate and seek entertainment using social media. In this section I examine African American use of various websites, blogs, Twitter, Facebook, YouTube and other communication links that meet a specific racial/cultural need. Additionally, I attempt to reveal some of the reasons certain sites meet cultural needs.

Communication for Another Generation

"Most of history's great charismatic leaders who started movements that enacted change were young people, many of them in their early 20s and 30s". McNeal (2011) notes that if another generation of leaders is to be groomed, they will have to be reached by using methods different from those used in the past. Older leaders are encouraged to use the technology and style of the younger generation. Whereas in the past, going to churches to reach people might spread the message quickly, the NAACP Chairman of the Board, Roslyn M. Brock, points out that, "We can't just mail out fliers or rely on word of mouth. People are communicating with their hands online" (McNeal, 2011).

Not all African American social media use is focused on African American-to-African American communication. The Centers for Disease Control (CDC) and other health-based organizations reach out to African Americans to provide information on diabetes, hypertension and HIV. One system established to talk to African Americans about HIV is "iknow". According to the CDC, "iknow" is a social media effort designed to encourage 18–24-year-old African Americans to talk about HIV online and off (Centers for Disease Control, 2010). In order to establish a dialog on this topic, the CDC used performers like Jamie Foxx, Ludacris and Marvelyn Brown to develop video and audio public service announcements for this audience. The CDC attempted to reach African Americans using Facebook, Twitter, a new website and text messages.

Indeed, African Americans are communicating online. Many younger people read news online and utilize blogs as sources of news with the same credibility as they afford traditional news services (pers. comm. with Ball State NABJ members, January 2012). According to boyd and Ellison (2008, p. 211):

> Social network sites are web-based services that allow individuals to (1) construct a public or semi-public profile within a bounded system, (2) articulate a list of other users with whom they share a connection, and (3) view and traverse their list of connections and those made by others within the system.

This definition carries a slightly different set of goals and expectations. Use of the word "networking" normally implies an opportunity to initiate relationships. While boyd and Ellison (2008) do not believe that most of the social network sites originated with the goal of bringing people together to form relationships, one might not feel as confident of that position when reading how and why African Americans use SNS. One might accept that some users just want to be heard, others can certainly see how some sites are used to lead to face-to-face encounters for either business or pleasure. In the next section, we examine digital options for African American expression. Users express their thoughts on how effective those options are and what outcomes they lead to.

> It's a good way to express your culture. When you go to my page, there are black R&B songs [....] In college, the population of black people is very low. It's a good way to stick together, connect with people who are more like you.
> *(Dave, 18, African American, cited in Correa & Sun, 2011)*

Blogs

In 2004, Technorati, Inc. reported almost 4.2 million weblogs worldwide (Rosenbloom, 2004). Today there are millions of blogs. Since 2006, however, blogging has fallen in popularity among teens and young adults but has maintained increased attention among older adults (Lenhart, et al., 2010). According to Pew (Madden & Zickuhr, 2011), since 2005, roughly 1 in 10 online adults has maintained a personal online journal or blog. Approximately 12% of the African American population uses blogs (Vernon, 2010). It is safe to assume that at least one million blogs are by or about African Americans.

Among the earliest developed websites was Black Planet, created in 1999. In its first iteration the site allowed combinations of personal, professional and dating profiles. Black Planet is the most popular networking platforms among the Black online community (Georgieva, 2011). Black Planet offers members the opportunity to create and participate in online communities. African Americans are reading and responding to comments on: BlackBloggersConnect.com, Seeing Growth.com, BlackFather.org, BlackBloggersNetwork.com and many more (Jackson, 2011).

Twitter

Approximately 25% of Twitter users are African American. Twitter has become another tool for advocacy. A blog about Twitter and Obama entitled "Obama winning on social media: Could Twitter 'blackness' be the reason?" (Reid, 2011), notes that Obama has a 69% approval rating among people who use Twitter and posits that Twitter is disproportionately African American. The same article notes 14% of African Americans use Twitter at double the percentage of Caucasian American Twitter users and exceeding the 9% Hispanic American tweeting community.

Twitter users are more interested in connecting with public figures such as politicians, celebrities and athletes. According to the Pew Research (Madden & Zickuhr, 2011), African Americans and Hispanics (11%) are more interested in hearing from these kinds of speakers than Caucasian tweeters (4%) (Smith, 2010).

Adam Sharp, manager of Twitter's government and politics bureau, pointed out that Twitter has affected the population in three ways (see Showell, 2011). First, Twitter gives voters direct access to real-time information. Second, candidates can directly communicate with voters, thereby creating relationships. Third, because of Twitter, candidates and voters don't have to have money to access a platform to communicate.

African American performers have had to learn the power of Twitter in some new ways. While they learned quickly that Twitter could lead people to watch their performances or buy the products they were selling, they have not always understood the ramifications for encouraging others to follow them. In February 2012, Oprah Winfrey encouraged her 9 million followers on Twitter to tune into her cable channel OWN on premiere nights (Stelter, 2012). That simple request broke one of Nielsen's ratings rules regarding coerced viewing efforts. Winfrey took the post down the next day after talking with Nielsen. Her ratings were marked with an asterisk for the time of day that her message was posted. The asterisk suggests "possible biasing effect." Because Twitter is still relatively new, there are concerns about its power that must be taken into consideration.

Besides Nielsen's concern about how Oprah used its service, African Americans have their own concerns about how the technology is and is not used on their behalf. News departments around the country have changed from their original retrenchment of having reporters use blogs, email and Twitter to making it mandatory as a marketing technique for each reporter and anchor. Reporters now post updates on stories they have covered or are continuing to cover. WSLS-TV reporter Scott Leamon commented, "In order to get more people to watch your story, tweeting lets them know you're out at the scene. If you're not using Twitter or Facebook, your game is antiquated" (Artwick, 2010). Recognizing that Twitter has such import with viewers, African American viewers question why many stories about them are not included in those tweeted or added to Facebook. The Trayvon Martin case garnered attention on all forms of communication. African Americans and others used Facebook, Twitter, blogs and the website Change.org to air their frustrations. MSNBC host Melissa Harris-Perry tweeted opinions about this case (Eversley, 2012b). Almost immediately after the February 26 shooting of Martin, the conversation began simmering on Twitter. But it was nearly three weeks later, on March 17, 2012, after the release of 911 tapes, before the story exploded on Twitter, blogs and in the mainstream media to become the first story of the year to get more coverage than the race for president.

Rashad Robinson, executive director of ColorofChange.org, believes social media provides an outlet for those who feel ignored. The Martin case brought in the thoughts of more "previously ignored people" than any other topic to hit their website (Eversley, 2012a). Michael Baisden, host of a syndicated radio talk show, likes social media because he believes it is a communication forum that is "just me and them and so they're getting their information" (Eversley, 2012c). Baisden credits social media with publicizing other cases that have direct political implications for African Americans including the case against Troy Davis, a Georgia man who was ultimately executed for a murder that many people believed him innocent of, and for the Jenna Six case against six Black teens in Jenna, Louisiana. Twitter and Facebook encouraged people across ethnic groups to wear hoodies and carry Skittles, from the very proper Marian Wright Edelman who founded the Children's Defense Fund, to former Michigan governor Jennifer Granholm, Current TV's host of *The War Room with Jennifer Granholm* (Eversley, 2012c).

Twitter can be profound in terms of connecting with others and giving African Americans the feeling of being part of a family. Tyrell Coley found out just how many people were drawn to what he had to say when he created "(hash)femalesneedto." Within hours his site became the number one topic on Twitter. Responses indicated that most responding were African American women talking about subtopics such as "learning that sex is not love." Coley had 3756 followers in 2011 and continues to initiate comments that cause others to follow him (Washington, 2011).

Anjuan Simmons started using social media for professional reasons and found himself using Twitter to find "a Black face to connect with" (Washington, 2011). Like Simmons, a number of African Americans just want to know that they are not alone. The short messages that they receive confirm their place in the world.

Myspace/Facebook

Myspace was once the bastion of African American social media use. When the total Myspace use was 18% of all social media users, 16% of its users were African American (Finn, 2011; Pew Internet & American Life Project, 2011). Perhaps the fact that it was available first caused the great attachment. Just as television programmers concluded that there is no network loyalty, social media researchers are finding out that in most cases, there is no social network loyalty either. After the success of Myspace, Baltimore-based Urban Communications decided that there should be an African American site devoted to issues of interest to the African American collegiate experience. Prior to the birth of this site, it was a portal on the Historically Black Colleges and Universities network. Ourspace had intended to announce its availability to majority students as well. However, it never reached the volume of users it had expected. After Facebook hit its stride, 92% of all social networking users chose to communicate using it (Madden & Zickuhr, 2011). For this author, across race, students began asking to do their group work assignments using Facebook rather than Blackboard or email because they kept their Facebook accounts open all the time. Even African Americans chose to leave Myspace for Facebook.

One might see the move from Myspace to Facebook as digital gentrification or white flight. In its prime, in 2006–2007, Myspace was the teen online place to be. African American teens were no different. Student members of a medium-sized Midwestern university's chapter of the National Association of Black Journalists talked about their passion for Myspace. This was their first opportunity to communicate with people everywhere about everything. Then, to quote them, "It got old." One student noted that, "I grew past that line of conversation. It was so childish" (pers. comm., March 28, 2012). According to boyd (boyd & Ellison, 2008), while African Americans were still in love with Myspace, Caucasians began to escape due to its "ghetto environment." Caucasians flocked to Facebook. African Americans followed. Since there was no immediate exodus by Caucasians, this may cause researchers to examine whether the exit was racially motivated or culturally motivated. Perhaps the class of friends in Myspace was lower than that of those who joined Facebook.

Although Facebook does not require demographic information when users register, it has attempted to identify ethnic groups among users. When Facebook launched in 2004, students from elite universities were the primary users. Diversity was not a concern. By the end of 2005, only about 7% of Facebook friends were African American (Swift, 2009). Using what they call Friendship Diversity, they made an educated guess on members' ethnicity based on the members' last names (Benton, 2009). In 2009, Facebook estimated 11% of its users were African American. At that time, researchers believed that the percentage of African Americans and other minority groups using Facebook reflected their presence in the population base. According to Vernon (2010), 53% of online African Americans use Facebook at least once weekly.

Predominantly African American Facebook sites also exist. Sites such as the Largest African American Facebook Group and Black Women are Beautiful are among the largest all African American sites (Swift, 2009). Research on African Americans on Facebook is a bit convoluted. Some articles combine blogs that started in Facebook with true Facebook communities. Black Planet statistics appear in some Facebook research as does Radio One's Facebook group (http://www.socialnetworkingwatch.com/2008/08/radio-one-creat.html).

YouTube

In 2010, 7% of the African American population visited YouTube weekly (Vernon, 2010). According to the Pew Internet & American Life Project, minority users exceed all others in YouTube use. The report indicates that African Americans and Hispanics were the most active video consumers on line.

A Google search of African Americans' use of You Tube suggests that African American women are the primary users of and posters to the website. Of the first 50 websites listed, at least 15 were directly focused on hair care or hair styling. Additionally, others were focused on makeup and beauty issues including African American rhinoplasty. Besides the need for physical enhancements, African American postings also presented a number of Black History posts as well as news issues followed by African American singer sites and other music sites. One area that seemed to have male domination was the use of Def Poetry Jams. African American males had a clear desire to be heard for their creative efforts.

LinkedIn

Although LinkedIn remains a popular site, its greatest support comes from Caucasian males. According to the Pew Internet Study, LinkedIn has the oldest average age of users, 40 years old, and has twice as many male as female users. While some reports suggest that 10% of LinkedIn's members are African American, the Pew Study suggests that only 2% of its members are African American (Finn, 2011).

Beyond the Basics

While giving a keynote address at MediaPost's Social Media Insider Summit in Key Largo, Michael Wiley, chief social media officer at Publicis, told attendees that it was time to move on from the ordinary social media (Facebook, Twitter, LinkedIn and YouTube) to what lies ahead (Mandese, January 24, 2012). Wiley cautioned attendees to remember that although Facebook and the others have attracted a large following in a short amount of time, new vehicles for communi-cation are coming up quickly that may have a greater impact. Some of the communication links mentioned already resonate with the African American community: Klout, Social CRM, Gamification, Cause-Marketing Re-Imagined and ascending Content Platforms such as Pinterest, Tumblr and Instagram. The effect of Klout, Tumblr, Pinterest and Instagram are discussed below.

Klout

Although Klout has not yet proven itself to be prominent in the list of African American social media sites, it is gaining support among young professional African Americans. Klout, a privately held company based in San Francisco, California, purports to measure the influence its members have across the social web by analyzing social network user data and identifying influential individuals (see http://klout.theresumator.com/apply/dzMHRc). Klout analyzes the impact of opinions, links, and recommendations of others who have been identified as influential. Klout uses innovative tools to allow companies to interact with those seeking recognition or jobs. Brands such as Disney, Audi, Nike and Fox are using this tool. A Google search of Klout and African Americans suggested that a number of potential employees, book club members, shoppers and employers are using Klout to find those with like interests. The search even revealed a group of people who want to avoid using Klout to find employees.

Tumblr

Tumblr is a blogging platform that allows users to post texts, images, videos, links, quotes and audio to their tumblelog. There is a definite African American presence on Tumblr. A Google search of African American users of Tumblr suggests the majority of the readers of Tumblr are concerned about issues related to being African American, political perspectives, fashion, and those who are interested in the Black inclusion of athletes in sports.

Pinterest

Pinterest allows users to pin photos or images of almost anything on a board. Some people use Pinterest to plan weddings and redecorate their homes. It is even used for such mundane activities as organizing recipes and keeping a stamp collection (Hu, 2012). Pinterest, like Facebook, allows you to see what other people are pinning to various sites. Skewing 60% female, Pinterest is growing fastest in topics related to women's lifestyle, home décor, fashions and cooking magazines (Sass, 2012). As Dvorak (2012) notes, Pinterest comes along at a perfect time, "just as the novelty of Facebook is fading."

African Americans are gravitating to Pinterest. Dvorak, who is not African American, calls it digital crack for women (Dvorak, 2012). African American blogger for the Daily Dot, Lauren Rae Orsini blogged that there were statistics on the age and gender of Pinterest enthusiasts but no statistics on race. She wanted to try to get something concrete about African American use of Pinterest. Toward that goal, Orsini contacted an African American, Harlem-based, social media marketing strategist, Mike Street, to see if he could clarify what the actual level of support was for Pinterest among African Americans. Street's examination of African Americans identifiable on Zoomsphere found only a few African Americans.

African Americans have a presence on Pinterest. Topics that suggest an African American presence include natural haircare, black fashion designers and models, Black historical figures and recipes (Orsini, 2012).

Instagram

Instagram is a photo-sharing social networking site launched in October 2010. Users can take pictures, use digital filters and share their pictures on multiple social networking sites (Frommer, 2010). In May of 2012, Facebook announced it was acquiring the company for $1 billion (Shaw, 2012; Stern, 2012).

African Americans gravitated towards Instagram. An examination of African Americans and Instagram suggests that famous people from the President of the United States to Rihanna to Chris Brown and the Old Spice African American spokesperson use Instagram. Topics covered on Instagram range from numerous photo essays on African American women, vanity pictorial essays to celebrity sightings. Only a few entries had negative things to say about Instagram. The writer of Blackperceptions.com was concerned that Instagram was not set to be as easy for mobile phone users as for desktop users (Blackperceptions.com, 2012).

The Value of Social Media for African Americans

African Americans and Hispanics like social media because both groups believe social media allows them to get information out. I began earlier in the chapter with a quote on developing leaders in the African American community and noted that even traditional organizations devoted to reconciling wrongs recognize that social media can lead to change. African Americans and others recognize that use of social networks is conducive to facilitating political participation (Scheufele & Nisbet, 2003; Shah, McLeod & Yoon, 2001; Scheufele & Shah, 2000).

Recent voting data suggests that African American youth are the racial/ethnic group most likely to vote in elections (Tisch, 2008), and Vernon (2010) suggests that African American and Hispanic teens spend 13 hours a week on various types of media.

In an analysis of African American youths' interest in politics and use of media, Artwick (2010) concluded that African American adolescents are more likely to engage in civic activities, politically participate in online and offline settings, and take part in a political consumerism, or both boycott and buy-cott. Additionally, African American adolescents were also more likely to talk about news, follow the news, and demonstrate overall interest in news. Considering that so many researchers have either concluded that race is not a factor in civic engagement or that African Americans are less inclined to participate in the process due to financial challenges and feeling left out of the decision-making process, perhaps there is much to learn about the value of social media and its ability to galvanize all participants.

From downloading videos to texting friends, media consumption is an integral part of teenagers' lives. What will this mean for those young African Americans participating in the political process? The John Kony story has galvanized another generation of young and future voters to participate in the political process at a grassroots level. There may be a similar effect for African American youth because of social media.

African American Misuse of Social Media

Perhaps one of the biggest complaints about African American use of social media is that too many African American business owners fail to use Facebook and Twitter as marketing opportunities (Dupé, 2011b). In a November 13, 2011 blog, Dupé complained that too many African American businesses did not use Facebook to their marketing advantage (2011c). According to Dupé, it is not only African American businesses that miss this opportunity but also African American churches, day care centers, barbershops, beauty salons and restaurants. His suggestion is that Black business owners should at least buy books on Facebook marketing or take a course in it (2011a).

It is safe to say that African Americans are engaged in a number of social media options. While plenty of research exists on blogs that focus on health issues such as AIDS and diabetes, more research would be useful in learning how they use social media for marketing purposes. Knowing how effective online referrals are for African American males and just how effective joining a product's Facebook group is could lead to the development of better targeted advertisements and the development of better products for the African American community.

Next, readers will find a discussion and analysis of Asian American use of technology and social media. The section includes an analysis of Asian American use of social media as well as look at how much time they spend and what they do when they are using social media. This section also examines the use of Global Social Media Tools and their viability. Readers will be able to consider the ways Asian teens and young adults use social media.

Asian American Use of Social Media

Cyworld, a Korean SNS fulfills cultural expectations about relationship maintenance by introducing features that support both the collectivistic traditions and increased individualism.

(Correa & Sun, 2011)

Analysis of Asian Americans can be a bit challenging. One might assume that use of a communication technology is based on a desire to communicate. Friends and students from traditional Asian cultures point out that relationships mean everything within the cultures of the various countries. Once Asians become part of the American culture, one has to seriously examine how much computer-based communication is about relationship building and maintenance and how much is about business.

Crouch (2010) found ethnic and cultural groups use tools in similar patterns, no matter the group. The author found cultural and ethnic groups that live within a different nation or surrounding used social media to connect globally and or they use social media to communicate within their own community.

Discussing Asian Americans' use of social media would be incomplete if one only examined those people born in the United States of Asian ancestry or naturalized as American citizens. Additionally, there are a number of countries of heritage that should be included if we say we are fully discussing Asian Americans. Indeed, 48 nations are considered Asian-based on the United Nations' divisions. So, in the spirit of honesty, the groups included in this section need to be articulated. This section looks heavily at Chinese and Chinese American use of social media. Because the Chinese have the largest number of social media users in the world, it is difficult to not include them both domestically and internationally. Among the other groups included were Japanese Americans, Korean Americans and Filipino Americans. On occasion, the technology of the country of heritage will be discussed. This is due to the fact that a number of Asian Americans either keep in touch with the country of heritage due to family relations or develop relations with others in those countries as a method of maintaining or developing a relationship with their heritage. Covering 48 nations' uses of social media is better handled in a book all its own than in one book chapter, unless that chapter is part of an encyclopedia.

Asian Americans Online

Asian American Internet users are better educated and earn more money than most other Internet users (Spooner, 2001). Asian American Internet users, on average, are more likely to have a college degree than other races and ethnic groups. More than half (52%) earned bachelor degrees or higher, compared to 38% of Caucasian Internet users. Almost one-third (29%) of African American Internet users and 26% of Hispanic users have similar levels of education. It might stand to reason that higher levels of education would lead to higher incomes. For Asian Americans who go online, almost 34% earn $75,000 or more. This reflects a slightly higher income than the average Caucasian Internet user in that 29% of Caucasians earn that much. That figure is significantly higher than African Americans and Hispanics earn. Only 18% of Hispanic online users earn $75,000 and 17% of African Americans online users earn that much.

Asian American online users are also the youngest of the major ethnic groups; 63% are between the ages of 18–34. Only Hispanics come close in that 61% of Hispanic users are in this age group.

Discussions of Asian American use of social media should begin with their presence on the Internet. According to the Pew Internet and American Life Project (2011), Asian Americans may not be America's largest minority but they certainly have a significant online footprint. When it comes to computer use, with six million English-speaking Asian Americans in the United States, 78% use computers. Approximately 75% of the Asian Americans surveyed say they have used the Internet and 70% said they are on the Internet daily (Madden & Zickuhr, 2011). With more than five million Asian American users, their presence exceeds Internet users of any other ethnic group. The Asian American footprint is 58% male, 42% female. This is compared to the general Internet gender split which is 50–50. On a daily basis, 70% of Asian Americans use the Internet. Other ethnic groups tend to have a much lower daily online rate. Fifty-eight percent of Caucasians use the Internet daily compared to Hispanics (48%) and African Americans (39%).

Asian American men and women have similar rates of daily use. Some 71% of Asian American men and 68% of Asian American females use the Internet daily. The percentage of Asians online daily could be attributed to the length of time they have been online. Asians were identified as veteran Internet users because they have been using the Internet for over three years. Only 34% of the online population has been online for over three years. Yet 49% of Asian Americans who use the Internet are veterans. Nearly 80% of the Asian American online users have been online for over two years.

In examining the gender breakdown of Internet use among Asian Americans, one would learn that Asian American men engaged in the Internet early. Asian American males are considered the most experienced ethnic or racial user group on the Internet. Some 49% of Caucasian online users began using the Internet more than three years ago. Among Asian American males, 55% have been on the Internet for more than three years. When looking at those who have been on the Internet for two or more years, 89% of Asian American males have been online. In examining the percentage of ethnic groups who are novices or who have been online less than six months, only 4% of Asian Americans are novices.

The Asian American female is also leading in many areas of Internet use. Nearly 40% of Asian American women are Internet veterans. Approximately 72% of the remainder of the online Asian American women have been online for more than two years. Unlike their male counterparts, Asian American females are not as productive on the Internet. Just under 10% are novices. Although that figure is twice as large as the male novice population, Asian American females represent the smallest percentage of Internet novices. Caucasians reflect 15%, Hispanics reflect 20% and African Americans reflect 23% of the Internet novice population.

Once online, Asian Americans tend to stay online longer. Nearly 40% of Asian Americans stay online for two or more hours. Of those who stay online longer, 15% stay online for four or more hours. Based on the Pew Study (2011), nearly 29% of all those who are online on any given day will stay online for two or more hours each session.

Not only are Asian Americans likely to log on daily, they also acknowledge logging on several times a day. While 64% of Asian Americans surveyed acknowledged going online daily from their homes at least once, 32% indicated that they go online from their homes several times a day. An analysis of the overall Internet population suggests that only 51% goes online at least once each day from their homes. The Asian population exceeds the norm in this area as well.

Just as Asian Americans enjoy daily use of the Internet at their homes, they also log on regularly at the office as well. Of those surveyed, 71% of the Asian American group said they go online at work at least once a day. Compared to the total Internet population, 67% of all Internet users go online once a day from the office.

Asian Americans are also likely to be smart phone owners. While 31% of US owners have chosen smart phones, penetration is higher among mobile users who are part of ethnic and racial minorities. According to Kellogg (2011), younger ethnic minorities are more likely to be smart phone owners. Only 27% of Caucasian mobile users own smart phones. Additionally, Apple's iOs is the favorite operating system among Asians/Pacific Islanders; 36% who own smart phones, own iPhones.

Asian American Online Behavior

Like most other groups, Asian Americans use email regularly; 61% use email on a daily basis. That compares to 51% for Caucasians, 39% by Hispanics and 32% by African Americans. Asian Americans have experienced most Internet activities at the same rate as other ethnic groups. Their daily Internet activities include checking the news online, getting financial information, getting information regarding hobbies and getting political information.

Wiltshire & Grannis (2011) published the Pew Internet report on Asian Americans and technology. Their research indicates that Asian Americans' use of social media exceeds other ethnic groups in most areas. Asian Americans are more likely to read the news online than any other group. With 21% of the overall Internet population getting its news from the web, 34% of Asian Americans use the web for that purpose compared to 22% of Caucasians, 20% for Hispanics, and 15% for African Americans. Asian Americans surpass other ethnic groups in obtaining political news and information online by more than 10%.

Asian Americans often go online to transact business, whether they are purchasing products, buying investments or handling their banking needs. More than half of Asian American online users (54%) have bought items online. Asian Americans and Caucasians are pretty close to making online purchases at the same rate, 54% to 49%. However, more Asian Americans buy items online on a day-to-day basis than any other ethnic group. Compared to other ethnic groups, a larger portion of the Asian American population uses the Internet to take care of banking or other financial activities. According to Nielsen (2009), Asian Americans were the largest demographic group using online banking. Some 75.3% of the Asian Americans surveyed bank online compared to 67.4% of non-Asian households. Although income and age were intervening variables, when analyzing use of the Internet for banking compared to ethnicity and income levels, Asians continued to stand out compared to other groups (Nielsen, 2009).

Asian Americans are more likely to use the Internet to make travel plans than any other ethnic group. In this category, African American, Caucasian and Hispanic online users all tie in the percentage of people who make travel arrangements online at 36%. Asian Americans, however, often pay attention to the time booked, the activities that must take place and the convenience of departure and arrival times. Some 46% of those surveyed said they chose to make travel plans online.

Asian American Use of the Internet for Entertainment

Asian Americans use the Internet for entertainment, but less than other ethnic groups. Almost 60% of Asian Americans admit surfing the web for fun on a daily basis, but African Americans and Hispanics (72%) lead in this activity. Caucasians (62%) also use the web for fun more than Asian Americans by a slim margin.

Nearly 32% of Asian American Internet users acknowledged chatting online at some time. For those who visit chat rooms on a daily basis, 11% identified with the practice. In that area Asian Americans surpass other ethnic groups two to one. Asian Americans are more than twice as likely to IM (instant message) friends as they are to meet them online.

The length of time Asian Americans spend online could be attributed to the fact that 34% of Asian Americans read their news online. Asian American men tend to use the Internet for financial activities and shopping, while Asian American women tend to use the Internet to listen to their favorite music and doing fun activities on the Internet.

Asian American Social Media Use

Crouch (2010) discusses global social media tools. These tools allow ethnic and cultural groups to stay in communication on a broader scale. Facebook, Twitter, LinkedIn and Tumblr are tools of the trade from an American perspective. Because Asians, like other ethnic groups with roots in other countries, are able to expand their options for communication, we should also consider similar communications links such as Weibo, Youku, Cyworld and others. We will keep in mind that some global social media tools are language-specific or culture/ethnic-specific. This section examines Asian American use of traditional American-based social media first then considers global social media tools.

Facebook

A blog posted on the 8Asians site "Ernie" posted an article indicating that Facebook's most common users are young Asian American females. Ernie attributed this comment to a Nielsen report indicating that this typical user would be between the ages of 18–34, living in New England, making less than $50,000.00 and having earned a bachelor's degree (Ernie, 2011). Yet 71% of Asian Americans use Facebook at least weekly; only 14% use Myspace weekly. A full 80% of Asian Americans are online, which is the highest rate among ethnic groups in the U.S. That suggests almost all Asian Americans using the Internet also use Facebook.

YouTube

A slight majority of Asian Americans (51%) use YouTube weekly. While television screens may not offer many options for Asian-oriented viewing, there is an abundance of Asians on the Internet. *The New York Times* reports Asians are finding their venue on the Internet. The impact of YouTube is not directed towards one Asian national group but rather most Asian American racial/cultural combinations. In an interview with the musical group, Legaci, Kai Ryssdal pointed out that fans were in love with Justin Bieber. What only a few people realized is that the four backup singers behind Bieber are Filipino Americans (http://www.marketplace. org/topics/life/asian-americans-find-spotlight-youtube). Ryssdal pointed out that not many Asian Americans and very few Filipino Americans were recognized in the music industry. He pointed out that Legaci had tried to break through the music industry by traditional means. When they kept hitting walls they decided to use YouTube and enter using grassroots methods.

Asian American parents often encourage their children to pursue traditional careers that offer security and better starting salaries (Hilburn, 2011). Like many young adults, Asian American young people are escaping to YouTube to show the world what they really want to do. YouTube star David Choi is one example. Choi pointed out that becoming a doctor or a lawyer was too stereotypical for him. Choi chose YouTube as a place he could share his talent for the world to render a verdict on his skill set. In the fall of 2010, Choi had almost one million subscribers to his YouTube channel, putting him near the top of YouTube performers.

Choi pointed out the challenges of being a Korean-American performer in the United States. He talked about being sandwiched in between parental expectations of being the hard-working, over-achieving model minority and trying to let New York and Hollywood know that there are singers who look different from their last superstar that really can bring in audience members. Choi began posting his videos in 2006 but actually gained fame in 2004 when he won the John Lennon Songwriting contest. Choi's parents learned of his notoriety from church members who told them they had seen their son on YouTube.

Clara Chung had a similar experience. Also Korean American, Chung was discouraged from pursuing a career in music. Because she had originally planned to attend culinary school, her parents knew she would not be following the path to traditional careers. YouTube gave her access to other Asian American singers.

Not limited to music, Asian Americans have been able to use YouTube as a vehicle for other forms of expression. Kev Jumba performs a comedy routine that makes fun of Asian American parental issues. He has nearly two million subscribers (Considine, 2011). Ryan Higa, a Japanese American, has over 4.1 million subscribers to his comedy act. He was identified as having the most subscribed-to YouTube channel (Hillburn, 2011).

At the time of writing, the Asian American woman with the most-subscribed channel on YouTube is a Vietnamese-American in Los Angeles. Michelle Phan has 1.5 million subscribers who watch her videos on makeup and beauty tips and tutorials (Considine, 2011). Phan's Internet success helped her land a job as a Lancôme spokeswoman. Phan believes that YouTube and the Internet offer more strong Asian roles than other media options.

Other Asian Social Media Options

While mainstream social media options resonate with Asian Americans, they also have other channels for communication that are becoming more and more popular with nonAsians as well. Ameba, Cyworld and QQ are very popular with Asian Americans and Asians in Asia as well as all Asians with American friends.

Ameba

Ameba is a Japanese social media site that operates as a microblogging service like Twitter but is in the Japanese language. This social networking site is similar to Wordpress in the United States (Georgieva, 2011). To be competitive, Ameba has a Twitter clone called Ameba Now. Users can perform gaming activities by using Ameba Pico. Ameba Pico users can create avatars, visit virtual places and chat with others.

Cyworld (Korean)

Cyworld was one of the world's most successful Social sites until the advent of Facebook and Twitter (http://www.Koreatimes.co.kr/www/news/biz/2011/11/123_99587.html). Cyworld, a Korean social networking site, is continuing to make a comeback in its efforts to be global.

In 2001, Cyworld was Korea's social networking leader. Minihompy, a Cyworld feature, became the "go to" location for SNS lovers. Cyworld flourished before blogs and microblogs became popular. Minihompy allowed users to present an online image that they could control. However, by 2005 when they decided to go global, they had not factored in the features that Facebook had built in to their systems. This may have caused some Cyworld users to become Facebook users. Cyworld closed its U.S. service in 2009.

Cyworld has 26 million users compared to 4.48 million Korean Facebook users. When Cyworld reemerged in the global market, it offered operations in six languages and a universal platform. Cyworld is keeping the format that made it popular but adding options that give users a bit more privacy yet lead to greater communication and relationship building.

Mixi

Japan also offers a social media option similar to Facebook. Mixi was founded in 2004. According to Bloomberg, by February of 2011, Mixi had a customer base of 22 million users (Georgieva, 2011). Mixi offers real-time check-ins and tagging information when used through mobile devices.

QQ

QQ, based in China, is the world's largest social Internet site (http://stockson wallstreet.net/2011/01/the-worlds-biggest-social-network-qq-chinas-facebook). In January of 2011, QQ identified 650 million accounts compared to Facebook's 575 million accounts. QQ was created because the Chinese government blocked Facebook. Because of QQ's success, China has turned into the world's largest market for both Internet and mobile phone users. QQ started out as an instant messaging site and has added multiplayer online gaming, ringtone downloads and social networks like Qzone. QQ now offers an online bank for use in other e-commerce and online venues.

Ushi

Ushi is the Chinese version of LinkedIn. Ushi means "outstanding professional" in Mandarin. Many Chinese social network clones exist by copying the original site. Ushi was started by a LinkedIn user who happened to meet the founder of LinkedIn. While traveling to Tokyo-Narita airport, Hansen Lu (who does business as Dominic Penaloza) met Reid Hoffman, the founder of LinkedIn. At the end of the bus ride Penaloza decided that China should have something comparable to LinkedIn (Seligson, 2012).

Ushi's actual startup date is debated. Chen (2010) identifies the private beta testing only invitation as going out in March of 2010, whereas Seligson (2012) identifies Ushi's startup date as February 2010. This confusion is probably because Penaloza also created another social networking site with Yue Zhang and Jinfu He in 2009. At that time, the team created WorldFriends, a dating site. By October of that year, Ushi had 60,000 members (Chen, 2010). Today, Ushi has 600,000 members and adds about 100,000 new members a month (Seligson, 2012).

Other Options for Asian Social Media Communication

Communicating with Asian friends can be challenging. While Facebook reaches millions, it does not easily reach any friends in China. The Chinese government, concerned about political stability, has blocked Facebook use in China because of the openness of communication and, from their perspective, inappropriate lines of communication that might be crossed. Although a number of technologically gifted people know how to breach the Great Firewall, many have to be careful about doing so too often. Rather than not allow 500 million netizens the privilege of doing what others around the world are able to do, the Chinese government has blocked the social media options that might be problematic and replaced them with similar options made in China. This section presents the most popular social media options and compares them to their American original. Included in this section are Sina Weibo, Renren, Youku, Diandian and Douban.

Sina Weibo

Weibo was launched in August 2009 by Sina Corp. Sina Weibo is China's version of Twitter. Former journalist and accountant Charles Chao approved the creation of this product even though the government was very wary of microblogs. By October 2010, Sina Weibo had 50 million users. When Chao saw how successful Facebook was, he made the effort to attract more movie stars, singers, famous business owners and media figures.

Sina Weibo's forerunner, Fanfou, was taken offline during the anniversary of the Tiananmen Square crackdown. Sina Weibo has found its niche. Whereas Fanfou created concerns that it could be the place where people who complained about the government gathered, Weibo meets a similar need with government approval. Sina Weibo is considered a "sandbox for cynics" (Epstein & Yang, 2011). It is considered an incubator for subversive Internet memes, meaning that poorly performing politicians are often mentioned on this site.

Numerous competitors have emerged since Sina Weibo found success. Tencent's QQ, Hong Kong's Phoenix and even the Communist Party's People's Daily all try to compete but none of them have found Sina Weibo's success. Although Chao anticipated the continued success of Sina Weibo, the company plans to start monetizing in a few years to allow for greater interest in the product. Sina Weibo has the feel of Facebook. Users stay on longer than Twitter users. It is traded on NASDAQ now and is expected to have a value of one billion dollars by 2015. Yet with all these accomplishments, Sina Weibo still has the same concern as its predecessor, Fanfou. There are still topics not seen on Weibo; items that the government might find challenging do not appear. Chao says that he has 100 employees who monitor what is printed 24/7. Critics believe that he has many more.

Renren

Renren Inc. (RENN) is considered by many to be the Facebook of China (http://seeking alpha.com/article/490251-5-reasons-why-we-believe-renren-is-the-most-attractive-social-media-stock, April 11, 2012). RENN is also a video-sharing website, a leading social commerce site and an online game center. It offers a daily deal site called Nuomi.com.

Financially, Renren has room to grow. In April of 2012 RENN's market cap was identified as just over two billion dollars compared to Facebook's anticipated IPO in the $75 to $100 billion range (http://seekingalpha.com/article/490251-5-reasons-why-we-believe-renren-is-the-most-attractive-social-media-stock, April 11, 2012). By the May 2012 reports, BBC News reported that Renren saw more losses than originally expected (www.bbc.co.uk/news/business-1868128). Renren said that it has shown an increase in the number of monthly unique users. By March of 2011, Renren had 31 million unique users.

Youku

Victor Koo, the founding president of Youku, launched the site in 2006. Although it is considered a clone by outsiders, Koo describes Youku as a platform that offers both professional and user-generated online video content (http://www.youku.com/about/en/youku_faq). The average Youku user is on a page for ten minutes. The company started with a focus on user-generated content but they have determined that only about 30% of its content is user-generated now.

Youku considers itself ahead of its competitors based on superior streaming speed. Their users offer self-developed technology and a self-operated video content delivery network (CDN). Studies also show that the users have a better experience with their system than other sites. Youku has the largest network of film, TV and music partners with over 2,000 partners and an active user base called "paike," the most active users who talk about hot topics and produce time-sensitive videos.

Like several Chinese developing social media companies, YouKu does not like to discuss its efforts to compete. It does note that it plans to make its money by advertising revenue. Representatives say that they work with 350 top-flight Chinese and international brands. Youku sees itself as the place to offer cost-effective brand messaging. Additionally, Youku says that they make a smaller amount of money selling limited subscription services for special content and mobile content offered through China's 3G network. They have found success working with advertisers such as HP, Dell, Lenovo, Canon, Nike, Adidas, Pepsi, Coke, Ford and Google.

So far, Youku has been given two licenses. One license allows it to operate a video-sharing website which allows Internet users to upload, via download. This license allows Youku to transmit videos of all types except films and TV serials to customers' homes, computers and cell phones. Like QQ, administrators are easy to contact so that police officials do not break rules.

Diandian

In China's efforts to keep all social media options available to its citizens, it only seems natural that it would create a product similar to Tumblr, a US light-blogging platform. Tumblr is also blocked by "the Great Firewall" that keeps American and other social networks locked out of China's portals. Diandian was created by Jack Xu who formerly worked for Renren.

Diandian is a lite-blog focused on mass users and their original UCGs (user-generated content). A beta version of Diandian uses the same dashboard design as Tumblr. It lacked a Directory and Goodies section but allows users to Text, Photo, Blog and Video. The beta version cloned 80% of Tumblr's capabilities. According to Techrice.com (Lukoff, 2011), the Chinese tend to clone 80% of a product and start to localize other options on the sites to meet the needs of Chinese netizens.

Douban

In China's efforts to make sure Chinese people can find all social media options at home, China allowed the creation of Douban. Douban.com is a popular Chinese site for book lovers, movie enthusiasts and fans of various types of music (Georgieva, 2011). Douban is globally one of the most visited sites. Members of the Douban community interact with brand pages, polls, forums and discussions.

Summary

We began this section with a concern about whether Asian American social media use was based more on the need to communicate or the need to build and maintain relationships. An examination of the tools used to communicate socially would suggest that Asian Americans have the desire to communicate using the latest technology to stay abreast of the news and take care of their business and professional needs. Beyond that, Asian Americans enjoy using social media to share their personal and entertainment interests with friends around the world. While their Japanese and Korean friends experience some challenges in how the technology will affect their ability to communicate, their Chinese friends continue to find ways to circumvent the obstacles that reduce their topics for conversation. Regardless, social media will aid in Asian American communication needs.

The New Digital Divide

The research clearly points out that people of color have been the focus of discussion on the digital divide. Research contributed during the last two decades of the 20th Century and the first decade of the 21st Century focused on the lack of connectivity among the rural population, and the lack of technology available to African Americans and Hispanic/Latinos. During the first decade of the 21st Century, the changes in technology and expansion of social media options have affected the statistics reflecting who the digitally empowered are. Indeed, it is the type of social media options that is causing the new divide.

During the first decade of the 21st Century, African Americans and Hispanic/Latinos lacked the technology that would have allowed them to use the latest social media options. Their lack of computers seemed to deny them access to various types of communication (Graham & Smith, 2010; Pew Research, 2010). The development of smart phones and other android-based technology placed devices that did everything that a desktop computer could do and more in their hands. Caucasians still have more broadband access than do African Americans and Asians, but African Americans and Hispanic/Latinos are now buying laptops and tablets at similar levels. Yet this newer technology created a slight new problem.

Job applications are increasingly being made available online. Most job applicants apply for jobs by using a desktop or laptop computer and printer. Not having easy access to the combination can create a problem for those seeking employment, applying for scholarships and entering competitions. Although use of library technology ameliorates the problem, it remains one of the last vestiges of the great divide. This lack of technology affects African Americans and Asians (Washington, 2011). Because of media meshing, the use of two media simultaneously, it is difficult to tell how much of a problem this lack of technology really is. Based on data collected in the latter part of 2011, Nielsen reported that 88% of U.S. tablet owners use their tablets while watching TV at least once a month while 45% do the same daily (Winslow, 2012). Research presented in this chapter suggests that African Americans and other ethnic groups support smaller-sized technologies.

This new problem, such as it is, makes clear that we have, in fact, bridged the great divide. Although Asian Americans were never victims of the divide, African Americans and Hispanic Latinos are much less severely affected by it. Many American eateries now offer free Wi-Fi and coffee shops now see having customers spend hours in businesses just so they can use their free Wi-Fi service as an acceptable way of doing business. Now prospective employees just have a slight inconvenience in their efforts to find out whether an employer wants her or his services. According to Robinson (McGrath, 2011, p. 43), "[T]he digital divide is not really a divide. It's a digital difference, I think, in many ways in how people do engage online and how they get online."

But now there is now a bridge across the great divide.

References

Adams, J., & Roscgino, V. J. (2005). White supremacists, oppositional cultures and the world wide web. *Social Forces, 84*(2), 759–778.

Artwick, C. G. (2010). White, Black and missing on Twitter: Social media highlight disparities in news coverage of two missing Virginia women. *Howard Journal of Communications*, March/April, 224–246.

Attewell, P., & Battle, J. (1999). Home computers and school performance, *Information Society, 15*(1), 1–10.

Barber, H. M. (2011). Blacks are more social online than other groups. Retrieved March 24, 2012 from: http://www.bet.com/news/national/blacks-are-more social-online-than-any-other-groups.html.

Benton, A. (2009). Number of African-Americans on Facebook mirrors US makeup. Retrieved from: http://www.blackweb20.com/2009/12/17/number-of-african-americans-on-facebook-mirrors-us-makeup/#.ULyvq4bOHSg.

Blackperceptions.com (2012, June 10). Instagram for those who don't already know, Retrieved from: http://voices.yahoo.com/instagram-those-dont-already-know-1142 4116.html?cat=9.

boyd, d. m., & Ellison, N. B. (2008). Social network sites: Definition, history and scholarship. *Journal of Computer-Mediated Communication, 13*, 210–230.

Brunsting, S., & Postmes, T. (2002). Social movement participation in the digital age: predicting offline and online collective action. *Small Group Research, 33*(5), 525–554.

Castells, M. (2001). *Internet Galaxy.* New York: Oxford University Press.

Castells, M., Fernandez-Ardevol, M., Qui J. L., & Sey, A. (2006). *Mobile communication and society: A global perspective.* Cambridge, MA: MIT Press.

Centers for Disease Control (2010). Raising the volume of young African-American voices in the fight against HIV. Retrieved from: http://www.cdc.gov/nchhstp/newsroom/docs/iknowFactSheet-FINAL508c.pdf.

Chakroborty, J., & Bosman, M. M. (2005). Measuring the digital divide in the United States: Race, income, and personal computers. *Professional Geographer, 57*(3), 395–410.

Chen, L. (2010). Professional social network Ushi is China's answer to LinkedIn. Retrieved June 15, 2012 from: http://venturebeat.com/2010/10/19/professional-social-network-ushi-is-chinas-answer-to-linkedin/.

Considine, A. (2011). For Asian-American stars, many web fans. Retrieved from: http://www.nytimes.com/2011/07/31/fashion/for-asian-stars-many-web-fans.html?_r=1&p.

Correa, T., & Sun, H. J. (2011). Race and online content creation. *Communication & Society, 14*(5), 638–659. Retrieved from: http://dx.doi.org/10.1080/1369118X.2010.514355.

Cothey, V. (2002). A longitudinal study of World Wide Web users' information searching behavior. *Journal of the American Society for Information Science and Technology, 53*(2): 67–78.

Crouch, G. (2010). Culture and ethnicity in social media. Retrieved from: http://www.mediabadger.com/2010/06/culture-ethnicity0in-social-media/.

Diani, M. (2000) Social movement networks; virtual and real. *Information, Communication, and Society, 3*(3), 386–401.

DiMaggio, P., Hargittai, E., Neuman, R. W., & Robinson, J. P. (2001). Social implications of the internet, *Annual Review of Sociology, 27*, 307–331.

Dupé, K. A. (2011a, June 21). Get inky with it. Retrieved from: http://whereareblacksin technology.blogst.com/.

Dupé, K.A. (2011b, August 7). Facebook marketing. Retrieved from: http://whereare blacksintechnology.blogspot.com/.

Dupé, K. A. (2011c, November 13). Reality TV that truly matters. Where are Blacks in technology? Retrieved from: http://whereareblacksintechnology.blogspot.com/.

Dvorak, P. (2012). Addicted to a web site called Pinterest: Digital crack for women. Retrieved from: http://www.washingtonpost.com/local/addicted-to-a-web-site-called-pinterest-digital-crack-for-women/2012/02/20/gIQAP3wAQR_story.html.

Epstein, G., & Yang, L. (2011). Sina Weibo. *Forbes Asia*, 7(3): 56–60.

Ernie (2011) Facebook's most common users are Asian American young adult females. Retrieved from: http://www.8asians.com/2011/09/21/facebooks-most-common-users-are-asian-american-young-adult-females/.

Eversley, M. (2012a). Trayvon case shows more Blacks tapping power of social media. Retrieved from: http://www.usatoday.com/news/nation/story/2012-03-25/trayvon-martin-social-media/53777510/1.

Eversley, M. (2012b). Social media vaulted Trayvon Martin case into spotlight. Retrieved from: http://content.usatoday.com/communities/ondeadline/post/2012/03/social-media-vaulted-trayvon-martin-case-into-spotlight/1#.ULyv-obOHSg.

Eversley, M. (2012c). Black, Hispanic Americans using social media in larger numbers, experts say. Retrieved from: http://www.thehispanicinstitute.net/node/5015.

Finn, G. (2011, June 16). A portrait of who uses social networks in the US (and how social media affects our lives). Retrieved from: http://searchengineland.com/a-portrait-of-who-uses-social-networks-in-the-u-s-and-how-social-media-affects-our-lives-81653.

Frommer, D. (2010, November 1). Here's how to use Instagram. *Business Insider*. Retrieved from: http://techometr.com/a/detail.do/id-2f73e64c-5a06-4536-8bc1-ae76ee41d378.

Garafalo, R., Herrick, A., Mustanski, B. S., & Donnenberg, G. R. (2007). Tip of the iceberg: Young men have sex with men, the internet and HIV risk. *American Journal of Public Health*, 97(6), 1113–1117.

Gates, H. L. (2000, January 12). Black to the future. *Education Week*. Retrieved from: http://www.edweek.org/ew/articles/2000/01/12/17gates.h19.html.

Georgieva, M. (2011). The ultimate list: 24 of the world's largest social networks. Retrieved from: http://blog.hubspot.com/blog/tabid/6307/bid/15931/The-Ultimate-List-24-of-the-World-s-Largest-Social-Networks.aspx.

Graham, R., & Smith, D. (2010). Dividing lines: An empirical examination of technology use and Internet activity among African Americans. *Communication & Society*, 13(6), 892–908.

Hargittai, E. (2002). Second digital divide: differences in people's online skills. Retrieved from: http://firstmonday.org/issues/issue7-5/hargittai.

Hargittai, E. (2004). Classifying and coding online actions. *Social Science Computer Review*, 22(2), 210–227.

Hargittai, E. (2006). Hurdles to information seeking: spelling and typographical mistakes during users' online behavior. *Journal of the Association of Information Systems*, 6(12), 1–25.

Hargittai, E. (2007). Whose space? Differences among users and non–users of social network sites. Retrieved from: http://onlinelibrary.wiley.com/doi/10.1111/j.1083-6101.2007.00396.x/full.

Hilburn, M. (2011). Asian-Americans buck stereotypes, find fame on YouTube. Retrieved from: http://www.voanews.com/content/asian-americans-buck-stereotypes-find-fame-on-youtube-129113898/165018.html.

Hu, M. (2012). What is Pinterest? Illuminasians spotlight on the Asian American market. Retrieved from: http://www.illuminasians.com/pinterest/.

Jackson, W. (2011). African Americans; Technology and social media. Retrieved from: http://jacksonville.com/opinion/blog/400553/william-jackson/2011-12-27/african-americans-technology-and-social-media.

Kellogg, D. (2011). Among mobile phone users, Hispanics, Asians are most likely smart phone owners in the U.S. Nielsenwire. Retrieved from: Retrieved from: http://blog.nielsen.com/nielsenwire.

Klout. (2012). Klout measures your influence on your social networks. Retrieved from: www.klout.com.

Lenhart, A., Horrigan, J., Rainie, L., Allen, K., Boyce, A. Madden, M., & O'Grady, E. (2003). The ever-shifting Internet population: A new look at Internet access and the digital divide. The Pew Internet and American Life Project. Retrieved from: http://www.pewinternet.org/Reports/2003/The-EverShifting-Internet-Population-A-new-look-at-Internet-access-and-the-digital-divide.aspx.

Lenhart, A., Purcell, K., Smith, S., & Zickuhr, K. (2010). Social media and mobile internet use among teens and young adults. Pew Internet & American Life Project, February 3, 2010. Retrieved from: http://pewresearch.org/pubs/1484/social-media-mobile-internet-use-teens-millennials-fewer-blog.

Lukoff, K. (2011). China's top 15 social networks. Retrieved from: Techrice.com/2011/03/08/chinas-top-15-social-networks/.

Madden, M. (2003). America's online pursuits: The hanging picture of who's online and what they do. The Pew Internet and American Life Project. Retrieved October 27, 2004 from: http://www.pewinternet.org/pdfs/PIP_Online_Pursuits_Final.pdf.

Madden, M., & Zickuhr, K (2011). 65% of online adults use social networking sites. A project of the Pew Research Center. Retrieved from: http://pewinterest.org/Reports/2011/Social-Networking-Sites.aspx.

Madigan, E., & Goodfellow, M. (2005). The influence of family income and parents' education on digital access: Implications for first year college students. *Sociological Viewpoints*, *21*, 53–62.

Mandese, J. (2012, January 24). Beyond the ordinary (A.K.A. Facebook and Twitter), *Online Media Daily*.

McGrath, M. (2011). Technology, media and political participation. Retrieved from: http://www.wileyonlinelibrary.com.

McNeal, N. (2011, October). Cultivating the next generation of leaders: New leadership calls for new tactics. Retrieved from: http://www.ebony.com/search/CULTIVATING+THE+NEXT+GENERATION+OF+LEADERS.

MediaPost. (2012, March 26). Men are more likely to visit LinkedIn and Wikipedia. Retrieved from: http://www.scribd.com/doc/64651329/Nielsen-Social-Media-Report.

Morahan-Martin, J., & Schumacher, P. (2003). Loneliness and social uses of the internet. *Computers in Human Behavior*, *19*(6), 659–671.

Mossberger, K., Tolbert, C. J., & Gilbert, M. (2006). Race, place, and information technology, *Urban Affairs Review*, *41*(5), 583–620.

Nielsen. (2009). Blog. http://blog.nielsen.com/nielsenwire/consumer/asian-americans-most-active-users-of-online-banking/.

Nielsen. (2010). African-Americans, women and southerners talk and text the most in the U.S. (n.d.) Nielsenwire, Retrieved from: http://blog.nielsen.com/nielsenwire/online_mobile/african-americans-women-and southerners-talk-and-text/.

Nielsen (2011). *The state of the media: Social Media Report: Q3 2011*. Retrieved from: http://blog.nielsen.com/nielsenwire/social/.

Ono, H., & Zavodny, M. (2008). Immigrants, English ability, and the digital divide. *Social Science Quarterly, 36*(4), 1135–1155.

Orsini, L. R. (2012, June 23). How the black community is embracing Pinterest. Retrieved from: http://www.dailydot.com/society/black-community-pinterest/.

Ourspace: Like Myspace for black people (2009). Retrieved from: http://www.screenshots.com/ourspaceourplace.org/.

Page, K. & Uncles, M. (2004). Consumer knowledge of the world wide web: Conceptualization and measurement. *Psychology and Marketing, 21*(8), 573–591.

Pew Internet and American Life Project. (2011). Retrieved from: http://www.pew internet.org/.

Pew Research. (2010, January 20). Generation M2: Media in the lives of 8–18-year-olds (pdf). Retrieved from: http://www.kff.org/entmedia/mh012010pkg.cfm/.

Pew Research Center Project for Excellence in Journalism. (2011, March 30). Retrieved from: http://www.journalism.org/commentary_backgrounder/special_report_howblogs_twitter_and_mainstream_media_have_handled_trayvon_m.

Reid, J. A. (2011). Obama winning on social media: Could Twitter "blackness" be the reason? Retrieved from: http://thegrio.com/2011/12/15/obama-leads-on-twitter/.

Rheingold, H. (1993) *The Virtual Community*. Cambridge, MA: MIT Press.

Rieh, S. Y. (2004). On the web at home: Information seeking and web searching in the home environment. *Journals of the American Society for Information Science and Technology, 55*(8), 743–753.

Rosenbloom, A. (2004). The Blogosphere. *Communication of the ACM, 47*(12), 32–33.

Sass, E. (2012). Pinterest now third most popular social media site. Retrieved from: http://www.mediapost.com/publications/article/171946/pinterest-now-third-most-popular-social-media-site.

Scheufele, D. A., & Nisbet, M. C. (2003). Being a citizen online: New opportunities and dead ends. *Harvard International Journal of Press-Politics, 7*(3), 55–75.

Scheufele, D. A., & Shah, D. V. (2000). Personality strengths are social capital: The role of dispositional and informational variables in the production of civic participation. *Communication Research, 27*(2), 107–131.

Seligson, H. (2012). Ushi links in Mainland China. Retrieved from: http://www.forbes.com/global/2012/0116/companies-people-dominic-penaloza-linkedin-connecting-china.html.

Servon, L. J., & Nelson, M. K. (2001). Community technology centers: Narrowing the digital divide in low-income, urban communities, *Journal of Urban Affairs, 23*(3–4), 279–291.

Shah, D. V., McLeod, J. M., & Yoon, S. (2001). Communication, context and community: An exploration of print, broadcast, and internet influences. *Communication Research, 28*, 464–506.

Shah, D. V., & Scheufele, D. A. (2006). Explicating opinion leadership: Nonpolitical disposition, information consumption, and civic participation. *Political Communication, 23*, 1–22.

Shaw, L. (2012). Facebook acquires Instagram for $1B. Retrieved from: http://www.thewrap.com/media/article/facebook-acquires-instagram-1b-36888.

Showell, A. (2011, December 2). Social media gets political. Retrieved from: http://www.bet.com/news/politics/2011/12/02/social-media-gets-political.html.

Smith, A. (2010). Technology trends among people of color. Pew Internet Commentary. Retrieved from: http://pewInternet.org/Commentary/2010/September/Technology-Trends-Among-People-of-Color.aspx.

Spooner, T. (2001). Asian-Americans and the Internet: The young and the connected. Pew Internet & American Life Project. Retrieved August 2, 2011 from: http://www.pew internet.org.

Staggers, G. (1984) Talkin loud black oral tradition. Retrieved from: http://www.yale.edu/ynhti/curriculum/units/1984/4/84.04.05.x.html.

Stelter, B. (2012, February 13). Nielsen chastises Oprah over a twitter plea, *New York Times*, reprint, online.

Stern, J. (2012). Facebook buys Instagram for $1 billion. *ABC News*. Retrieved April 27, 2012.

Swift, M. (2009). Facebook mines census data to track its diversifying users. *San Jose Mercury News*. Retrieved March 18, 2012 from: http://phys.org/news180270572.html.

Tisch, J. (2008). Turnout by education, race and gender and other 2008 youth voting statistics. Report for the Center for Information and Research on Civic Learning and Engagement. Retrieved from: http://www.civicyouth.org/?p=324.

Townsend, A. (2011). Today, we know more about who is using Twitter. *Techland*. Retrieved from: http://techland.time.com/2011/06/01/today-we-know-more-about-who-is-using-twitter.

Vernon, K. (April 19, 2010). Minority mobile and social media use by the numbers. Retrieved August 15, 2011 from: http://everywhereallthetime.com/?p=272 Minority and Social Media by the numbers.

WARC (2012, March 26). African Americans warm to social brands. Retrieved from: http://www.warc.com/News/PrintNewsItem.aspx?ID=29624.

Warschauer, M. (2003). *Technology and social inclusion: Rethinking the digital divide.* Cambridge, MA: MIT Press.

Washington, J. (2011, January 19). For minorities, new digital divide seen. *USA Today*. Retrieved from: http://www.pewinternet.org/Media-Mentions/2011/For-minorities-new-digital-divide-seen.aspx.

Wiltshire & Grannis. (2011). Asian-Americans and technology. Retrieved March 18, 2011 from: http://www.pewinternet.org/~/media/Files/Presentations/2011/Jan/2011%20-%20pdf%20-%20Asian%20Americans%20-%20DC.pdf.

Winslow, G. (2012). About 45% of all U.S. tablet owners simultaneously watch TV and while using their tablets every day. Retrieved April 5, 2012 from: *Broadcasting and Cable*, http://www.broadcastingcable.com/article/482762-Nielsen_Heavy_Tablet_Usage_ While_Watching_TV.php

13

THE SOCIAL MEDIA INDUSTRIES

Summary and Future Directions

Alan B. Albarran

After reading the previous twelve chapters, you, dear reader, are likely to have more questions about the social media industries than when you started investing your time in this volume. For what it's worth, as Editor, I feel the same way. We have a far from complete understanding of the social media industries, no doubt due in part to the nascent stage of development. There is perhaps some frustration because we have little, if any, actual data to digest as to how these firms that make up the social media industries are performing. Very few social media firms are public companies, and the few that are public have not had a long enough history to truly gauge their economic impact and performance as an industry.

But there are some things we can take away from these chapters by drawing a synthesis of the material, and by understanding that more research will be needed on this subject. In no particular order, here are a few of the main propositions one can pull from the insights offered by the contributors to this volume.

- The social media industries are unique in that there are few barriers to entry (so starting new firms is relatively simple), sites that meet the demand of consumers are widely popular, but very limited business models exist, and there is no clarity as to how these sites will make money aside from traditional advertising. Many business analysts outside the social media industries question the long-term potential of social media from a finance/investment standpoint. A few companies are making money. The majority are not. The dependence on advertising as the primary means of support is a huge issue.

- Social media's strength as a marketing tool is widely known. Miller's Chapter 5, written from the perspective of a social media marketing professional, emphasizes the importance of strategy and audience engagement in forming social media campaigns. As the social media industries continue to develop and refine their role as a form of marketing, this will help the industries in their effort to attract additional revenue streams beyond advertising.

- Consumer demand for social media is one of the industry's great strengths. We know how Facebook alone would be one of the three largest countries in the world if it were a nation, but as this volume attests, there is also strong growth occurring in the United States for people over 35, and among the key ethnic groups of Latinos, African Americans, and Asian Americans. Coupled with strong global growth, the social media industries are in strong demand by consumers.

- Clouding the growth of social media as an industry is a number of ethical concerns. In Chapter 7, Beasley offers many examples of ethical concerns broached by social media. Questions over ethical practices by corporations can quickly damage public opinion and create public relations nightmares. Social media by its participatory nature raises numerous questions and issues over the ethics of social networking sites, so consumers play a role in this area as well. Ethical issues can damage the goodwill in an industry and also limit potential growth.

- Privacy issues surround many aspects of the social media industries, as detailed by Lee in her examination of the topic in Chapter 9. Privacy issues have led many individuals to close profiles and walk away from SNS because of fears as to how personal information will be used by the firms involved. Privacy issues will continue to pose challenges to the social media industries and could affect economic performance, especially if new controversial policies are introduced.

- In terms of theoretical issues, there is much to be learned about social media and its tangled "web" of relationships between firms, audiences, advertisers, marketers, and other constituencies. As Pérez-Latre's Chapter 3 illustrates, social media is impacting human communication and communication between individuals and industry. Social media needs further exploration not just from a business perspective, but from other theoretical orientations as well.

- The social media industries will continue to impact the development and distribution of media content, whether created by traditional media or in the form of user-generated content. Schackman's Chapter 6 details how the social media industries are delivering original content, and how users have moved into roles as gatekeepers and curators of content.

- Traditional news media has been dramatically affected by the growth of the social media industries. Standley's Chapter 8 offers a slice of original research detailing how news media organizations have both embraced and adapted social media in their newsgathering efforts. Social media has emboldened the concept of the "citizen journalist." Social media has also established itself as a key source for breaking news.

- Social media is everywhere. Social media is a global phenomenon that is yet to reach its full potential. Social media has impacted many areas of society, and has proven to be a catalyst in organizing individuals and groups in terms of politics, social initiatives, and activism.

Moving Ahead: Researching the Social Media Industries

How then should the scholarly community address future research on the social media industries? Clearly there are multiple paths available to researchers. Trying to research the social media industries is itself a daunting task. Here are a few suggestions, again drawing on a synthesis of ideas generated by the contributors to this volume:

- In examining social media as a set of industries, going forward, researchers will have more data to monitor trends in terms of evolving market structure, conduct, and performance. What will be interesting to study is how social media evolves outside this traditional paradigm. How will firms respond to new competitors who enter the market? How will innovation and new technology affect the development of social media as a whole? Will the social media industries find new revenue streams beyond advertising, and, if so, what will they be?

- Social media is primarily driven by consumer demand, and most likely more of those consumers will access social media via mobile devices. As such, the study of social media must also consider the development of the mobile media industries, and how it will impact social media. Soon we can expect to see mobile devices that we wear. Google is one company experimenting with a pair of glasses that will access the Internet, take pictures and video, and offer other features.

- Social media's impact on traditional media will continue to be an important research topic. How social media evolves in the distribution of content products and news is of particular interest. As more and more content moves to the web, how will social media be affected? Will social media firms enter the content markets by actually creating original content?

- Because of their growth and first mover advantage, Facebook, LinkedIn, Twitter, and YouTube have tended to attract most of the scholarly attention among social media firms. What we need are case studies of other social media firms, so we can better understand their development, their strategic planning, and the markets they are trying to capture.

- Likewise, we need case studies and essays exploring "best practices" among firms outside of the social media industries who use social media for marketing, promotion, and public relations activities. This would be particularly helpful to those of us training future generations of social media practitioners, to help identify needed skill sets and opportunities for careers.

- Legal and ethical issues associated with social media deserve more scholarly attention. Litigation is rather common across social media and technology firms, usually over topics like patents. The courts will continue to have a role in monitoring the industries and taking action as necessary. Ethical issues are all too common across the media industries, and in the early development of the social media industries, we've seen a number of ethical concerns raised.

- The social media industries need to be examined across levels of activity. The individual level should be looked at in conjunction with the nation-state and global levels to truly assess impact. Social media functions across these levels, yet most research tends to focus on only a single level. Multi-level research is challenging, and can be expensive. But to understand the social media industries as a global force, researchers will have to move in this direction.
- Finally, we need more theoretical development in researching social media. It has become trite to offer this suggestion, but it is true in this case. We do not have developed theories specific to the social media industries. Theoretical development will help us better understand how social media fits in within the broader spectrum of communication, and delineate how it will contribute to the larger body of knowledge.

The social media industries are functioning at a very early age in their life cycle. As such, this volume can hopefully contribute to a baseline of research about the social media industries. Clearly, there is a lot of work still to be done and more research and investigation are needed as the social media industries move through the industry life cycle.

Speaking on behalf of the contributors, we hope this volume will help spur your own ideas and thoughts on the social media industries, and serve as a heuristic tool to inspire your own research efforts. Thank you for the opportunity to share some of our research on this fascinating emerging set of industries with you.

AUTHOR INDEX

SUBJECT INDEX

Page numbers in **bold** refer to figures. Page numbers in *italic* refer to tables.